The Practical Ruskin

The
Practical
Ruskin

ECONOMICS AND AUDIENCE
IN THE LATE WORK

Linda M. Austin

The Johns Hopkins University Press
Baltimore and London

© 1991 The Johns Hopkins University Press
All rights reserved
Printed in the United States of America

The Johns Hopkins University Press
701 West 40th Street
Baltimore, Maryland 21211
The Johns Hopkins Press Ltd., London

The paper in this book meets the minimum requirements of American
National Standard for Information Sciences—Permanence of Paper for
Printed Library Materials, ANSI Z39.48–1984.

Library of Congress Cataloging-in-Publication-Data

Austin, Linda Marilyn.
The practical Ruskin: economics and audience in the late work / Linda
M. Austin.
p. cm.
Includes bibliographical references and index.
ISBN 0-8018-4162-3 (alk. paper)
1. Ruskin, John, 1819–1900. 2. Economics—Great Britain—
History—19th century. 3. Ruskin, John, 1819–1900—Political and
social views. 4. Ruskin, John, 1819–1900—Aesthetics. 5. Arts—
Economic aspects. I. Title.
HB103.R8A87 1991
330'.092—dc20 90-23911

In Memory of My Father

Thoughts hardly to be packed

Into a narrow act,

Fancies that broke through language and escaped;

All I could never be,

All, men ignored in me.

    —Robert Browning, "Rabbi Ben Ezra"

Contents

Preface

This book really began a decade ago with a feeling rather than an idea. I had decided to write my doctoral dissertation on John Ruskin's experiments with various genres, but I avoided most of the writing after 1869, for its variety and manic energy dazzled and confused me. At that time most other scholars had too, possibly for the same reasons. The exhilarating word painting of *Modern Painters* and *The Stones of Venice* was gone. In its place was an intricacy, even an incoherence of thought (in *Fors Clavigera*), a flat repetition of his famous aesthetics (in the Oxford lectures), and in everything an embarrassing personal note—admissions of mental breakdown and failure. By the writer's own testimony, then, the late work provided no material for those interested in Ruskin's methodical construction of a moral aesthetic. I returned to *Fors* a few years after, however, wanting to feel what I can only express as its aura of difference, and I found something new in these letters and in other works of the seventies and eighties. It was a relationship with readers not present in *Modern Painters* or *The Stones of Venice,* and it surfaced, I decided, from the effort to be practical, to break through the conventions of the letter or the lecture, to rupture language into some kind of action, or, if that seemed impossible, to view the writing itself as a deed. Of course the effort resulted in digressive and obscure letters, in fragments, and in flat, schematic lectures. They are interesting, if forbidding, because what Ruskin tried to do was so difficult. In a number of his "professional practices," including essays, letters, a museum, and accounts of publishing methods, Ruskin himself declares his position unbearable, his task a failure.

I have attempted in the chapters that follow to analyze and clarify Ruskin's position and task. What I call the late work—from 1869 on—came after the essays on political economy and bears the influence not only of the reformist ideas Ruskin published but also of the traditional social and economic thought he had rejected. As an unstated but understood set of ideas, it penetrates his late aesthetics, and it does so because it explained to him the change in aesthetic values and the mounting power of mass audiences. Economics and audience are symbiotic elements in this study, and their interplay reveals why Ruskin advertised himself as a failure in the last two decades of his life. He was writing to an audience he felt had been corrupted by a modern industrial economy, but to a certain extent he himself had internalized and was using many of its principles and values. This accounts for the frustration and confusion in his work, its tone of wildness and despair.

Parts of chapters three and four first appeared as "Labor, Money, and the Currency of Words in *Fors Clavigera*," in *ELH* 56 (Spring 1989):209–27. In the book that grew from this essay, I tried to assemble both the late-nineteenth-century audience and the contemporary sense of economics as two equally important contexts for Ruskin's last, tortuous efforts. I thank David G. Riede for helping me to balance these elements. He read the manuscript, as well as preliminary studies, with care, and I am grateful for his encouragement and advice over the years. I also thank Brian Maidment and Martin Wallen for their help, Jane Warth of the Johns Hopkins University Press for her careful editing, and Mallory McNease for proofreading. My work has received generous institutional support from the Oklahoma Foundation for the Humanities and Oklahoma State University. A National Endowment for the Humanities Summer Institute at the Yale Center for British Art gave me the opportunity to use the university's collections of nineteenth-century periodicals. The John Rylands University Library allowed me to study and quote from its collection of Ruskiniana, and I appreciate the hospitality of its staff.

The Practical Ruskin

Introduction:
Economic and Aesthetic
Contexts

In the last fifteen years of his public life, John Ruskin merged his two main preoccupations, art and political economy, into an economic view of aesthetic value. This view was never circumscribed and stated as a theory, as were his ideas of beauty in volume two of *Modern Painters* or his definitions of wealth in *Munera Pulveris*. Rather, the economic aesthetic was assimilated unannounced and unexplained in his work. The aesthetic is, therefore, an economic *discourse* because, as a series of embedded ideas, it informs his general view of art production and reception. For example, the discourse is evident in newspapers, pamphlets, and letters, and it permeates his writing on the fine arts, myth, and literature. By nature a group of unwritten assumptions, this discourse is practical, not theoretical: never emerging as a declaration, it appears only in the course of the main arguments and often motivates the points Ruskin makes with such urgency and conviction. For instance, in his last years he pressed for a society of commerce and work based on cooperation, dedication to spiritual and moral life, and shared standards of beauty because he suspected that values had become fragmented and subjective. And he affirmed orthodox theories of production and even pursued them, in Marxian fashion, to their dire implications for all workers, because he sensed a disturbing shift in economic studies toward consumption.

The book's title refers to work of the 1870s and 1880s that harbors economic thought at a crucial point in its development from the eighteenth-century labor theory of value to the current primacy of demand. The latter economy highlights the role of the consumer and seems to have influenced or reinforced Ruskin's sense of audience. It emerged as a premise that Alfred Marshall and Philip Wicksteed called "marginal utility" in the nineties, but it had insinuated itself into Ruskin's writing two decades earlier.

At that time, increasing rates of literacy and cheaper materials created new audiences for books and periodicals and expanded the volume of reading matter available. Whereas in 1814, the first edition of *Waverley* had sold 6,000 copies in six months, in 1871, the penny edition of *Oliver Twist,* in weekly numbers and monthly parts, sold 150,000 copies in three weeks.[1] These figures probably underestimate the number of readers, because one book, whether bought or borrowed, could pass through many large households, including members of the staff. The acceleration of production no doubt obliged Ruskin to face new readers for his own work, and their heterogeneous and largely unknown nature suggested the possibility of subjective value. In this way, larger audiences may have forced current economic thought into Ruskin's writing. Conversely, the aura of economics, both traditional and revolutionary, in aesthetic matters—often evident simply as vulgar commercialism in the art market and the Royal Academy's Picture of the Year, for instance—may have propelled him toward new readerships. The causal relation between the two forces, economics and audience, is in Ruskin's work reciprocal, and an understanding of them as the conditions in which he wrote is crucial to my argument. In this chapter, I shall describe the state of economic theory, prevalent taste, and the market for art and literature, especially as Ruskin perceived them. I then shall sketch the economic and philosophical sources of his strategies for reaching and educating a large audience of varying tastes and backgrounds.

AUDIENCE AS CONTEXT

Ruskin's reaction to public demand for an explanation of art's truth and value created disjunctions in the sense of audience throughout the texts. Sometimes the readership inscribed in a work differs from the one addressed. This discrepancy is apparent in *Fors Clavigera,* as well as in the early Oxford University lectures, especially the first one.[2] At other times, Ruskin focused on readers he had limned indirectly, usually through the art and literature he saw available for sale or viewing. Generally, these readers showed an ignorance of, or lack of interest in, the literary and iconological conventions that had informed his most famous books. These people carried their own frames of reference to the verbal and visual arts. Ruskin believed that all of them were mobile and ambitious, and the narratives presuppose social models a rung or two higher than the level that the context and occasion indicate.

For example, the undergraduates whom Ruskin envisions in his Inaugural lecture are at the top of a class hierarchy, bred to be gentlemen, whereas in reality they most likely were a much more composite group, the children of artisans and earls.[3] The workers of Great Britain to whom Ruskin speaks in *Fors* are not the masses he evokes in his dedication, but a narrower and exclusive group, ranging from the upper-middle classes living in the country to skilled artisans. Indeed, much of what Ruskin said in his letters and lectures outside of Oxford appealed to the *rentiers,* or those aspiring to that class.[4] These people did not work at all, but lived on the profits and savings of their ancestors. Almost all of them were women, as Ruskin knew; his obvious fondness for female readers came as much from his desire to attract a leisured class as from his displaced, and much-discussed, psychological and sexual motives.

Despite his fabrication of an ideal audience from the motley one before him, Ruskin often did try to attract a broader audience by conceding to popular taste and to the power of popularity itself. In his final productive years, he was more and more aware of the gulf between his aesthetics and mass preferences. This gulf was evident in both sales figures for original pictures and the market for reproductions. Not only were businessmen disregarding his and other critics' canons of taste and paying high prices for the paintings they liked, but workers were buying prints of them to decorate the walls of their modest rooms. In an increasingly inflated and frenetic market, dealers satisfied and stimulated the desires of all but the lowest classes by reproducing popular originals as engravings.

The availability of prints allowed people from almost all social levels to enter the art market. For example, George Baxter's highly finished copper or steel engravings cost from three to ten guineas in 1838 when, according to a contemporary account, "people of quality" bought them to commemorate Queen Victoria's coronation; by the year of the Great Exhibition they were advertised as "cheap artistic pictorial illustrations" for "the millions."[5] Landseer's animal paintings, fancy dress portraits, and narrative paintings with an obvious message attracted both the middle and lower classes, who bought them in the progressively cheaper forms of copper engravings, steel engravings, woodcuts, lithographs, chromolithographs, and, eventually, photographic heliogravures. In the 1870s, workingmen's clubs could purchase, on the installment plan, steel engravings for two guineas. By the 1880s, chromolithographs sold for a shilling. A source of profit, they also served as advertisements for the actual paintings and thereby increased attendance at exhibitions.[6] The mutual dependence of painting and print in the mid- and late-nineteenth-century art market indicates the growing influence of mass taste.

The history of Luke Fildes's *Applicants for Admission to a Casual Ward* demonstrates the way a reproduction could usurp the status of an original. This painting, which sold in 1883 for £2,500 to the cotton merchant Thomas Taylor, actually appeared first in 1869 as an illustration in the *Graphic*.[7] Called *Houseless and Hungry,* it was a more accessible form of the acclaimed painting, although as a print it lacked what Walter Benjamin calls *aura,* the "unique phenomenon of distance" of an authentic work of art.[8] In contrast, *The Casuals* had this distance, and allure for viewers: it was only the fourth picture in the history of exhibitions at the Royal Academy that needed a rail to protect it from crowds of spectators.[9] But though it was one-of-a-kind, the picture was not, in a strict sense, the original, but a reproduction of the print. Whereas unapproachability is "a major quality of the cult image," according to Benjamin, "the technique of reproduction detaches the reproduced object from the domain of tradition."[10] In this case, *Houseless and Hungry* had authenticity without distance. As a printed and highly available image, it suggested that mass, rather than cult, perception had begun to define tradition.

Ruskin understood that the cheapness of reproduction would base taste on fashion rather than longstanding tradition. At the time he was writing, the standards of the affluent middle classes determined the most popular subjects for prints. Buyers of expensive oils, as well as those of Baxter prints and illustrated magazines, looked to the visual arts for a message. Compositional values meant little to them (indeed, Ruskin was one of the few critics in the 1870s to explain color, line, and chiaroscuro to the average viewer). Fancy dress portraits were in great demand: the rich commissioned and purchased them; the poor cut them from magazines or hung sixpenny photographs of themselves. J. R. Green, the social historian, wrote of commonly seeing "the array of little portraits stuck over a labourer's fireplace."[11] People preferred domestic over religious or historical subjects, and English over Continental painting. Although the nobility often bought French and Belgian artwork, the newly rich maintained their "illusion that modern English painting was the culmination of all the painting that ever was," comments Gerald Reitlinger, describing the narrow boundaries of Philistine taste. To buy Pre-Raphaelite paintings, he says, "was to invite the reproach of being artistic, the greatest insult which could be hurled at a middle-class family in the classic age of the British matron, when to admire Botticelli was to be thought a cissy."[12] Both popular taste and reproduction were *domestic,* in the double sense of the word. Prints suitable for hanging on the walls of working- and middle-class homes depicted or evoked things English: family life, landscapes, animals, even Anglicized versions of the ancient world. While at Oxford, Ruskin gradually acceded to this preference for English painters and English subjects. He began his first term in 1870 with explanations of the formal properties of art, including sculpture, and with social histories of medieval and Renaissance Italian art, but he ended his second tenure thirteen years later with celebrations of domestic painting and domesticity in lectures on Alma-Tadema, Kate Greenaway, and John Tenniel, among others.

In short, the variety of subjects Ruskin attempted, and his willingness to consider popular illustrations, woodcuts, and various sorts of engravings show that he grasped the impact of both reproduction and exhibition on the whole market of art, which included viewers, artists, and objects. He was aware of the way the media changed aesthetics in the total sense of the word, both as popular taste and, profoundly, as a mode of sensory perception. The alteration of tradition, the diminishing importance of originality, the commercial success of domestic subjects, and the domestication of painting were all trends he simultaneously embraced and rejected. His dual role as a moral aesthetician and a political economist gave him a missionary zeal for attracting a wider audience whose tastes he sometimes shared and often tried to accept. However, this popular aesthetic inevitably threatened his own authority as a critic and educator, as well as the values on which he based his analyses and judgments.

ECONOMICS AS CONTEXT

As an attribution, "popular" suggests fleeting worth. It implies that values themselves are fickle. In granting popular art legitimacy by admitting it, in effect, to Oxford, Ruskin accepted a subjective and shifting basis for value. At other times, he relied on a criterion that was both objective and absolute. His vacillation between unstable and fixed values parallels his ambivalence between the two competing economic theories that governed thinking in the 1870s. These were the labor theory of value and the new utilitarian school centered on demand. Much of my argument in the chapters ahead relies on an understanding of Ruskin's attitude toward each, so I will now sketch his official and inadvertent positions.

Essentially, labor was the bulwark of his aesthetics to the end of his public life. The concept also dominated nineteenth-century economics. Introduced by Aristotle, fortified by John Locke and the French Physiocrats, promoted by David Ricardo, and affirmed by John Stuart Mill, the labor theory was not seriously challenged until the last quarter of the century. According to Alan Lee, the concept permeated nineteenth-century thought as both "a body of conventional science" and "conventional popular wisdom." Considered "essential" in the instruction of the "lower orders," it was part of the curriculum of the National Schools by 1848 and a compulsory subject in men's training colleges from 1863 to 1885.[13] Even Karl Marx's revolutionary *Capital* confirmed that labor was, as Adam Smith declared, the "real measure of the exchangeable value of all commodities."[14] The significance of labor expanded through the century. Whereas Ricardo had excluded nonreproducible commodities such as rare wine, books, and paintings from his discussion, Mill defined labor as both muscular and nervous, thereby bringing works of the imagination and intellect within the domain of the theory. Marx abstracted "labor" into *labor power* and viewed both from what then seemed an anamorphic perspective, that of the individual body.[15] The worker's plight grew from the unequal relation between *labor power,* or the amount necessary for subsistence, and the actual labor exchanged, the constituent value of the goods. The latter was always more, ensuring a surplus value for the manufacturer and the exploitation of the worker.

Ruskin's reading of economic theory was scant; he did not read *Capital,* for instance, which appeared in English in 1886, when his public life was ending. Yet his writing on aesthetics suggests many of the features of labor theory. As I shall discuss in chapter three, he measured the value of a painting by the actual time a great artist spent creating it. The qualification "great" does, of course, separate Ruskin's conception of labor theory from that of the orthodox economists. It indicates genius or imagination, qualities outside the scope of economics. However, in Ruskin's economy, such genius merely becomes the condition under which labor theory operates. Furthermore, although Ruskin never detected a gap between wage and the exchangeable value of a product, and never traced the surplus to a specific agent, as a writer and artist himself he perceived the discrepancy between *labor power* frequently sold as the worker's potential or reputation, and the grueling hours he spent sketching, explaining, and describing. His own exploitation was in one sense figurative because his return did not take the form of poor wages, but of a paltry response. In another sense, though, his dilemma was just as physical as the factory worker's. There runs through *Fors* a mounting horror at the gap between his mental and bodily efforts and his meager subsistence from confused or hostile readers.

Subsistence as reception of meaning is an analogous illustration of Marx's labor theory. But as I shall argue in chapter five, the analogy is one Ruskin assumed, with numerous precedents for doing so. The most important was the Judeo-Christian concept of salvation through suffering. A biblical version of labor theory appeared as early as 1856, in volume three of *Modern Painters,* according to Nick Shrimpton. "For there are two classes of precious things in the world: those that God gives us for nothing—sun, air, and life . . . and the secondarily precious things which He gives us for a price."[16] Ruskin's continuing, implicit conviction that this price was dear, that work—whether industrial or rural, manual or creative—was an emptying rather than a fulfilling activity, fit the Christian paradigm of action. Self-effacing and fatal, the idea was akin to biblical examples of self-mortification and sacrifice. From the material conditions of his own work, he inflated labor into a governing abstraction resembling Judeo-Christian ethics. This is the Feuerbachian inversion that in 1953 Pierre Bigo claimed Marx had maneuvered, in which the "phenomenology of the Mind has simply been changed into that of labor."[17] The idea of deferred remuneration for labor echoed and survived Ruskin's waning belief in Old Testament theology.

Ruskin's identification of himself as a laborer, his borrowing of Ricardian economics in order to describe his own suffering, his abstraction of payment into the reception of his message, and his sense of his writing as a commodity were therefore natural extensions of labor theory as it developed from Smith to Marx.[18] Epitomized in Western metaphysics, the Christian paradigm is built into the economic discourse, which habitually "characterizes both the external economic and moral results of our action as earnings," observes Georg Simmel. He continues:

> Thus, in order for the moral ideals not to deny the moral earnings, the structure of myth among peoples everywhere allows their religious founder to conquer a "temptation" and every Tertullian holds the glory of God to be greater *si laboravit*. Just as the real moral value connects with the restriction that is overcome in a contradictory impulse, so too does economic value connect in the same way. If man performed his work in the same way as the flower performs its flowering or the bird its singing, then no remunerative value would be attached to it.[19]

In *Munera Pulveris* (1862), Ruskin raises the possibility of pleasurable exertion, which turns this dialectical model into an organic one.[20] Under this schema, labor in the fine arts exemplifies the same sort of natural performance as the bird's or the flower's. "The Nature of Gothic" in 1856 celebrates the joyous efforts of the artisan. Certainly Ruskin did not choose Ricardian labor theory as an ideal. The concept was, rather, the paradigm for actual work he had done or witnessed, imaginative as well as manual.

By the 1870s, the ideal of labor had receded, and the seeds of the biblical labor theory buried in the nostalgic paean to the artisan in volume three of *Modern Painters* had grown into a full-scale Ricardian model in which suffering and death inhere in all work. Industrialized labor, with its division of tasks and numbing repetitions, substantiated this view. One of the few sources of Ruskin's ideas, Smith had reached the same conclusion at the end of *Wealth of Nations,* when he commented that a worker's "dexterity at his own particular trade seems . . . to be acquired at the expense of his intellectual, social, and martial virtues."[21] Ruskin eventually came to see all labor within this sacrificial paradigm, partly because he himself was breaking down physically and mentally (he finally collapsed in 1878). In addition, his fear of consumption—a great unknown—and his need as a writer to retain control of his work forced him to insist that demand for labor equalled actual production. One of his chief objections to Mill's *Principles of Political Economy* focused on the confusing statement that a demand for a commodity was not a demand for labor.[22] In maintaining the opposite, Ruskin asserted the supremacy of production over demand and the producer over the consumer in all estimations of value. Ironically, his position echoed that of Mill. One commentator explains the dilemma of Mill, an economist of labor theory confronting new ideas about the role of demand:

> Because of Mill's disinclination to develop a full-fledged theory of consumption in coordination with the theories of production and distribution, these ideas [of utility] failed to be absorbed into the mainstream of the classical tradition as modified by Mill's *Principles*. Mill's reluctance had its point because the development of the theory of the consumer along the principle of marginal utility would have undermined the labor theory of value, as it did later. Since Mill wanted to adhere to the structure of the classical system of which the labor theory of value formed the capstone, he was compelled to neglect the suggestions made by Bentham and by the Oxford and Dublin economists.[23]

Marginal utility would have upset the entire system, and as an economist Mill was essentially an interpreter of the often-difficult Ricardo. In contrast, Ruskin's commitment to labor theory was more emotional than intellectual. A metaphysics of labor filled the void that agnosticism was opening, and it bolstered a critical reputation that the newly literate may not have understood or adequately regarded. The primacy of demand diminished the importance of his work, whereas orthodox economic theory had granted Ruskin and all artists a certain status. Even in Marx's theory, the worker was the purveyor of value, and being a victim was better than being overlooked. Therefore, during the last fifteen years of his career, Ruskin had to advertise himself as a Ricardian martyr to maintain his control of aesthetic meaning and value.

Despite this sense of his own weakening authority, Ruskin was much more willing than Mill to discuss the effect of consumption. Perhaps, as Jeffrey Spear suggests, this is because of his long experience as a consumer himself within the art market.[24] *The Political Economy of Art, The Queen of the Air,* and *Fiction Fair and Foul* do reflect the unsettling effects of demand on meaning and value, even though Ruskin ignored the theoretical developments that were accounting for this influence.

The main proponent of demand-based economics in England was William Stanley Jevons, a review of whose early work Ruskin summarily rejected.[25] The roots of the idea lay in utilitarianism, an anathema to both Ruskin's mentor, Carlyle, and to another self-professed social and moral historian, Dickens. For Jevons's economics borrowed the notion of units of pleasure and pain from Jeremy Bentham, as well as ideas of scarcity from Thomas Robert Malthus. Through mathematical equations involving reciprocal ratios, Jevons deduced the actual existence of a subjective and relative theory of value. This was—or would have been, had he read of it—a double blow to Ruskin: instability had acquired the status of fact. According to Jevons, the effects of pleasure and pain—both expressions of utility—are not intrinsic qualities, but "a circumstance of things arising out of their relation to man's requirements."[26] This subjective or circumstantial utility is *marginal* in the sense of *final* or *least:* it refers to the least-wanted portion of a good, what he calls "the degree of utility of the last addition, or the next possible addition of a very small, or infinitely small, quantity to the existing stock."[27] Jevons arrived at this principle from observing that market prices contradicted the labor theory of value. To his eyes, demand affected price, not costs of production. In fact, no costs of production figure into value at all; it is private and unstable. Moreover, value is not the signified of price, as the Ricardians, including Mill, supposed, for price only indicates *market* value. If a commodity originally priced at $300 sells for $150, its value is not simply $150 if the buyer *would* have paid more; $150 is its present market value, but it may be worth $300 to the purchaser. In this light, value in marginal utility theory denotes how much more one is willing to pay. It has become not only an individual but a comparatively invisible or psychological phenomenon, founded on demand rather than supply.

The elements of value radically shifted with the advent of Jevons's theory in the early 1870s and its development in the work of British economists Alfred Marshall and Philip Wicksteed two decades later. Whereas the orthodox economist had separated exchange- from use-value, Jevons and his successors merged them. In the dawning Victorian economy of consumption, notes Asa Briggs quoting Wicksteed, "'a vast number of things which I desire' entered into a 'circle of exchange' based on choice."[28] Because the economy now centered on demand, the value of a product did not reflect the value of production. Rather, the value of production derived from the value of the product. Labor, no longer a direct determinant of value, became an indirect influence: the quantity of labor affected market- or exchange-value only through its influence on supply, which in turn set the conditions of abundance or scarcity in which personal desire operated.

TEXTUAL SOLUTIONS

In the following chapters, I shall argue that both value and meaning in Ruskin's late writing reflect the transition from orthodox labor theory to marginal utility. And both, as I have said above, are correlatives of the pluralistic, expanding audience that somehow marks all of the texts. At times Ruskin erases the problems resulting from unknown and unknowing readers by gradually excluding them in favor of an ideal audience he creates. At other times, he tries to engage them by *leveling down* (a contemporary expression) through diction, explanation, or familiar examples. *The Queen of the Air,* the lectures on English art of 1883, and some addresses to public groups embrace unknown audiences and unstable values with critical ease; *The Queen* in particular displays an interpretive freedom gone in *Fiction Fair and Foul.* The latter is typical of Ruskin's hostility toward new economics and new audiences. Ruskin alternates between engagement and withdrawal during the period I examine. Often within a single text he recoils from a readership he has been trying to attract just when he realizes that he is jeopardizing his claims of absolute truth or of a fixed value of art. Sometimes, as in his plans for a museum, the subject of chapter eight, he does not see that he has obscured the very audience he thinks he addresses. Because contrary impulses usually undermine or confuse his strategies, his attitude toward his readers can seem bewildering. For this reason, a brief discussion of the economic and philosophical sources of Ruskin's solutions to the problems of addressing a heterogeneous audience will be helpful. I sketch the sources below.

The economic vision Ruskin offers his readers and followers in his industrial experiments and in various texts like *Fiction Fair and Foul* reverts to the archaic value system of the Physiocrats, which fixed all value on land and the labor on it. In 1776 Smith had rejected most tenets of the theory, and, by the late-nineteenth century, it no longer had any relevance to Britain's already flagging industrial economy. In this context, a land-based economy seems escapist and fanciful, filled with conservative, even primitivistic, elements. One of the most pervasive in Ruskin's texts is preindustrial saving. In the idyllic accounts of work he presents in *Fors*, in prefaces to fairy and folk tales, and in plans for a library of great works, Ruskin replaces the interest-gathering capitalist with the peasant hoarder as a model for the reader and writer. Indeed, Ruskin recommends and practices various sorts of stockpiling—of money, goods, and meaning—in order to stop the constant dispersal and transformation of material and aesthetic value. In the 1870s, one could "hoard" land by not treating it as industrial or residential real estate. Thus, Ruskin claimed that farming was the only productive and, by implication, moral use of land.

This concrete and figurative miserliness seems less fanciful in historical context. For Ruskin developed these models in an age of agricultural depression, when land to him had become the commodity of ultimate value, and the country was surviving on finance and foreign imports, particularly from the undeveloped world. In this light, the Guild of St. George reestablished land as the base of an economy that in reality was depending more and more on investment—"invisible" income rather than measurable goods. As a solution, then, the guild was a misreading of a contemporary situation, for the Great Depression of 1873-96 resulted from a market surplus, not a lack of food; the diminishing costs of transport had made food cheap, especially in urban areas throughout Europe.[29] Ironically, in setting up the guild to buy property, Ruskin evinced a domestic form of the imperialism that drove the financiers. His speculative side was in part disguised by a physiocratic notion of land as capital, and by the language of social reform.

Ruskin thought of his enterprise as cooperative rather than capitalistic and even called himself a "Communist," a word he probably knew from Mill's description of English socialism in the *Principles*. This brand of communism promoted community property, but it also accepted social inequality, grounded on principles of justice rather than accident such as inheritance.[30] With this conviction that society must be both cooperative and hierarchical, he redefined archaic terms of honor and privilege such as *lord* and *inheritance* to merge social and moral ascendancy. But his obsession with the words in countless texts from *Sesame and Lilies* in 1865 to his essay on picture galleries in 1880 conjures the antiquated social differences that had faded with the agrarian culture at least two generations before.

In addition to these terms, Ruskin loaded his description of physiocratic economies with vaguely moral words such as *spirit, truth,* and *life*. His experiments in publishing, his cottage industries, and his land purchases were all romantic returns to nature, and followers, including E. T. Cook, wrote of them as antiscientific, antitechnological ventures. Simplifying production and promoting natural processes were part of a new metaphysics in which health, goodness, and truth blended. His efforts resemble those of many proto-Marxists—most markedly of later European intellectuals such as Karl Mannheim, Georg Lukács, and Arnold Hauser, who, like Ruskin, made collectivism and the culture of the Middle Ages their ideal. In retrospect, Ruskin's ideas seem portentous because they were later assimilated into Bolshevism. At the time, however, these ideas looked like conservative efforts to regulate all forms of production and consumption. And although the ideas stressed healthy living, they were neither reformist in their approach nor humane in their focus. Instead, they exemplified the older and mythical England, which the newly moneyed classes were trying to imitate. The fashion for a rustic culture spread through architecture, sports, even literature. Renewed attention to thatched cottages and hunting, as well as Arnold's bucolic packaging of Wordsworth in the popular anthology of 1879, typifies the merry England of the middle-class businessman's imagination.[31] In 1937, the *Master's Report of the Guild* expresses the same romantic and elusive vision: "We must hold fast to the values he [Ruskin] has taught us to cherish, as we seek the revival of England as essential to the health of our people, as we strive to promote the education of young and old in the training of hand and eye, heart and brain, mind and spirit, in reverence for beauty and truth, and in fellowship with others."[32]

In practice, these goals were not good business. For example, neither the land-purchasing scheme nor the spinning and weaving projects flourished.[33] Yet the bad business practices of the guild, its romantic trappings, and its image as a philanthropic group obscure the capitalistic basis of its beginning. Ruskin started the guild to buy land. He was convinced that England's resources for farming and forestry were vanishing, and he acted mainly from what today we would call survivalistic fear. St. George's must be seen within his enduring worry over an economy of scarcity, which his reading of Smith's *Wealth of Nations* and his physiocratic leanings would have aggravated. Unlike Marx, Ruskin did not apply scarcity to the lack of demand for labor. For a promoter of an ethical, altruistic society and a Malthusian, he is uninterested in the effects of an economy of scarcity on human beings. Instead, he is eager to save the land and to produce durable goods. In the published accounts of his industries, disciples portray the work force as a highly select labor aristocracy of skilled artisans. Only in private correspondence do the humane effects of the guild appear: disciple Egbert Rydings once grumbled that most of the employees at St. George's Mill on the Isle of Man were charity cases; philanthropy was not Ruskin's chief intention.[34]

One could argue that regreening the land and controlling the market were humanitarian goals because they would have relieved the plight of workers. Rydings' revival of archaic machinery—for example, the spinning wheel—would preclude the alienation and objectification of the modern laborer. Yet Ruskin did not see these as solutions to human suffering. He launched his social schemes even as he came to associate exploitation and sacrifice with all kinds of labor. The Christian and Ricardian perspectives from which he viewed work both function within an economy of scarcity. Marx's description in 1844 of generic labor expresses the Ruskinian view: "The more the worker by his labor *appropriates* the external world, hence sensuous nature, the more he deprives himself of *means of life* in a double manner: first, in that the sensuous external world more and more ceases to be an object belonging to his labor—to be his labor's *means of life;* and secondly, in that it more and more ceases to be *means of life* in the immediate sense, means for the physical subsistence of the worker."[35]

Marx's idea of double appropriation—that labor consumes the sensuous world and thereby robs the worker of his own means of living—has dire consequences in an economy of scarcity. In a very literal way, the concept pervades *Fiction Fair and Foul* and *The Queen of the Air,* among other texts, in which Ruskin describes land, sky, and water as the waste of a nature consumed by factories and concomitant industrial growth, a nature in which no healthy work is possible. Those laboring within a world that in effect their work already has used up must move to untouched land. Because *all* labor feeds off nature in this double way, working without machines will merely slow the rate of appropriation, creating the semblance of a cyclical, harmonious relationship with nature. Ruskin's project can only work, then, if it fails—that is, if St. George's can increase its landholdings and real estate but keep its membership relatively small. The illusion of abundance will then be maintained, as will the organic connection between human beings and nature.[36] Within an economy of scarcity, acquisition and exclusivity ensure the survival of the guild, which today thrives as a tiny but rich organization.

Ruskin inflates scarcity beyond its agronomical significance in Malthus and Smith and its implications for the body in Marx into a concept of physical lack governing all estimations of value. He does not succeed in formulating a convincing theory of aesthetic valuation based on this concept partly because he clings to an incompatible sense of absolute worth. The only truth in an economy of scarcity is the inevitability of the limit, whether production or consumption sets the value. Ruskin never admits this, but the course of his writing, especially in *Fors,* verifies a universe of scarcity. Having extended the labor theory

to the creation of nonreproducible commodities, he views the artist's resources as objective and external to the creator, just like Marx's "sensuous nature." Imagination, like physical energy and skill, is not to him infinitely replenishable. As a result, increased production of words and images often means circulating the same thing under different, sometimes even the same, signifiers. To prevent a flooded market and an exhausted worker, Ruskin asserts but refuses to explain the presence of an absolute meaning and intrinsic value for art. Exclusivity and retention, his legacy to the guild, confer the highest value on the rare or unexchangeable object.

Accordingly, his crucial statements about aesthetic truth and value are retentive and romantic, despite his commitment to art education. Throughout the first series of Oxford lectures, he asserts the Hegelian notion that all art expresses its own internal laws, that the "search for physical accuracy is merely the external operation, in the arts, of the seeking for truth in the inner soul" (20:228). Such a statement assumes a hermeneutics of total, unchanging equivalence, in which anything can mean everything else. Louis Althusser describes the effects of the Hegelian aesthetic in this way: "[Hegel's model] presupposes in principle that the whole in question be reducible to an *inner essence,* of which the elements of the whole are then no more than the phenomenal forms of expression, the inner principle of the essence being present at each point in the whole, such that at each moment it is possible to write the immediately adequate equation: such and such an element (economic, political, legal, literary, religious, etc, in Hegel) = the inner essence of the whole."[37]

The educational, historical, and monetary models Ruskin created during the 1870s and 1880s all functioned within this anagogic universe. He relied on a spatial schema to withdraw from the demands of a heterogeneous reading public and a economy of constantly changing value. The organic resolution of differences in meaning and value was, of course, hardly practicable, for it relied on the mystical authority of the artist critic and the metamorphosis of contemporary readers into synthetic audience with the same material background, knowledge, and values.

Last resorts in a sphere of uncontrollable demand, these models also grew from Ruskin's stationary and romantic idea of history. The notion had served the polemic of *The Stones of Venice*, in which a golden age of trade and religious faith, as well as its passing, became a paragon and a warning for industrial England. Similar analogies occur in *Val d'Arno*, the lectures of 1873. The glorification of tribal communities and a sense of history as cataclysmic rather than evolutionary evade implicitly opposed, current assumptions. The notion had been voguish in midcentury, particularly in the work of Oxford historian Thorold Rogers. As Alon Kadish points out, the proponents of a golden-age theory perceived all contemporary reforms "as the restoration of ancient rights." Naturally, in doing so, they "established class antagonisms and conspiracy as historical phenomena which were likely to recur."[38] As in *The Stones of Venice*, warfare among Italian city-states in *Val d'Arno* is a natural process, and class distinctions, with the attendant strife and misery, likewise appear inevitable. This romantic view furnishes another reason for Ruskin's attention to landscapes and cityscapes rather than to specific human abuses: the attacks on existing conditions and attempted reforms maintain the "natural" separation of classes. Ignoring current dialectical views of history, Ruskin seeks a stationary state through analogies and retention, theoretical as well as monetary.

These remedies for a fragmenting culture were conservative; they derived from ideas and methods that were decades, even centuries old. Yet amidst this nostalgia and mythologizing is a vibrant sense of the world of facts, for Ruskin also records the way he sees aesthetics operating in the public sphere. With reluctance and anger, he depicts the sort of billiard-ball causality between monetary base and cultural superstructure which some critics argue remains a valid explanation of the changes resulting from nineteenth-century publishing and readerships.[39] At bottom, he is cynical about the actual production of value; it is uncontrollable and fleeting, and it results from the enormous demands on the laborer within a world of limited material, physical, and mental resources. Consequently, the worker is condemned to exploitation and the art object to continuous revaluation and debasement. As a political economist,

Ruskin was certain enough of this dismal process to inflate it into an implicit law; his concepts of labor and exchange are sublated into abstractions, absolutes of sacrifice and change.

The links between the romantic solution and mechanical system, and the way they subvert each other in Ruskin's final work, are the focus of the next seven chapters. Chapter two characterizes the university audience of the 1870s and 1880s in order to explain Ruskin's choice of lecture topics and the tone and imagery of his written addresses for readers inside and outside of Oxford. Chapters three and four delineate the economic model he presented piecemeal through comments about labor and studies of money; the latter become one of his most complex attempts to teach art to a newly literate audience. Chapter five shows the effects of the economic discourse on his readings of art and myth, especially the way his hermeneutics and his notion of value had absorbed an aesthetic version of exchange-value. The operation of these ideas in Ruskin's writing and projects for the laboring classes are explored in the three remaining chapters. The political economy Ruskin had invented in the early sixties has little to do with any of these subjects, for it had not permeated his habitual perception and understanding of art.[40] Instead, this political economy was undermined by the economic discourse, signs of which are everywhere. It constitutes the orthodox thought he rejected and the new theories he dismissed. It frames his observations, and it turns his final work into a drama of economic transitions.

Ruskin at Oxford: The Problem of Audience

When Ruskin joined Oxford University in 1870 as Slade Professor of Art, he was famous as an aesthetician, a philosopher, and a critic of perception and taste. Yet it was his political economy, rather than *Modern Painters,* that was already part of the university curriculum. Benjamin Jowett, who became Master of Balliol College in the same year, used excerpts from *Unto This Last* and *Munera Pulveris* to convey to students his vision of an egalitarian Oxford representing social and intellectual diversity. To some extent, the university had the broad constituency Jowett wanted. A typical entering class of the 1870s comprised a high proportion of public-school men and a large number of Scots, as well as many privately educated students who depended on scholarships and would have to find jobs—in private schools or the civil service, perhaps—immediately after graduation.[1] Confronting a mixed, but often cliquish, student body, Ruskin promoted his own ideal of a unified Oxford, one resting on social differences it would eliminate. Whereas Jowett hoped that the earl and the artisan would learn from each other and enrich university culture, Ruskin assumed that all artisans wanted to be earls. His Inaugural lecture, in particular, appeals to ambition rather than class loyalty. Likewise, his later lectures during the semester offer aspirants elitist material, including the moral aesthetic from *Modern Painters* based on a small canon of great artists, and art history as a record of nationalistic movements and military conquests.

In his first series of lectures at Oxford, Ruskin effaces the composite audience, but, in the late 1870s, he tries to reckon with its perspective. Aware of the power of popular taste in the market, particularly exhibitions, he engages readers who have developed standards with no reference to the principles in *Modern Painters*. The art he now discusses ratifies middle-class satisfaction, rather than ambition. However, such contentment rests on the same vision Ruskin conjures for the undergraduates: a preeminent but rural, hierarchical, and static country of some vaguely recent past that both grew from and contrasted with the England, as well as the Oxford, of the 1870s and 1880s.

OXFORD: EXTENSION AND THE INAUGURAL LECTURE

Ruskin came to Oxford at a time when the universities were competing for influence and jurisdiction throughout the country. Following Cambridge, Oxford began offering extension classes in various cities in 1878, but, as early as 1857, it had established a Middle Class Examination providing a common standard by which students in middle schools could compare themselves. In 1872, a joint board of both universities began inspecting the work of public schools through three kinds of examinations and offering successful students certificates that signified "something like a degree" and possessed "a definite university value."[2] The board hoped that, with encouragement, promising students would bring their certificates to Oxford. Because many institutions—including the Civil Service Commission, the College of Surgeons, and the Royal Institute of Architects—used these certificates to replace all or part of their own entrance exams, the two universities were now, W. R. Ward comments, "indirectly governing the standards of entry to professions whose education they had either let slip, or had never undertaken."[3] Starting in the 1860s, the university attempted to increase the demand for its degree by expanding its resident audiences, too, and Oxford's matriculation had increased by 50 percent from 1862 to 1872. New kinds of students appeared with the reduction of residency requirements in the early 1870s; and in 1870 women were admitted to the Associate in Arts examination.[4]

With the German institutions as their models, both English universities changed policies that had connected them with specific professions or classes. In 1871 Cambridge and Oxford abolished the Tests, which were religious exams restricting posts and emoluments to Anglican graduates. They considered ways to obscure the universities' image as a place of privilege and to enhance their reputation as centers of inquiry. At Oxford, prizes granted to nonresident fellows for life, as well as the open scholarships frequently given to wealthy matriculants of little intellectual distinction, were increasingly seen as a waste of money, especially when these funds could be used to enhance the university's reputation as a center for research. With these changes in the 1860s and 1870s, Oxford inched toward a more intellectual, less elite standard of education.

The debates over these new policies were often long and complicated, but in the end Oxford, as well as Cambridge, was compelled to change by the growing access to higher education outside its halls. Independent colleges had appeared in provincial cities, including Sheffield, Leeds, and Liverpool. As an Oxford *University Extension Report* of 1866 shows, the university realized that the training of clergy was passing from its hands: there had been 319 fewer ordinations in the last eight years than in the preceding eight, but 674 new parishes in the last ten years.[5] In order to attract candidates who could not afford the often extravagant expenses associated with university life, committee members proposed various ways to reduce the costs of living and even the temptations to spend money. Both Cambridge and Oxford began offering courses in other cities, and the *University Extension Report* outlined a plan for affiliation with the new institutions in these places. The ethos of the ancient universities began to alter slowly in response to a new middle-class patron who was willing to circumvent Oxford and Cambridge altogether in pursuit of higher education.

The issues of extension and endowments created a problematic relationship between Oxford and potential students, particularly the working-class intellectual or radical. For example, Christopher Harvie notes that the controversy over the Tests "necessitated an appeal to national politics, and reinforced an alignment with Nonconformist radicalism: for nine years it linked the universities, Liberal politics, Nonconformity and the intellectual world of London."[6] Because no one, on matriculating, had to sign the Articles, there was, as records of an 1866 report on the religious Tests show, "no legal obstacle . . . to the admission of Dissenters, *as students* at either [university]."[7] But even though the question of the Tests became part of election programs after 1867, neither university began instantly to draw a population it had for years excluded. The "nonconformist world at large cared very little for admission to universities, and especially to Oxford, which was known to be full of Puseyism and other bad influences," writes Ward.[8] University men and their families did become involved in local programs such as the temperance and public-health movements and the school boards, and their intervention may have united Oxford with some townspeople, but cooperation, according to Harvie, was intermittent.[9]

The university pursued new territory and working-class students with missionary zeal. It considered its extension movement a way to convert radicals from revolutionary socialism to gradual reform. Fittingly, one of its first and most publicized courses was in political economy.[10] However, both universities' support of the Charity Organization Society (C.O.S.) alienated the working classes. The C.O.S. coordinated private charity and regulated public almsgiving with the Poor Law. It consisted largely of liberals and members of the university, who no doubt favored the workhouse test and the curtailing of outdoor relief, for the dismal financial position of the colleges had resulted from the rise in the poor rate during the agricultural depression. Self-interest thus lay at the basis of the policy, bolstered as Harvie describes it, by an economic philosophy of free markets: "University liberals enforced the Poor Law not from any hostility to the working classes but because they saw outdoor relief as a threat to the independence of the individual and a distortion of the working of market economics."[11] This practical allegiance to laissez-faire economics and the concomitant myth, which Ruskin also espoused, of the free man and woman, estranged the university from the working classes even as it extended its domain through lectures, affiliation, and supervision in middle schools and colleges. [12]

In one way, Oxford's extension and efforts to endow research stressed individual achievement rather than social qualifications and thus signaled a new philosophy of education. The reform of the Greats course was another milestone in the university's quest for, and accommodation of, new audiences with new demands; it replaced a survey of classical literature, ancient history, and philosophy with a more concentrated, thus more "professional" curriculum. [13] However, in another way these changes also exemplified opposing directions of university growth. For as it moved toward the provinces and opened itself to a heterogeneous group of students, the university also began to redefine its intellectual values in a manner that isolated it from the socioeconomic forces that were expanding its audience. Oxford was becoming a "separate, internally satisfying world," remarks Harvie; "the need to go beyond it, into the political world, for a life which was meaningful and responsible diminished." [14]

During his two terms as Slade Professor—from 1870 to 1878 and from 1883 to 1884—Ruskin wrote and lectured with an idea of audience which reflected this ambivalent movement in the university. The tone of his lectures, his etiology of aesthetic value, and his judgments of particular works of art parallel the extension movement, the specialization of curriculum, and the diversion of endowments in their missionary attitude toward, and isolation from, the lower levels of the student market.

In his Inaugural lecture at Oxford, Ruskin outlines an aesthetic mission and posits an audience that reflects the social tensions within the university itself. He begins by applauding recent reforms in the curriculum that offer students more practical knowledge earlier than did the old program of study based on "abstract branches of literature and philosophy" (20:18). He stresses, however, that the universities are not training apprentices or professionals. Instead, they still are forming gentlemen who, he explains in a long footnote appended to one of the drafts of the lecture, compose a "captaincy" over the poor. Their moral dispositions are both "gentle" and "noble," he stresses, characteristically endowing virtue with social distinction; he will continue to combine the aristocracy and the gentry throughout his writings as interchangeable signifiers in his social metaphors of ethics. The chief duty of Oxford graduates is to "feed and clothe" the underclass "by leading them in disciplined troops to fruitful labour by land and sea" (20:19n.3). The military and imperialistic rhetoric in this lecture, which Ruskin wrote *not* to offend officials at Oxford, is pronounced (though Jowett thought it in "very poor taste").[15] "Reign or die," he tells his listeners. England must "found colonies as fast and as far as she is able, formed of her most energetic and worthiest men;— seizing every piece of fruitful waste ground she can set her foot on" (20:42). Recalling this exhortation at his own inaugural lecture, Slade Professor Kenneth Clark cringes at his predecessor's "doctrines of conquest, dominion, and obedience."[16] Ruskin's words seem so ominous not only because in light of them Oxford's extension becomes class-colonizing but also because such imperialistic motives looked particularly sinister in 1947, the year Clark wrote his speech. Indeed, both the progressive social forces that drew Oxford into the provinces and the intellectual ambitions that fortified it against social and political turbulence (at least in theory) were forms of the imperialism that Terry Eagleton correlates with the rise of academia in the late nineteenth century.[17]

Ruskin's cultural imperialism was directed toward class rather than international relations, but, like the larger imperialistic movements of the country, it sought to eliminate cultural difference. In the ideal of a homogeneous Oxford, the lower levels would assimilate and disappear. Ruskin accomplishes this goal in the Inaugural by stirring nationalistic feelings in his audience, then associating this Englishness with the upper classes. In this way, listeners connect national loyalty and chauvinism with their own social ambitions. For example, he calls the English the "race mingled of the best northern blood" (20:41) and education "not the equalizer, but the discerner, of men" (20:20). Aesthetic values seem to be hereditary, and only "noble races" can enjoy their country's natural beauties (20:36). Here, Ruskin suggests that this nobility inheres in the whole English nation, not simply the upper classes. He seems sincere; if he truly believed that the aesthetic faculty lay only in certain bloodlines, he would not have tried for the next fifteen years to educate the ineducable.

However, as the examination of Turner and Giorgione in volume five of *Modern Painters* years before had shown, he believed that surroundings condition individual sight and define pleasure. If environment governs what and how people see, social class would be as deterministic as genes. Ruskin expresses this belief most clearly ten years after the Inaugural in the first essay of *Fiction Fair and Foul,* but now, in a conciliatory mood, he resorts to the idea of national characteristics to resolve social divisions. Like another contemporary study of perception and taste, Matthew Arnold's *Culture and Anarchy,* his writing presents a fabricated notion of "the English" to obscure class differences, which are the real and obvious subject.

The class chauvinism of the Inaugural, which Clark understandably links with Fascism, is also the early rhetoric of the social welfare state. The really troublesome issues in England in the nineteenth century were domestic, not foreign, and Ruskin transferred foreign-policy jingoism to the current unmentionable: class conflict. In retrospect, his appeal seems distasteful to us, but the public then felt comfortable with the aggressive, monarchical rhetoric—Ruskin used it because it was acceptable. His tone, of largesse and noblesse oblige, applies to a privileged few. Yet it is precisely the composition of the group who actually heard Ruskin's speech that makes its feudal politics unsuitable, because these Oxford students did not all represent the social elite whom Ruskin addressed. Most likely, many were sons of newly rich manufacturers. These scions of industrialists and tradesmen were modeling themselves after aristocrats such as Albert Edward, the Prince of Wales. The gentlemanly ideal was for them and Ruskin an ethic circumscribed by class. "The Ethos of later-Victorian Oxbridge, a fusion of aristocratic and professional values, stood self-consciously in opposition to the spirit of Victorian business and industry," comments Martin J. Wiener. "It exalted a dual ideal of cultivation and service against philistine profit seeking. Businessmen were objects of scorn and moral reproval, and industry was noted chiefly as a despoiler of country beauty."[18] When Ruskin blames the economic distress of the middle classes on *"living always up to their incomes"* and *"imagining that they can subsist in idleness upon usury,"* he attacks their simulation of inheritance through the manipulation of capital (20:40). Yet when he states a few lines later that the current economic depression will compel English families "to learn that food can only be got out of the ground," he evokes an agrarian economy linked in the minds of his audience with the gentry. Ruskin does not say that they themselves should work the land. His passive construction hands the labor of farming to an unnamed agent. The place of the English families is left equivocal; it easily could be construed as supervisory. On the surface, then, Ruskin's censuring of recent wealth as interest from investments accumulated through the surplus value wrested from laborers could have offended his audience. But many in the group were not the industrialists but their sons, and they were intent on using their patrimonies to finance an archaic lifestyle. Ruskin encouraged them to change the basis of their economy, not their position in it.

"The late nineteenth-century British man of business, like any third-generation figure, viewed the entrepreneurial aggressiveness of his grandfather with distaste," notes Louis Menand.[19] Ruskin's message suited an audience at the perhaps inevitable stage of disaffection from fathers and grandfathers who encouraged the atavistic ideals of their children. The contempt for making money and for industry and machines that runs through this and succeeding lectures appealed to the self-hatred inherent in all bourgeois ambition. The allusions to and metaphors of monarchy and of the Anglican Church in the Inaugural imply a rigid sense of hierarchy that the newly rich associated with the lives of warriors and eighteenth-century gentlemen. It was a world that had vanished forever but one that Oxford undergraduates and Ruskin, the son of a sherry merchant, tried to revive under transformed conditions. Toward the end of the Inaugural lecture, he offers them two alternate bases for new societies, signified by the archaic military image of the oriflamme. Which one, Ruskin asks, "shall we plant on the farthest islands,—the one that floats in heavenly fire, or that hangs heavy with foul tissue of terrestrial gold"? (20:42). In such heated, jingoistic rhetoric, "heavenly fire" suggests the missionary energy of England's colonizers, and the "tissue of terrestrial gold" they are to reject implies the infrastructure of the capitalistic economy that now supports them. The sentence intimates that "gold" and "heavenly fire" are separable, that cultural values can be divorced from the economic structure of a society.

This passage is wishful thinking, for in his examination of political economy in the 1860s and his diatribes against interest and capital throughout *Fors Clavigera,* Ruskin presupposes that the economic builds in all value, aesthetic and moral. The mechanical view of economic conditions as a causal force does not inform the exhortation above, but neither does it prevent the England of the Inaugural from becoming a nation of shared standards, for the newly rich audience it inscribes is eager to adopt the official culture that Ruskin the established art critic offers. Aesthetic value, he tells the undergraduates, is a combination of the artist's labor and the market, and the latter is a "vast and new patronage" by persons of "sudden" wealth. These people are "earnest and conscientious" purchasers who "would be glad to promote the true interests of art in this country" if they knew them (20:24). This hope, the basis of his educational schemes, lies in the belief that the recently empowered class knows or can learn the correct cultural values, that they have the seeds of English nobility. They lack only exposure: beauty—of landscape, for instance—"can only be enjoyed by cultivated persons; and it is only by music, literature, and painting, that cultivation can be given" (20:36). It is this assumption that makes the Inaugural characteristic of the imperialistic and missionary attitude of various university extension programs and that earned it the praise of officials. The speech presents a relatively fluid nation in which people strive to be a rigid, static one. Its progressively hortative tone makes Ruskin's faith in the enduring values of a hierarchical society, as well as his belief in the educability of the middle classes, seem at bottom wistful.

This optative mood reflects the composite audience Ruskin saw as he wrote. The Inaugural suppresses its members by correlating their social ambitions with a vision of a unified, traditional culture. Thus, with the aspiring squire in mind, he could depict the marketplace as an arena of total equivalency in the best of all economic worlds: "It is one of the facts which the experience of thirty years enables me to assert without qualification, that a really good picture is ultimately always approved and bought, unless it is wilfully rendered offensive to the public by faults which the artist has been either too proud to abandon or too weak to correct" (20:24–25).

Yet five years after the Inaugural, in discussing a popular painting by Elizabeth Thompson at the Royal Academy, he is surprised to like it: "I thought what the public made such a fuss about *must* be good for nothing" (14:308). Arguably, the "public" he conjures here differs from the capitalistic "aristocrats" he addresses in his first speech at Oxford. If this is true, then Ruskin's sense of audience in his Oxford lectures, at least in his initial speech, has little to do with his vision of the public outside the university, for the latter group's good taste is the exception rather than a rule by the mid-1870s. Ruskin effaces this view with his metaphors of medieval heraldry and various images of hieratic hierarchies at the end of the lecture, but elsewhere he betrays his dismal faith in economics as the etiology of value. He believes, in short, in the mechanical model: that the system of production and exchange creates the audience for art. Now the public, a collective term for gradations of both middle and lower classes—debased products of their material and economic conditions—has not only bad but also unredeemable taste.

The economic view of value, which Ruskin carries from his study of political economy in the 1860s, grows more distinct during the 1870s. By his second tenure at Oxford, he perceives university audiences as much less exclusive, much more susceptible to fashion, than he had during his first term and consequently, perhaps, his attitude toward them grows hostile. Whereas in the Inaugural, he speaks in league with listeners of the virtues of the national mind, in a notorious lecture of November 1884, he shows them a picture of a pig as a "type" of the honest Protestant (33:509). In fourteen years, many things have embittered him. Yet the Inaugural lecture is probably an unfair standard by which to measure Ruskin's sympathy, because its conception of both England and the English is necessarily optative. Ruskin had to begin his tenure at Oxford with what Pierre Macherey calls "a subjective pact, according to which a general tacit confidence would be established between the author and his potential readers before even the mediation of the actual work." Macherey thinks a pact such as this is illusory, in part because it "assumes" an "imaginary site which precedes and prepares for the work."[20] This imagined place, which made the Inaugural lecture possible, was an Oxford characterized by class aspiration and denial. Ruskin's desire for such a place relied on a vision of a holistic world in which economics and culture still reflected each other, but in which social mobility and shifting demographics did not change dominant tastes and values. Evidence itself of class fluidity and tension, his desire perpetuated an organic view of history that was conveniently Calvinistic: the ambitious middle classes, elided in the Inaugural by the "noble" English race, somehow already had the aesthetic and ethical values they were at Oxford to acquire.

LEVELING UP OR DOWN

When in his second lecture of 1870 Ruskin spoke to his audience of "our duty" to anchor belief in "rational" proofs of the Divine (20:60), he was separating listeners who understood myth and metaphor as figures from unsophisticated, literal readers outside of Oxford and, most likely, of the middle classes. These simple readers mistook images as evidence of reality, and Ruskin's idea of the way to reach this group differed from the method he used to engage university students in his early years as Slade Professor. The New and Revised Edition of these lectures on art, which appeared in 1887, contained the following note: "I have expunged a sentence [from lecture two of 1870] . . . having come to reverence more, as I grew older, every simple means of stimulating all religious belief and affection" (20:60).

The omitted sentence condemns allowing "undisciplined fancy" to stimulate ideas of divinity. Since 1846 Ruskin had used "fancy" in a traditional and faintly pejorative way, as an illustrative and arbitrary invention: it "sees the outside" whereas the imagination "sees the heart and inner nature" (4:253). By 1887 he seems willing to provide naïve readers with the verbal and visual outside even though they may mistake it for the inner and divine. In effect, his retraction condones any means to evoke or explain the abstractions of the spirit, even if it becomes a mimetic rather than a figural image in the eyes of readers.

Producing signs in bad faith—because they are conscious fictions—seemed by the late nineteenth century a legitimate way to educate the newly literate working classes. Mayakovsky would use it to create a proletarian art in the early years of the Russian revolution. This sort of reaching down never became a national trend in Great Britain, but merely part of a perpetual dilemma. One letter of 1883 in the *Oxford Magazine* presents alternative ways of educating the lower orders:

> The ideal of an old fashioned Democrat is "a Government of the people, by the people, for the people"; he does not think all communities are ready for such a form of Government, but this is always his ideal, so that measures tending to educate and train the masses for political life are most welcome to him. . . . A Tory Democrat's ideal of Democracy is a very different thing, viz., "a government by the best for the good of all"; in other words the ideal Democracy of a Tory Democrat is an Aristocracy. . . . In order to bring the masses up to this high standard . . . [the previous correspondent] proposes simply to "level them up." The old-fashioned Democrat, the Radical in Birmingham, "levels down," whilst truly cultured Democrats (Tory) "level up."[21]

In *Praeterita* Ruskin defines himself as a Tory "of the old school;—Walter Scott's school, that is to say, and Homer's" (35:13); he had, remarks Clark, "a contempt for democracy in all its forms" although the form in which Ruskin derides it is always industrial capitalism, with its "law" of laissez-faire competition and its production of surplus value.[22] His family's own roots in trade and in evangelical Christianity brought him closer to the lower end of the middle classes than his professed Toryism suggests, but his position as a wealthy and preeminent art critic allowed him to surmount his class origins and cultivate others as he had been cultivated—by leveling up. The Oxford correspondent's description of the Tory Democratic ideals match Ruskin's: the choice of feudal and hieratic images in the Inaugural lecture, and later of Carlyle, Plato, and Napoleon III as educational authorities most likely looked autocratic to the working-class portion of Ruskin's intended audience.

Unlike Arnold, however, who was a candid advocate of leveling up, Ruskin ostensibly believed in leveling down in matters of culture, particularly when he addressed audiences outside of Oxford. The method seemed to him the only practicable way to educate Birmingham radicals and laborers to appreciate and understand the great books and paintings that exemplified a nation's taste and perception. Obviously this sort of leveling down maintained the Tory Democrat's ideal of government, because it converted the masses to the aesthetic of the ruling classes. Ruskin may have been fooling himself as well as his audience, but his efforts to adopt popular perception to "educate and train the masses" did in some sense level down.

For example, political economy now colored his notions of artistic value in a way, he thought, that the general public understood. He was familiar with the generally accepted labor theory of value and extended it to artistic production, which he equated with other kinds of work. I will discuss the strain of Ricardian labor theory in Ruskin's late aesthetics in later chapters. For now, I want simply to note that Ruskin applied the conditions and consequences of modern labor to both painter and bricklayer and that this was a common equation by midcentury. As Helene E. Roberts explains, "To the critics writing for the Victorian periodicals the artist seemed not so much a lonely genius . . . but a producer of goods that . . . if purchased, would embellish the home and bring pleasure to its inhabitants."[23] The National Institution of Fine Arts expressed this view. Its first catalogue in 1847 announced, "A picture, a statue, and a shawl are made for exchange."[24] The public's view of painting as furniture, the power of the various societies, especially the Royal Academy, to decide place on the wall and even to "varnish" or touch up canvasses, and the growing importance of picture dealers throughout the century all diminished the control of artists over the execution and sale of their work and conjured in the public's eye a vision of an art market rather than an individual creator. "Liberal" or free art—art which in Kant's aesthetic must not be exchanged—"cannot produce itself, in its freedom," says Jacques Derrida, "without the very thing that it subordinates to itself, without the force of mechanical structure which in every sense of the word it *supposes*—the mechanical agency, mercenary, laborious, deprived of pleasure."[25] Ruskin and others certainly sensed that this agency empowered everyone in the art-market, including the consumers. Marion Harry Spielmann, editor and art critic for the *Graphic, Pall Mall Gazette,* and the *Magazine of Art,* adopted what Julie F. Codell calls an "economic language" for the popular press, just as Ruskin applied the labor theory of value to art.[26] By applying part of the economic discourse to aesthetics, he conceded to popular perception.

In his attempts to attract the general public to a canon of great books and pictures, Ruskin, like Arnold, was practicing what then seemed ethical indoctrination. Unlike Arnold, however, he fabricated a homogeneous society and superstructure that would develop from a revolutionized economy, one more like the Birmingham radical's than the Tory Democrat's. Like cooperative labor, this culture would not unite but reconcile the various antipathetic classes of England. Erasing the sentence that contained "undisciplined fancy" from the New and Revised Edition of his *Lectures on Art* exemplifies one way to fabricate this culture. Arguably, in this instance Ruskin merely has acknowledged the effectiveness of putting concepts into familiar images and words, and such translation represents for the Tory Democrat the best way to level up because it circulates the same ideas and values behind different terms. However, in using a tactic which he knew resulted in popular misreading, Ruskin was not preserving the traditional concept intact; instead, he was modifying signs. Allen Hoey has remarked that "value alters with usage, for each utterance is dually diachronic: grounded in a particular moment, it is nonetheless influenced, even determined, by all prior usage and at the same time exerting pressure on future usage."[27] In this way when Ruskin tried to form a cooperative culture by manipulating visual and verbal signs, he inadvertently leveled down, for like the artist, he could not control the reception of images.

During the 1870s and 1880s, Ruskin tried in various ways to draw readers from the working classes, but in his official position at Oxford he had to capture the interests of a more exclusive group. Therefore, in his catalogues and critical notes he addressed or discussed the middle and lower classes, while as Slade Professor, he sought a more exclusive following. Even with this division, the university's undergraduates did not constitute the homogeneous body he often pretended they were, and the advertised topics of the lectures of 1883–84 indicate a slight leveling down to a middle-class group of nonspecialists.

Whereas the first series (1870–78) included technical lectures on landscape and sculpture and medieval histories of Tuscan art and heraldry, the second series (1883–84) concerned contemporary English painting and drawing. In the Spring of 1883, he spoke about artists whose paintings were then hanging at the Royal Academy or had appeared at the Grosvenor Gallery's Winter Exhibition. His discussion of Rossetti was timely. The artist's death the year before had prompted exhibitions and critical retrospectives of his work and the Pre-Raphaelite *corpus* in general. Cosmo Monkhouse had written a long review of the Trist Collection at Brighton, and in the same year Sidney Colvin had traced the artist's development.[28] Later in the term, Ruskin spoke of John Leech and John Tenniel, whose illustrations of British political and social life appeared regularly in *Punch,* and of Kate Greenaway and Helen Allingham, whose drawings of children and country landscapes recalled a vanishing place and time.

Ruskin was fond of these artists, and the essays generally have a sympathetic tone. His criticism displays what he described in his *Academy Notes* of 1875 as a "fixed criterion of separation between right art and wrong" (14:262). Virtues are balanced with defects: Greenaway's illustrations are too decorative but delicately engraved and colored (33:344); Alma-Tadema's draughtsmanship is accurate but his architectural color and shade "insufficient" (33:319). Yet in written form, anyway, the lectures are thin; most critics today ignore them. Their significance, I think, lies in the fact that a "professor with the power of popular utterance," as the *Oxford Magazine* described Ruskin, had chosen to give them at all. [29] His doing so reflects his overall effort to extend his audience beyond undergraduates and art students by capitulating to trends in art criticism.

Generally, the lectures of his first tenure came closest to a British *Künstgeschichte*. Compared with European art critics, the English were indifferent to art history in the nineteenth century, and apart from the *Fine Arts Quarterly Review,* which lasted only four years (1863–67), no British periodical or critic focused on technique and iconography. [30] Ruskin still mentioned formal properties in his lectures of 1883, but *The Art of England* focused on popular subjects. Because Greenaway, Leech, and Tenniel were primarily illustrators, their work was accessible and probably familiar to those who did not or could not visit exhibitions. Their subjects, moreover, were generally domestic. In discussing them, Ruskin was seriously treating reproducible art which the vast middle classes could bring into their homes on pages of magazines, books, and newspapers. He had discussed the mechanically reproducible arts before in 1872 in his lectures on wood and metal engraving, but then his examples were European (Holbein, Dürer) and his tone often suspicious. Engravers worked with "mechanical tricksters" who overproduce for a public that wants to own representations of the familiar (22:387–89). Compared with an engraving by Holbein, the lines of a cover of *Punch* are unsubtle, hurried, conventional—all "to catch the vulgar eye" (22:357–58). In 1883, he still condemns the "mischief" of mechanical reproduction, noting that the woodcut requires little work or skill and often expresses "ideas of ugliness or terror" (33:353), but he devotes a session of measured praise and criticism to illustrators in *Punch.* The choice of subject and often balanced treatment underscore Ruskin's efforts to tap popular taste with domestic content and media.

Of course the term *popular,* when attributed to painting,

still describes the preferences of a relatively small group. For example, a nontechnical magazine such as the *Art Journal,* aimed at cultivated persons, probably had a circulation of no more than a few thousand.[31] Exhibition at the Royal Academy could make an artist's reputation, but academy members, rather than the public, chose the paintings and decided their placement (Ruskin wanted to open this professional enclave and have the public elect Royal Academy members [14:478]). Because all Royal Academy members were guaranteed eight hangings on the line in every exhibition, popularity was predetermined by and confined to a small group. Still, within this limited field, public taste evaded the judgments of artists and critics and ultimately created a demand for certain kinds of work, demonstrating the reciprocal influence of artist and public in the art market. This is evident in the *Pall Mall Gazette*'s poll of 1886 for the best pictures at the Royal Academy. The categories the *Gazette* used indicate the importance of subject in both artistic production and public perception. There were contests for the best landscape, water-color, historical, and religious painting as well as for the best portrait, animal picture, and "best prettiest baby." In reporting the results, the *Art Journal* suggested that public taste was susceptible to the "preaching of the *Pall Mall Gazette*": of fifteen hundred voters, it added without irony, only three "named correctly ten of the pictures."[32] The censure of the *Art Journal* thus seemed to have little effect on many of those who attend exhibitions.

Many of the paintings selected, such as Frank Dicksee's *Memories,* (called "sentimental" in the *Art Journal,* which favored William Quiller Orchardson's *Mariage de Convenance*) most likely were produced with popular reception and eventual purchase of engravings in mind (Ruskin mentions this to the Royal Academy Commission in 1863 [14:483]). For example, at the start of his career, Luke Fildes asked John Everett Millais, the Pre-Raphaelite turned fancy-dress portrait painter, whether he should launch himself with a picture of the poor based on his *Graphic* illustration *Houseless and Hungry* or with a love idyll in Watteau dress. Millais recommended doing the latter. The successful painting, *Fair, Quiet and Sweet Rest,* hung on the line at the Royal Academy's Summer Exhibition of 1872.[33] With the

preferences registered in the *Pall Mall Gazette,* this anecdote
suggests the intimate economic relationship between painter
and beholder or prospective buyer. Frequently critics, supposed
arbiters of taste, had little influence on this relationship. Yet by
conceding to popular taste, Ruskin's lectures on Watts, Alma-
Tadema, and Burne-Jones set the critic and historian within this
sphere of reciprocal influence. In the *Gazette's* poll of 1886,
Alma-Tadema's *Apodyterium* received the most votes for classical
painting and for the best picture of all. By simply mentioning
this artist three years before, even with reservations, Ruskin was
acknowledging one of the most visible figures in the current art
scene and at last expanding his exclusive and dated repertory of
English artists.

Appropriately, attendance at the lectures of 1883 was better than it had been during Ruskin's first tenure as Slade professor. Whereas his lectures on landscape of 1871 were, he said,
too technical for women and his accounts of Tuscan art during
the thirteenth-century trade wars were sparsely attended, the
sessions on English subjects were crowded (22:xxix; 33:li).[34]
Three lectures—on Burne-Jones and Watts, Alma-Tadema and
Leighton, and Allingham and Greenaway—were delivered twice,
once for the Oxford population and once for non-residents, to
packed rooms. Anticipating a large showing, Ruskin decided to
admit persons by tickets. Members of the university and their
friends were supposed to have precedence for the first lecture;
others could go to the informal repetition (33:259). The plan
did not work well, and outsiders with tickets flooded the session
at the university. An anonymous writer in the *Oxford Magazine*
of 9 May, three days before the scheduled lecture on Burne-Jones
and Watts, complains of having to procure tickets and goes on
to state, "Surely all members of the University have prior claims
to those of the outside public."[35] In October of the same year
during the course on *The Pleasures of England,* an item under
"Notes and News" in the *Oxford Magazine* broaches the same
problem: "To prevent a crush, admission is to be by ticket, but
the notice says nothing about any preference to be given to
members of the University. . . . It is rather hard that the people
for whom the lectures are really delivered should be excluded by
the rush of ambitious outsiders."[36]

Most of the "ambitious outsiders" whom undergraduates wanted kept out were women; according to an article in the *St. James's Budget*, they formed half the audience at the first lecture of the term in March 1883.[37] Since the 1860s Ruskin had had an avid following of young female *rentiers,* and he courted them through the first term of his professorship with *The Eagle's Nest* (1872), which he said he wrote specifically for them, and with an outside project, *Proserpina*, a botanical handbook for girls; both this work and *Love's Meinie,* his lectures of 1873, often describe flowers and birds as primping young ladies. The outsiders whose presence the *Oxford Magazine* resents had therefore been interpellated in Ruskin's lectures and essays throughout the 1870s, but their large numbers at the lectures during the 1880s disrupted the scholarly community because they metonymically embodied the social movement that was changing Oxford itself. Ruskin was aware of the tension; during the second course of the 1880s, *The Pleasures of England,* he offered to sneak in a girl who could not get a ticket.[38] In addition, his term "informal" for the repeated lectures implies that his delivery, if not his content, would address a less knowledgeable or skilled group. Although Ruskin himself was always devising ways to expand his constituency and had planned a series on fashionable English art to attract more people, he had to gratify Oxford's sense of privilege and try to keep newcomers separate. In this way, he reinforced social distinctions and thereby undermined the concept of a national aesthetic and character around which he had organized the series.

Because Ruskin's delivery often was extemporaneous, it is impossible to know how the informal lectures were directed to a mass audience. Certainly the presentations at the university were less than scholarly. Eyewitnesses describe the sessions of Ruskin's last term as chaotic, filled with raucous undergraduates who expected an eccentric performance. Listening to Ruskin speak in one the last sessions, Hubert von Herkomer remarked, "It was painful to his friends . . . who so plainly saw how he played to the gallery, how . . . he seemed only to wish to arouse hilarity amongst the undergraduates, who did not know him."[39] As a passing comment in the *Oxford Magazine* hints, he made even the courses of his first tenure into "afternoon 'sensations'" rather than the technical discussions they seem in print.[40] In general, Ruskin's lectures were like revivalist meetings, writes Kenneth Clark.[41] All these accounts confirm the nature of the conflict between the university and its (largely female) outsiders: it concerned social rather than intellectual elitism, a fear that those pressing into the lecture hall would alter the mythical homogeneity of a group that comprised many parvenus to whose ambiguous taste a revivalist style might appeal rather than offend.

The versions of the lectures in the Library Edition, as well as contemporary writings on English art for audiences outside Oxford, evince this social separatism more markedly. References to national character and national art are dogged by insinuations of class tension. In his *Academy Notes* for 1875, Ruskin calls a foreigner's painting of a land- or city-scape a "secondary form" of beautiful art, because true renderings of national character must be made by natives: "your own people, as they live, are the only ones you can understand" (14:290). He is talking of *School Revisited* by G. D. Leslie, in which Victorian girls wear Georgian dresses—"English girls, by an English painter," comments Ruskin (14:290). In a retrospective letter about the painter Frederick Walker (1876), he develops the social and geographical determinism that, but for a few comments, he had suppressed in his first Oxford lectures. Class and physical surroundings have made many English people foreigners to each other, and Walker cannot depict common English country life because city living has conditioned him to see the country from a distance, as spectacle. "All those peasants of his are got up for the stage. . . . " In Walker's canvasses, Ruskin detects a "straining to express the feelings of a cockney who had never before seen a goose in his life, web-footed" (14:346–47). On the other hand, Edouard Frère, who had shown six pictures at the French Exhibition in Pall Mall in 1857, has the "simplicity of Wordsworth" (14:346). Whereas Walker's executions are "an agony of labour," Frère's bucolic scenes and figures look natural because "he lived in a village, loved it, and painted what he saw" (14:347, 346). (A few years later, living in the country would not guarantee this natural vision, and Ruskin would criticize Wordsworth for artificiality.) Ruskin also objected to the neatly clad mother in Allingham's watercolor, *The Clothes-Line* (1879); the subject should have been a "rough work-woman."[42] In general, though, Ruskin liked Allingham's "fair weather" paintings which efface signs of poverty from the landscape. In *The Old Men's Garden, Chelsea Hospital* (1876), she surrounds the back of an old veteran with two young women in graceful white dresses and a garden of flowers. The critic Tom Taylor compared the picture with Walker's *Haven of Rest,* and Allingham herself admitted the influence of Walker on her work.[43]

It is not clear, then, how Ruskin wanted the poor and the rustic depicted, and his ambivalence reflects his own position as a critic whom money and suburban life estranged from the subjects he tried to see with objectivity. He is surest about the sympathy of the early nineteenth-century painters William Henry Hunt and Samuel Prout, but his preference for these artists exemplifies his adoption of both a comfortably bourgeois audience and a romantic remedy for existing material conditions. Hunt's drawings, as well as Prout's, were the focus of an exhibition in 1879–80 which Ruskin helped arrange. In his catalogue, he notes that both artists, now out of vogue, created country views for the homes of the middle classes sixty years before. Both were "part of the characteristic metropolitan population" that endowed holidays in the country with "pastoral charm." Hunt "never painted a cluster of nuts without some expression, visible enough by the manner of their presentation, of the pleasure it was . . . to see them in the shell, instead of in a bag at the greengrocer's" (14:374). Even with this physical distance, neither Hunt nor Prout had the contempt for rural subjects Ruskin detects in work of the preceding age, which frames an aristocratic point-of-view. Rather than "polished flower pieces" that fill corners of European galleries, Hunt's primroses are "fresh from the bank," his hawthorns "white from the hedge" (14:377–78). Birds are not viewed from the sportsman's perspective, as potential food. With these remarks, Ruskin seems to imply that a native's or peasant's version of simple country life and landscapes would be truer, but he does not offer any sort of social realism as an alternative. The seventeenth-century Dutch genre school could not represent the "artless origin" of rustic life; the Dutch painter bought his flowers, but

Hunt "saw the flowers in his little garden" (14:378, 380). Indeed, as Ruskin describes him, Hunt was by birth as much a stranger to rural simplicities as Walker. Yet the "plebeian" vision of the older man at times sheds its metropolitan conditioning. He is in a sense one of Arnold's and Marx's *aliens,* whose "real sense of natural beauty" transcends physical and social conditions (14:378).

Hunt's is not a purely individual genius, however, but a *kind* of bourgeois vision possible at a time when the physical and mental distance between place or class was traversable. Along with Prout's, Hunt's "seemingly unimportant works . . . illustrate phases of our own national mind . . . even of national civilization—which coincide with many curious changes in social feelings" (14:376). Writing sixty years later, Ruskin can call both artists and their patrons middle class but praise the pastoral simplicity of their drawings as sealings of the rifts he now sees in current work, such as Walker's. The notion of a past utopia—the years of his own birth—in which city-dweller and villager, bourgeois and peasant, were not antagonistic strangers effaces any distance between Hunt's urban, bourgeois background and the countryside he painted. To the late nineteenth-century critic, the English artist in the early years of the century—years of mythical social unity and abundant natural beauty—can transcend his London address and his London sight. At a time of proliferating art schools such as South Kensington's and Ruskin's own at Oxford, the untutored metropolitan vision looks idyllic.

In this essay, Ruskin's allusions to English art and character—in short, culture—as a homogeneous, national phenomenon, thus entails the same nostalgic and utopian sentiments apparent in his Inaugural address and his lecture series of 1883–84. The military imperialism of this first lecture simply veils the cultural imperialism he would direct not so much toward other countries as other classes. If his Oxford audience could nationalize the new middle and lower strata, the future would operate like the fictional past. There, industrial laborers, entrepreneurs, and middle-men would revert to peasants and shepherds; *otium* would replace the aspiring mind and the laboring body. At the close of his lectures on landscape in 1871, Ruskin advises his readers, "See that your lives be in nothing worse than a boy's climbing for his entangled kite. It will be well for you if you join not with those who instead of kites fly falcons. . . . " (22:70). The following year, he dismisses the epic and religious painting of the German school at Dusseldorf, known for its detailed, almost anatomical treatment of subjects, in favor of a shepherd boy's deal carving of a dog.[44] "Happy these!" he begins, in pastoral cliché, referring to the young cottage artist, "so long as, undisturbed by ambition, they spend their leisure time in work pretending only to amuse, yet capable, in its own way, of showing accomplished dexterity, and vivid perception of nature" (22:186). In contrast, he hints at the current alienating forms of production: "But ignorance *dis*contented and dexterous, learning what it cannot understand, and imitating what it cannot enjoy, produces the most loathsome forms of manufacture that can disgrace or mislead humanity" (22:186). *Otiose* labor, furthermore, is effortlessly exchanged: Samuel Prout had "quiet" dealings with country printsellers: he supplied them with drawings in the "understood" size for the "understood" price. In turn, these works were always in "tranquil demand by the better class of customers" (14:402–3). This process replicates the contracts of preindustrial societies in which relations stayed unspecified and personal.[45]

Like the notion of English art, nationalistic language obscured the division in aesthetics among classes. Ruskin envisioned a country in which everyone could acquire the taste and perception that had typified a mythical, agrarian England in the years of his own childhood. For both him and his Oxford listeners, a country life of ease, whether the squire's or the peasant's, was a middle-class picture of such a past, and Hunt and Prout became its ideals. In this light, the social ambition he sees or projects onto his Oxford audience becomes the means to an end: in addition to leadership and conquest, their goal is *otium,* a cessation of labor and the industrial spirit signified by a return to nature. To those outside Oxford, he celebrates the same life at a lower level, without ambition. His lectures in 1883–84 in effect invited a wide audience to adopt this national aesthetic, but of course it was impracticable for the urban working classes or newly- and sub-literate masses. If Ruskin did broaden his constituency in the 1870s and 1880s, as Brian Maidment argues, he reached a composite group such as the one at Oxford who, having adopted attitudes it perceived as belonging to the landed gentry, looked on the similarly mobile working classes as an encroaching force.[46] In his nationalistic strategy, Ruskin thus ignored rifts in perception, taste, and understanding. Yet over and over again they break through his syncretic rhetoric and expose it as a wishful strategy. The poor remain a problem for realistic representation in works such as his *Academy Notes,* and women, his most enthusiastic converts, receive specific, thus divisory attention.

Ruskin's habitual assumption of national characteristics and ideals allows him to speak of a united nation and an aesthetic as though they were tacit. Yet his focus belies his assumption. As Fredric Jameson observes, the late-nineteenth-century attention to values arises from a perceived absence; they enter the language as concepts when they cease to exist.[47] The idea of a British nation was, in matters of culture, a forced and false hypothesis in Ruskin's writings, for he had brought from his studies of political economy a picture of the way society operated which explained new readerships and new values but modified his aesthetic and threatened his authority. Before his university and museum-going audiences, he used rhetorical and programmatic strategies to mend national divisions that in some way he wanted to retain.

Ruskin's Economic Model

Officially, the Slade professorship signaled Ruskin's retreat into art criticism after a failed venture into political economy in the early 1860s. As early as 1861, he wrote to his father, "I cannot write when I have no audience. . . . I believe the temper in which I wrote *{Unto This Last}* to be past, and as utterly and for ever as that in which I wrote the 2nd vol. of *Modern Painters*" (17:1). Yet he was at this time preparing essays on political economy for *Fraser's*. These papers, later called *Munera Pulveris*, met the same hostile reception as had *Unto This Last* in *Cornhill* and ceased after four installments. Understandably protective, he fostered the illusion that he had withdrawn into the hermetic studies of art and history by circulating reports in the early 1860s that his sole concern then was Turner and the Venetians (17:lxii). He was obstinate in the pursuit of his interests, however. As the letter reveals, he still considered the essays on political economy his best work and disparaged some of his most popular volumes, such as volume two of *Modern Painters*. During these years, he seemed at odds with his own reputation, especially when, after the fiasco with *Cornhill*, Smith and Elder compiled a volume of extracts of his earlier work. According to the publishers, the book met the demand of "a large circle of readers," but it furthered the author's renown as a word-painter, a reputation he resented (17:l). Although he had agreed to the project and suggested passages for inclusion, he disowned the completed volume. "Don't send the book of extracts to *any*body, that you can help," he wrote his father (17:li). As if to counter his persisting public image, Ruskin changed his audience to laborers in *Of Time and Tide* (1867) and *Fors Clavigera* (1871–84), epistolary works largely on social topics that presented him in correspondence with actual persons of the working classes. Of course Ruskin became Slade Professor with honest intentions and real enthusiasm for art education, including a planned drawing school. But the position induced an apparent split in his interests and audience: officially, Ruskin was an art critic and educator for the university and middle classes and, on the side, a social critic and political economist for working men.

Obviously the distinction was never this neat, and one sort of writing, like one kind of audience, spilled into the other. As early as the 1850s, Ruskin's discussions of art had been strongly ideological, more like cultural polemic. After *Unto This Last* and *Munera Pulveris,* economics became the detailed backdrop for Ruskin's focus on art. In the essays and reviews he wrote after the Inaugural lecture and often apart from his official work at the university, economics, in Pierre Macherey's words, formed a "site" that "preceded" and "prepared" for Ruskin's presentation of art to the heterogeneous readers of the 1870s and 1880s.[1] This economics derived only in part from the political economy Ruskin had proposed in his controversial essays. It also included the orthodox economics of the age in its nontechnical form, a discourse that his audience recognized and understood.

This discourse—the traditional assumptions about economics that Ruskin had internalized by the 1870s—supposedly did not apply to matters of aesthetics. David Ricardo, the most influential economist of the century, classified "rare statues and pictures, scarce books and coins, wines of peculiar quality, which can be made only from grapes grown on a particular soil" as nonreproducible commodities, and Ruskin had stressed the difference between art and marketable objects.[2] Things of beauty, he declared over and over, should have stable and lasting value. But increasingly he connected art and economics. For him the link was at times a bitter one: one selection of his essays was called *A Joy Forever,* trailed by the admonitory subtitle *And Its Price in the Market.* Often, though, Ruskin automatically considered art a reproducible commodity; certainly inexpensive methods of reproduction encouraged him to do so. By 1870 elements of orthodox economics had coalesced into an arena of thought or a "site" that subjected belief, perception, and taste—aesthetics in its broadest definition, as ideology—to a marketplace described by the century's political economists.

The most vivid picture of the "site" establishing an understanding between Ruskin and his audience appears in *The Laws of Fésole,* a revision of *The Elements of Drawing* which Ruskin wrote between 1877 and 1878 for the few students in his drawing school at Oxford and the Guild of Saint George. It is prefaced by an apparently tangential link between art and money. For the first exercise in making a circle, Ruskin proposes that his readers draw sixpence. The coin probably was the most available circular object he could find, and its use as money seems less important than its familiarity and convenience. It is no different from the pieces of a tea cup he tells students to sketch in an earlier lesson (15:363). Imagining the completed circle he comments, "It might just as well stand for the outline of the moon" (15:373). Both the china and the money tell the reader that anyone surrounded by ordinary objects can learn the elements of drawing. In addition, they suggest that heightened perception, as well as increased dexterity, comes from looking at common, accessible things. The students who cannot visit the Museum of Naples to copy an Etruscan vase or, in this case, the circle of the bas-relief on the Tower of Giotto can learn the same skill from drawing sixpence or the shards of a tea cup.

Ruskin was aware, though, that his use of sixpence implied more than the democratization of perception and artistry. It exemplified the intricate relationship of art and money:

> If any student object to the continued contemplation of so vulgar an object, I must pray him to observe that, vulgar as it may be, the idea of it is contentedly allowed to mingle with our most romantic ideals. I find this entry in my diary for 26 January, 1876:—"To Crystal Palace . . . with organ playing above its rows of ghastly . . . amphitheatre seats, with 'SIX-

PENCE' in letters as large as the organist,—occupying the full
field of sight below him. Of course, the names of Mendelssohn,
Orpheus, Apollo, Jullien, and other great composers, were
painted somewhere in the panelling above. But the real
inscription—meant to be practically, and therefore divinely,
instructive—was 'SIXPENCE.'" (15:373)

There is sarcastic resignation in this passage, and the tone
characterizes many of his digressive comments about the contemporary love of money and its corruption of the landscape and
of art. Money ruins art because in changing the landscape
through its primary manifestation, factories and suburbs, it
alters perception. Descriptions of paintings in the *Academy Notes*
of 1875, for example, frequently erupt in ferocious asides about
the principles of modern profit or "Art-produce," the "results of
mechanical English labour on English land" (14:276, 302–3).
These comments are always syntactically or visually marginal;
the above paragraph, for instance, is a footnote. Yet as digres-
sions, they constitute a continuing threat to the discourse of art.
Money may seem peripheral or outside the concerns of Mendelssohn, Jullien, the Tower of Giotto; yet it always is min-
gling, even invading culture's imaginary boundaries because of
its very ordinariness. It claims attention because of the importance of the everyday in Ruskin's own democratic program. As
the footnote implies, money underlies and subverts the organist's performance. Ruskin is vaguer about the location of the
composers' names than he is about the place of "SIXPENCE," for
money constitutes the base of the site of all such expression.

The scene in the Crystal Palace becomes a paradigm for the
production and value of the artwork in Ruskin's late writings.
The organist is situated between the "oriflammes" of musical
tradition and the price of execution, or artistic exchange in the
larger sense. Money, the universal equivalent symbolizing the
organist's labor, sets the value of culture in implicit relation to
all other commodities of the same price. At the same time, it
makes the performance itself contingent on monetary exchange.
As a signifier of labor in exchange, money produces the recital
and conjures the whole musical tradition the organist's performance encapsulates. Turning attention to money itself thus

becomes Ruskin's sardonic way of acknowledging the primacy of orthodox economics in his democratic arena of aesthetic value. The elements of orthodox economic theory thus become the new aesthetic terms that both threaten and explain the production, reception, value, and meaning of art in Ruskin's late work.

LABOR THEORY AND VALUE

Despite his now famous essays of the sixties, Ruskin himself was never a scholar of economics. In preparing his studies, he had probably read some of John Stuart Mill's *Principles of Political Economy* (1848), Smith's *Wealth of Nations* (1776), and Dugald Stewart's lectures on political economy (or perhaps his *Life and Writings of Adam Smith* [1793]).[3] All of them either anticipate or elaborate David Ricardo's first principle, that the "value of a commodity, or the quantity of any other commodity for which it will exchange, depends on the relative quantity of labour which is necessary for its production."[4] The labor theory of value was a commonplace by midcentury, and Ruskin could attack and perpetuate it in a diluted form without having read Ricardo's *Principles of Political Economy* (1817). Instead, he picked up the simplified discourse of Ricardian theory from newspaper editorials, lectures, and pamphlets that often disseminated simplified and perhaps inaccurate versions of the earlier economists' views.[5] Although Ruskin had not read *Capital* either, he had caught the philosophical implications of Marx's formulations, just as Marx, in *Capital,* had sustained the century's theory that "human labour . . . creates value" and that the labor-time necessary for production determines the "magnitude" of an object's value.[6] And without discussing Malthus, Ruskin conveyed a Malthusian fear of population growth and diminished productivity. Although the dire prophecies about famine had not come true by midcentury, he began buying property for his Guild of St. George, convinced that "healthy food-giving land, so far from being infinite, is . . . limited to narrow belts of the globe" (29:14). He based work on the land to eradicate the changes in production brought about by machines, which he could never accept, but which figured importantly in Ricardo's additions to the *Principles* (1821) and in Marx's development of labor theory.

In his public declaration concerning economics, Ruskin viewed the fundamental theories of the nineteenth century traceable to Adam Smith with moralistic contempt. The principle of laissez-faire created an inhumane society based on competition. The emphasis on production in Smith and Ricardo neglected use value and the kind of labor that should determine worth. *Fors*, like *Munera Pulveris* and *Unto This Last*, is filled with diatribes against labor theory's "economic man" who lives to accumulate riches and satisfy his desires. In both *Unto This Last* and *Munera Pulveris*, Ruskin asserts the importance of quality and the production of goods to "avail towards life" (17:84, 134–35, 152–54). Arched by traditional codes of Christian charity and chivalry, his whole economy lay outside conventional assumptions of the economic man who lived to gratify his own wants.

Ruskin did not contend with orthodox economics on its own terms and sometimes willfully misread Mill's *Principles*.[7] But the popular discourse of economics he set himself against likewise had become more and more irrelevant both to the realities of late-nineteenth-century life and to contemporary research. As recent critics have observed, the agrarian economy described in *Wealth of Nations* was an obsolete model for an industrial country, and much of Ricardo's *Principles* made sense only in the context of the Corn Laws.[8] The labor theory of value continued to dominate popular thought even as pioneering economists during Ruskin's tenure at Oxford were revising their ideas of the market; indeed opponents of Ricardo, such as Ruskin and Marx, merely affirmed the dominance of labor theory through their attacks. They operated, that is, within the discourse of economics. Marx's ideas, as Michel Foucault has observed, did not radically break with labor theory but elaborated its consequences.[9] As his attacks and his alternative political economy show, Ruskin sometimes was an unwilling adherent of labor theory, just as he was a frightened believer in Malthusian notions. The economy of scarcity, with its source of value in labor, became the rhetoric of the discourse he used as a populistic strategy to talk about art.

Many of his comments about ethics and aesthetics during the 1870s and 1880s suggest that he truly believed labor to be the source and measure of value for everything. As early as 1843, Ruskin finds labor one of the five sources of pleasure derived from art. In volume one of *Modern Painters*, he calls the "perception or conception of the mental or bodily powers by which the work has been produced" ideas of power, not labor, but he visualizes part of this force "exerted in the production" of art as manual labor (3:93–94). Increasingly Ruskin saw the artist as a species of the laborer and by the 1870s viewed, or wanted to view (the distinction is not always clear) the painter and writer within the whole community of workers, a picture realized in Ford Madox Brown's famous painting *Work* (1852–65). Here, as in Ruskin's perception, the artist belongs with the manual laborers rather than with the mounted gentry or the intellectuals Carlyle and F. D. Maurice, who supervise or watch others work in Brown's depiction.

During the 1870s, William Stanley Jevons at Owens College in Manchester and later, University College, London, was replacing labor with exchange as the criterion of value. The concept of exchange as the source of value introduced consumption and the demand it expressed as crucial variables of an economy. Because it admitted the influence of consumers, who to Ruskin were a growing and amorphous source of demands, exchange was more frightening than labor as a basis of value, and like many of his contemporaries, he clung to the earlier theory partly to resist the newer, more technical one. Marx of course had declared that though labor was the source and magnitude of value, exchange was the only way to *express* it. Through exchange, the inherent worth of "art-produce" manifests itself. [10] This notion was obvious to anyone who thought at all about value. Ruskin sensed it, and although his political economy separated the two forms into "wealth" and "effectual wealth" (17:153–54), the notion of value manifested only in exchange actually had an enormous effect on his work from *The Queen of the Air* in 1869 to his essays on fiction and poetry in 1880–81. Ruskin's conflict with exchange value in many ways resembles his ambivalence toward labor theory. Ruskin failed to suppress the idea of exchange value in his discussions of both meaning and taste because he could not articulate the absolute value of art apart from some kind of transfer from the artist to reader, beholder, or listener—in short, without considering consumption. And because he saw great differences between the object in and outside the marketplace, Ruskin often mentioned exchange or its arena, the marketplace, with a moral indignation that is absent in Marx's matter-of-fact definitions of value.[11]

Exchange, for instance, is the main action in his arrangement of the scene in the Crystal Palace. Likewise, other scenes are framed around exchange; it provides the basis for superstructural byproducts such as literature, music, and the fine arts. In his catalogue of the drawings of Samuel Prout and William Henry Hunt on loan at the Fine Art Society's Galleries in winter 1879–80, Ruskin focuses on a number of representations that center the life of the towns in marketplaces and commercial districts. Examples are Prout's *Amiens, Abbeville, Evreux, Strassburg,* and *Antwerp* (14:392ff.). All depict commercial streets, squares, or clusters against a cathedral looming in the background. This is, of course, a conventional angle from which artists portray town life, though one of Prout's, *Domo d'Ossola,* reverses the perspective and presents the avenue of exchange from the arches of the cathedral (14:422ff.). These drawings simply reinforced an accepted way of picturing society, which Ruskin undoubtedly knew, but he emphasizes the perspective in his comments. In *Strassburg,* the ostensible focus is the cathedral spire, but the "real subject of the drawing," he declares, is the shop. In the style of a Swiss cottage, it has an inscription, "Commerce de Jean Diehl," along the side (14:413, 416). The figures in the drawings, particularly in *Amiens,* are lounging or are in other casual or static postures. Despite the foregrounding of *Commerce,* no one seems to be buying anything; all is quiet and understood, like Ruskin's description of Prout's dealings with printsellers. These drawings, which preserved for Ruskin a vanished world, helped him resolve his problem with the primacy of exchange by recording while omitting all details of money and actual trade.

Ruskin felt more comfortable with labor theory because it at least provided a fixed standard of value; exchange built in fluctuation. And because labor theory dominated the nineteenth-century discourse of economics, it naturally penetrated his own writing. In *Fors*, he even parodies the theory by portraying himself as a commodity formed through the combined work of Spanish laborers who trod the grapes for the sherry that his father sold; of the sailors who shipped it, of the horse breeders who trained the animals that pulled the coach in which his family took their Continental tours; of the postillions who drove it; of the barons and monks who showed them their paintings, castles, and monasteries (28:391–92). Ruskin the critic is the sum of a synthetic "labor" that erases differences in manual and intellectual work. Here, Ruskin's "house-that-Jack-built" labor theory seems deliberately silly, but it informed sober arguments in similar ways. In a letter Ruskin reads and reprints in *Fors* with "amazement," Coventry Patmore claims that a woman's daily *toilette* and "trivial round" of visiting are comparable to manual labor, for "dressing becomingly and looking pleasant are a deal harder, and better worth doing, than brickmaking" (29:177). Labor justified for Patmore the primping his friend had gently attacked in *Sesame and Lilies*. The tone of these passages suggests how pervasive labor theory was, for in general Ruskin treated it seriously. In a letter he wrote during the fifties to T. E. Plint, a stockbroker from Leeds who was collecting Pre-Raphaelite paintings, he proposes using labor-time to set price:

> It has always been my notion that—putting bad work out of the question or wholly valueless, good work ought to be paid like other workmens, by its quantity. {sic} and that however much greater one man may be than another, he should not be paid by his greatness but by his labour. Rossetti is far greater than Brett. But Rossetti puts perhaps a weeks work only into one of his average drawings and gets forty or fifty guineas for it, while Brett spent simply his whole available Summer and . . . lodging and travelling expenses, on the picture of Val d Aosta for which he asked 450 [guineas]. [12]

The rhetoric of labor pervades the notorious feud between Ruskin and Whistler as well. During the trial, both sides link the value of Whistler's paintings to labor-time: "'Can you tell me,' asked the Attorney-General [Sir John Holker], 'how long it took you to knock off that Nocturne?' 'Two days.' 'The labour of two days, then, is that for which you ask two hundred guineas?' 'No; I ask it for the knowledge of a lifetime.'"[13] Labor is the implicit *source* as well as the *measure* of value in Ruskin's initial attack on Whistler "for flinging a pot of paint in the public's face" and asking two hundred guineas for the effort (29:160). Both Ruskin's term "flinging" and Holker's "knocking off" connote a romantic notion of spontaneous creation which is worthless in a society that valorizes the *amount* of work.

In distinguishing the kind from the quantity of labor in *Unto This Last* and in illustrating the distinction in *The Stones of Venice,* Ruskin formerly had rejected the criterion of quantity. In the "mean act" of labor, the "unhumanized" laborer bends the eye of his soul to the "finger-point . . . ten hours a day, that it may not err from its steely precision" (10:192). In his criticism of the Pre-Raphaelites, he showed that labor could become excessive and detract from painting; in "Pre-Raphaelitism" (1851), he accuses the group of "working too hard" (12:388). The comment has its roots in the contempt for copying he learned from Reynolds and other eighteenth-century aestheticians; the thought also appears in his derogation of the Dutch school in volume three of *Modern Painters* (1856). The precision of the Dutch genre painters, he quotes from Reynolds, is one "in which the slowest intellect is always sure to succeed best" (5:34). "Is not the evidence of Ease on the very front of all the greatest works in existence?" he asks in "Pre-Raphaelitism" (12:345). But like laboriousness, ease is a sort of negative degree of work that Ruskin used to evaluate the virtues and deficiencies of a painting. Both laboriousness and ease, then, were ways to measure labor-time through technical and representational detail. In this light, Ruskin's association in these earlier works of creative genius with spontaneity—really minimal labor—still affirms labor-time as the standard of value. Quality has little effect on comparative estimations of value; rather, it is a precondition of labor theory, as in the discussion of Rossetti and Brett. Assuming, that is, that artists are good enough, one then prices their work according to the amount of time spent. In this letter and throughout the 1870s generally, Ruskin reversed the relation between labor and value from an indirect to a direct proportion. Work became less romantic, merely a naïve act of the imagination. Writing or painting was seldom a fortuitous burst of inspired energy, done with *sprezzatura,* but a tiring, measurable, and time-consuming task. However, it still provided the framework within which Ruskin and contemporaries such as Patmore evaluated artistic production. In "The Nature of Gothic," it furnished the conceptual backdrop against which he detected the artist's "savageness," and at the Whistler trial it remained the source and measure—this time of the painter's violation. By then, it was preferable to exchange-value, a volatile criterion that implied that consumers of cheap novels and prints could control the manufacture of these articles and set their own aesthetic standards. Ruskin clung to a standard that was relatively fixed and familiar, though as he aged he saw its dark side.

A METAPHYSICS OF LABOR

Ruskin's growing reliance on quantifiable work as a measure of price or market value grew from his studies of a just and regulated economy, as well as the erosion of his orthodox religious beliefs. When Ruskin finally abandoned evangelical Christianity in the late 1850s, he looked for new authorities and new concepts in which to anchor fixed moral and aesthetic standards. He found them in Ricardian labor theory and in Greek ideas of social ethics, which for him simulated the role of doctrinal religion.

Conforming to Mill's idea, the concept of labor Ruskin carried to aesthetics from *Unto This Last* and *Munera Pulveris* encompassed both manual and intellectual activity. In explaining the total operation of a society, it therefore became the new Absolute in his system of value. Its syncretic, substitutive role is evident in a lecture he gave at the London Institution in 1882. In discussing monastic life, he turned the Benedictine abbeys at Cluny and Cîteaux into economic models. Cluny organized itself around jewelry-making, coined its own money and thereby became the "culmination of the power of the monastic system," a "Westminster Abbey and Bond Street in one" (33:244).

Cîteaux had an agrarian economy. It was a peasant society founded, like Venice, on a swamp near water to power a mill. Ruskin points out that in England the monastery usually has a mill: the place of production, even if meager, is the place of cultivation—both agricultural, mercantile, and spiritual. By describing Cluny and Cîteaux as fundamentally economic, not religious communities, Ruskin shows how a society founded on religious principles was based on some method of production. He does not, in this lecture, discuss whether or how these different economies follow a mechanical model and effect super-structures of belief, but he dwells on the productive processes themselves in order to assert their primacy over Christian myth. The legend that sets the beginning of Saint Benedict's ministry with the monk's mending a broken corn sieve is "just as impor-tant in [the saint's] life as the killing of the Nemean lion is in the life of Heracles" (33:236). Insisting on the centrality of the story of the corn-sieve in the *mythos* of the Benedictines (in its pub-lished form, the lecture becomes "Mending the Sieve" [1893] [33:190]), Ruskin commeasures farmers, innkeepers, and craftsmen with hermits and martyrs. Of course there have been other farmer-saints, so making Saint Benedict the apostle of peasants' agriculture and squires' farming machines does not counter the hagiographies (33:237). It simply shifts the empha-sis from Cistercian architecture, the advertised topic, to econo-mies and demonstrates, as the *Art Journal* reported, that the Church's "saints are no longer martyrs only, but workers. . . . Mysticism changes to real action; fancy to fact; belief passes into law."[14] Ruskin's digression, first into the myth of Saint Bene-dict with the corn-sieve and then into Saint Bernard's colonizing the wild land of Cîteaux, became for the anonymous reviewer in the *Art Journal* the metonymic leveling of aesthetics into pro-duction.

This lecture marked a public reversal that the *Art Journal* also recognized, for the history of Cîteaux in particular dis-proved a Calvinistic prejudice passed to Ruskin from his parents that Catholics took the most fertile land for their monasteries. By relating how the Benedictines actually cultivated marsh, Ruskin spurns what he calls "my dread of ritualistic devotion" and aligns himself with primitive if unorthodox Catholicism. [15] He does so not by embracing ritualism, but by portraying the Catholics as colonizers and laborers. In effect, he subsumes Catholicism into the base of his economic model of belief.

A lingering dread of Catholicism probably helped prevent Ruskin's final religious beliefs from solidifying into its orthodoxy, but his implicit commitment to the economic model left religion relatively ignored and, therefore, doctrinally vague anyway. That Ruskin perceived it as a byproduct of his economy is evident in his carefully written lectures on religion and morality in his first term at Oxford. In February 1870, he addressed the university audience for the first time since the Inaugural on "The Relation of Art to Religion." His statements reflected his recent reading in Plato's *Republic,* Aristotle's *Ethics,* and Max Müller's comparative mythology. Religion, or "the feelings of love, reverence, or dread with which the human mind is affected by its conceptions of spiritual being," is a form of mythology (20:49). This means Ruskin treats it as myth, which he regards as extended projective metaphor. This poetic approach was, remarks James Kissane, a popular method; by the late sixties, myths "had become dominated by a desire to see [in them] a flowering of human imagination rather than to reduce them to some primitive misconception or some primeval truth."[16] Similarly, in the religion without doctrine Ruskin presents in 1870, the Christian ideal is actually a "feeling" that grows from a "conception," and verbal or visual narratives of religion represent this emotion or belief through projective metaphors. As he argues, religious iconology uses actual figures or landscapes as models, but when it "induce[s] a belief in, the real existence of the imagined personage, contrary to, or unjustified by the other evidence of its existence," the realizations are "mischievous" (20:60). The "mischievous" metaphor has a reified or historical signified rather than an emotional one.

In this lecture, Ruskin tries to read religion in the way his contemporary Nietzsche tried to read philosophy—as a history of metaphor. [17] Both use a sort of inverted Platonic hierarchy in which the ideal is a product of representation. As a result, art cannot have the ties to religion that Ruskin's audience might conventionally conceive. It cannot reveal divine truths or ennoble them; it can only evoke metaphors through metaphors. An image of the Madonna, for example, may govern a conception of the Virgin (20:58–59). This, according to Ruskin, is how religious belief works for everyone, although the less intelligent will make the image historical, a figure of a real woman as she actually looked. But the demotion of religion into metaphor would, he knew, divide society into naïve idolaters and disingenuous believers, and consequently shatter any common system of values. He could not, therefore, abandon the Platonic ideal or invert it into a hermetic linguistic system. He had to find a replacement that would govern belief and value.

In the same lecture, then, he installs labor as the Absolute in the paradigm of representation. As I have discussed, he was at this time also picturing labor as the base of his model society. He now conveys this overdetermined function through a pun: it links both art and military power through a genealogy of physical action. "All the great arts . . . are founded first in mastery, by strength of *arm,* of the earth and sea, in agriculture and seamanship; then their inventive power begins, with the clay in the hand of the potter . . . and in the carpenter's work. . . . Nor is it without . . . strange significance . . . that the statue of Athena Polias was of olive-wood, and that the Greek temple and Gothic spire are both merely the permanent representations of useful wooden structures" (20:45–46).

Through the triple association of "arm" as imperialistic, agricultural, and artistic activity, Ruskin draws "one united system from which it is impossible to remove any part without harm to the rest" (20:45). "Arm" is the originary term from which he derives various kinds of work, like colonizing, farming, warfare, and creativity, both manual and imaginative. In this way, the ideal of labor overarches Ruskin's schema of aesthetics, and the practice of labor forms its ground. Ruskin arranges the relationship between the ideal, representation, and production to reverse the Platonic paradigm: at the top, the ideal realm of belief and value springs from representation, which in turn results from actual labor. Of course this only resembles Plato's model of perception in a tangential way, for though it contains the same elements, or versions of them (the ideal, representation, and the real [or labor]), it is causal, not just sequential. Moreover, as the cause or base, labor supersedes the ideal in importance; it is both practice and an idea itself— most completely in Marx's articulation, *labor power.*

The details of this mechanical model, in which base begets superstructure, come from Ruskin's reading of another popular and authoritative text, the *Ethics.* At the beginning of the same lecture, he quotes from Aristotle in order to base all fine art "in the actual *production* of beautiful form or colour" (20:46). But unlike Ruskin, Aristotle separates production, which character- izes art, from action. To him, "the reasoned state that is capable of action is also different from that which is capable of produc- tion. . . . Every art is concerned with bringing something into being. . . . And since production is not the same as action, art must be concerned with production."[18] He pursues the distinc- tion between production and action through his classification of practical wisdom or *phronesis.* Prudence is a "true state, reasoned and capable of action in the sphere of human goods."[19] It is not production like *technē* or art, says Aristotle, because "production aims at an end other than itself; but this is impossible in the case of action, because the end is merely doing *well.*"[20]

Ruskin's moral aesthetic had always ignored these differ- ences. In *The Stones of Venice,* art had been a kind of *phronesis,* an exercise in practical wisdom, an action. It had, of course, man- ifested the creator's striving for truth or wisdom. Ruskin con- tinued to assert this in the early Oxford lectures. The highest function of art is to "relate to us the utmost ascertainable truth respecting visible things and moral feelings" (20:46). The ver- sion of this truth or wisdom in the *Ethics* is *sophia,* to Aristotle "the scientific and intuitive knowledge of what is by nature most precious."[21] In this second lecture, Ruskin invokes the moral journey toward *sophia* when he states that the fine arts require "the exercise of the . . . heart and intellect" (20:46), equivalents of the intuition and scientific knowledge of *sophia.* But Aristotelian wisdom is an essentially "useless" truth because its objects, unlike those of *phronesis,* are not "human goods, i.e., things about which deliberation is possible."[22] Similarly, truth in Ruskin's lecture is really an absent ideal; it is the ultimate referent of art, but it is embodied only in *phronesis,* expanded by

Ruskin to include all action. By collapsing truth into action, and action into production or labor, Ruskin makes art more central to society than ever before. The artist in the economic model is not a "minor commodity producer," in Terry Eagleton's phrase, but a worker in a world structured and evaluated by work.[23] Production and action become two coeval forms of labor or the "strength of arm." Thus broadened, labor operates as the material source as well as its conceptual "product," the ideal of value.

Ruskin's choice of the *Ethics* as an authoritative text (which, typically, he freely revised) was appropriate, even expected, at the Oxford of this era. It was not only the most translated Greek text of the century, but the most taught—and read—book at the university. Its practical philosophy had accommodated various readings, and by the last quarter of the century it was providing an intellectual model of Christian virtues for those who had abandoned orthodox religious faith. Ruskin's loose interpretation of Aristotle resembled T. H. Green's, whose classes attracted many undergraduates. Like Green, Ruskin stressed Aristotle's treatment of virtue as a social formation. His definition of a practical aesthetic in which the ideal reifies itself into the acting subject, and *sophia* becomes simply a projection of *phronesis,* suited current interpretation. Besides being "eminently practical in content," remarks Frank Turner, the *Ethics* "upheld the social elitism so much a part of Oxford life."[24] The *Republic* became Ruskin's other source for the same reason. In it Ruskin discovered confirmation of his authoritarian stance toward all workers. He was, as I have said, aware that the figurative and the emotional realms were still literal and historical for many readers among the lower orders, while he assumed that their superiors believed through some sort of nonmaterial, nonliteral, a posteriori idealism (a posteriori because it resulted from the labor of representation). Because different classes perceived differently, social and economic hierarchies extended to the *Gemeinschaft* of readers he envisioned for art and literature as a whole. In the model of society he borrowed from the *Republic,* the leaders control the production of images through which the people form their beliefs and morals. In his second lecture, he translates from book three: *"Must it be then only with our poets that we insist they shall . . . create for us the image of a noble morality . . . or shall we not also keep guard over all other workers for the people, and forbid them to make what is ill-customed, and unrestrained, and ungentle, and without order or shape, either in likeness of living things, or in buildings, or in any other thing whatsoever that is made for the people?"* (20:48).

The deficiencies that Plato lists evoke standards for aesthetic production of a cultural aristocracy. The crucial point of the Inaugural—and the assumption of a few subsequent lectures—was the identity of those in whose hands power over the creation of such images and beliefs lay. Presumably, the potential governors sat before him at these first lectures: men and women, undergraduates, and other interested persons around the university who had read the announcements and procured free tickets. When one thousand copies of the first-term lectures appeared in print in July of the same year, purchasers with six shillings could also identify themselves as potential leaders. In this way, the heads of Ruskin's new Republic were self-selected, just as many of the Oxford undergraduates were self-made, or sons of the self-made. The essentially undemocratic message of the first few lectures suited an audience who had appropriated the interests of the aristocracy and could display those interests, but only in a utopian future or past in which everyone was in one sense or another a laborer. Thus the Platonic description of the artist's social duty appealed to the (illusory) ideology of a group who translated their social ambitions into intellectual elitism.

In the Oxford lectures, Ruskin's vision of England as a nation of laborers united all classes, but simultaneously it made them victims, for in the economic discourse all work takes all the worker's energy. Ruskin had claimed this in volume one of *Modern Painters* and most eloquently in *The Stones of Venice*. Mental powers such as imagination, ingenuity, and judgment are as taxing as bodily exertion; clearly Ruskin always traced the value of art to suffering in effort. This is why "The Nature of Gothic" captivated workers, why he became involved with teaching artisans at The Working Men's College, why he contradicted

Burke and based the sublime in the "deliberate measurement of . . . doom" and suffering (3:129). To prove a work excellent, we must prove the difficulty of its production, he writes in 1843; "the less sufficient the means appear to the end, the greater . . . will be the sensation of power" (3:123). The life and effort of the hand are evident in great works of art, he argues in *The Seven Lamps of Architecture*. Because to Ruskin every sort of work exhausts the body, artists as well as artisans share the fate of *homo oeconomicus:* he is, as Michel Foucault states, "the human being who spends, wears out, and wastes his life in evading the imminence of death."[25]

This paradigm of production, centered on the martyrdom of the worker, is Ruskin's new metaphysics. In 1870, he writes in his third lecture of the term, "No man can read the evidence of labor who is not himself laborious, for he does not know what the work cost" (20:78). All fine art, he observes in a later lecture, "requires . . . the whole strength and subtlety of the body" as it contends with the natural resistance of the material (20:304). The best realistic work demands exhausting effort of the maker in order to prompt a desire in the beholder for the real thing. The artifice, in other words, should be transparent, a conveyance for the idea it represents. And the artist must use all his or her strength to create this self-effacing object. In effect, the labor of the artist entails a sort of double erasure in which both the body and the creation disappear. In doing so they express the ultimate alienation of labor. This process does not startle or anger Ruskin because it replaces the familiar biblical paradigm of sacrifice of the chosen one for the people; the modern, Ruskinian worker striving for perfection is a variation of the Christian who must die trying for personal redemption. The use of alienated labor as the bulwark of a system of value refocuses the traditional pattern of Christian torture and sacrifice on the bodies of existing workers.

During his first tenure at Oxford, when Ruskin was writing scores of essays, catalogues, and correspondence, including *Fors,* he felt tired and overworked, and one might argue that he simply inflated his condition into a vision of alienated labor that filled the space left by the loss of literal belief in Judeo-Christian myths and adherence to church doctrines. Yet he went on to use the economic model to present the elements of iconology and art history to various audiences, elaborating his metaphysics of labor into a system of signs. The vortex of his economic model was money; it signified labor and provided the most convenient and prevalent example of reproducible art.

Money

The drawings of social commerce that Ruskin loved, as well as the pictures of it he himself framed in his writing, reveal a conception of society based on the economic model, in which art is a specific kind of transaction backed by an evaluative standard, labor. No wonder, then, that much of his writing during the 1870s is often about labor and what Marx called the universal equivalent of its exchange, money. It is doubly significant to Ruskin by the 1870s: as currency it indicates the value of a specific exchange of labor power, and as an object it often represents the cumulative labor manifested in the beliefs and *mythoi* of a nation. Thus it becomes an overdetermined sign in his late work: as currency, whether paper or metal, it is a receipt for available objects such as the organist's performance at the Crystal Palace; as a commodity or art object such as gold and silver coins or the sixpence the young artist uses to trace the circle, it is an emblem of popular myths and cultural values. These values and myths are, in turn, implicated in money's use. In this way, each transaction of money encapsulates a nation's economic base and superstructure of beliefs.

The multiple function of money allowed Ruskin to give his ideas about labor the status of metaphysical belief, but this versatility sometimes became problematical, especially in texts for the general public about iconology. In *Munera Pulveris,* Ruskin detects potential confusion in gold's dual function: "They partly neutralize, since in so far as the gold is commodity, it is bad currency, because liable to sale; and in so far as it is currency, it is bad commodity, because its exchange value interferes with its practical use. Especially its employment in the higher branches of the arts becomes unsafe on account of its liability to be melted down for exchange" (17:197–98).

These interfering signifiers especially intrigued Ruskin at a time when, with an economic paradigm of society, he resumed his study of art for a projected audience whose religious beliefs, education, and taste ranged widely. He saw in money an accessible art object he could use to explain iconologies and iconographies to people who did not visit museums. In discussing the engravings on coins, Ruskin could therefore treat them as found objects and continue what Carol T. Christ has called the aesthetic of particularity characterizing much Victorian sight.[1] However, like architecture, money—both paper and coin—was chiefly functional, and its aesthetic properties tended to become invisible in its use. Ruskin's treatment of the double function of money dramatized the shift from traditional to immediate and fluctuating iconologies and his reluctance to disclose the change, especially to his mass audiences.

ICONOLOGIES OF MONEY

In *Fors Clavigera,* his letters to laborers, Ruskin uses money to show how exchange value can obscure the treasured beliefs of a once ascendant ideology. This is evident in the popular use of the penny, which, with the shilling and pound, composes what he sardonically calls the "British Bible" (27:450). Possessors of the penny, which shows Britannia sitting on her shield, associate the image with the iron industry and the enormous commissions of manufacturers. It therefore suggests one of the means of its own accumulation, the ironworks. The reading, Ruskin implies, is preposterous and ignorant, but he does not correct it. It is one of many instances of bad faith in the letters: Ruskin supplies a debased iconography in a hostile attempt to level down to his listeners, not bothering to flatter them with the observation that historical distance has elevated a once accessible meaning.

Similarly, the "new florin" coined to replace the one of 1849 (called "godless" because it lacked the legend "Dei Gratia" [27:453n.2]) also functions as a tiny emblem book whose images and mottoes document the British spirit through history and myth obscured for the public in repeated exchange. The florin shows two heraldic devices: the first, repeated twice, contains four lions—one rampant—representing Scottish arms and enclosed by a tressure knotted with fleur-de-lis; the second shield contains the Irish harp. Together, they signify the history of the English and Scottish alliance with France, along with the chivalric code shared by the three nations. Ruskin does not explain the iconography of the harp and claims not to know the origin of the lion rampant but says he believes that the florin holds a breakable code. This is a vaguely taunting statement, which places truth out of popular reach. He reveals the meaning of as much of the imagery as he cares to or can, then leaves the rest vague or unexplained. Instead, he emphasizes the coin's practical value by contrasting the myths depicted on each of its sides. Looking at the penny, he mocks the average change-holder's inability to recognize national emblems ("Who, then is this lady, whom it represents, sitting, apparently, on the edge of a dish-cover?" [27:451]); examining the florin, he labels the all-too-readable legend on the reverse ("One Florin." "One Tenth of a Pound." {27:453]) the "war-cry" of "republican England," which in this coinage replaces the ancient motto of kings, "Honi soit qui mal y pense" (27:458). Ignorant of the historical significance of the engravings, the public substitutes its own familiar *mythoi* and thus brings money into the crowded arena of popular art.

In comments directed at the general public, Ruskin resists commercial iconology. In fact, he shows his ambivalence toward money for the dual function that attracted him to it as a pedagogical tool in the first place. After interrupting an arithmetic lesson at the Coniston school in 1884, he shows the children a sovereign and asks them the meaning of the royal arms, the harp, and the lion rampant. Answered with silence, he switches back to arithmetic, asks them the number of pence in a sovereign (240), the number of pupils in the room (35), and the number of pence allotted to each should the money be divided. When the children find division with fractions too hard, he figures that thirty children each could have eightpence even and suggests that five stand out (29:481–82). This rather mean lesson in charity illustrates his hostility toward public ignorance of the traditional iconologies and their view of money as merely a means of exchange, valuable in itself. Either he mystifies his audience through cryptic suggestions or he apes their readings.

To his Oxford listeners, Ruskin professed to accept fluctuating value; it became a scholarly issue. In his lecture on likeness in sculpture delivered in 1870, he says that finely executed art must "be didactic to the people" (20:300). To do so, its meaning must be reinvented by different ages, or its formal properties must be newly considered. At times, then, art must efface what it represents to endure (20:300). Theoretically, money would provide an ideal example of this, which is presumably why he chose to discuss it. But in *Fors,* Ruskin neither accepted his theory of a changing iconology nor fulfilled the art critic's, and Oxford professor's, duty to unveil what had become recondite or invisible about objects. He was unwilling to transfer his populistic ideas into actual interpretations for a readership he had identified as working class.

Even at Oxford, where Ruskin accepted the popular readings of money through a distanced, academic perspective, he could shun its obvious function as a means of exchange. In "The Tortoise of Aegina," the unfinished sequel to *Aratra Pentelici* probably drafted in 1870, he connects the birth of the Myrmidons, a transformation of ants into men, with the coming of a new tribe, but admits that it also could signify "sticks, leaves or dust" (20:387). Away from popular readers, he tolerates even the superficial associations of an untrained eye, then supplements these visual associations with a context from myth. The tortoise on a coin of Aegina may signify the lyres of Hermes and Orpheus: in its naturalized form, the lyre is "the concave of the cloudy heaven, and . . . that of the starry vault in which Hermes is lord of motion." The tortoise thus expresses movement as well as harmony of movement, and "pacification, or charming of all irregular impulse" (20:388). In this seemingly tolerant discussion, Ruskin omits an obvious reference. For the editors of the Library Edition, Cook and Wedderburn, note that the tortoise has semimythological and historical connections with commerce. It may symbolize Astarte, the Phoenician goddess of trade, or it may be an index of the island's barter, the tortoise shell, as well as its chief product, the tortoise-shell bowl (27:389n.2). The obvious, self-referential reading of the tortoise is missing from Ruskin's description. As a result, the engraving does not have the adaptability of the popular image and is not instantly consumable by the reading public.

Ruskin may have conveniently forgotten the tortoise's historical value as a former index of exchange because the coin no longer had monetary use. Yet perhaps the elevation of trade to the status of myth, with its own goddess, bothered him, for Astarte personifies currency's self-referential meaning. She functions as he thinks Britannia does on the new florin; the tortoise announces its own exchange value just as directly as does the florin's denominational inscription. Both of these coins are variations of monetary canting badges or *types parlants* that Marc Shell describes, simple representations that work not through allusion but through puns. For example, the *fiorino d'oro* of 1252 displays a *fiore* or flower blossom representing *Firenze* and has an explanatory description which states its value ("Det tibi florere, Christus, Florentiam vere").[2] Ruskin must have been aware of this tradition from looking at old coins like the *fiorino* of 1252, which he has engraved in the twenty-fifth letter of *Fors* (27:461), so in reading the coin of Aegina as a circulating sign of harmony and order he seems deliberately to ignore the traditional self-referential images on coins, especially because he states that he views the coming of money like the Aegenian coin as the end of mythic and the beginning of historical Greece (20:381). Perhaps Ruskin mystified a coin that he himself claimed had introduced the historical and that bespeaks the history of its use in trade because he wanted to connect the daily lives of people to a moral and metaphysical set of values. His interpretations implicate money and exchange in a society's higher beliefs and values, but because they do so through allusion, rather than through easily caught puns, many people, especially the uneducated and unobservant, are not aware of the elevated significance of their daily purchases.

As his economic model shows, Ruskin saw signs of trade and myth coinciding. He often combined them reluctantly, however, for one frequently obscured the other. In the scene at the Crystal Palace, musical tradition, represented by the names of real and mythological composers, looms over the exchange. It is, however, overshadowed in Ruskin's eye by the transaction of the performance. In general, the public's preoccupation with trade and ignorance of iconology prompted his resistance to historical images or monetary referents on coins. His nasty reticence before the schoolchildren, his esoteric analysis of the tortoise, and his contemptuous description of the British penny and florin exemplify what Fredric Jameson calls a "perceptual opacity" about money: as art it reflects an ideal realm of thought and emotion; as currency in the economic discourse, it signifies labor and exchange.[3] The functions correspond to the polarized realms of "heavenly fire" and "terrestrial gold" of his utopia in the Inaugural lecture, and in much of his art criticism one actually suppresses the other. The silver tortoises thus cannot be indexes of exchange while they represent lyres, even though he says that he tolerates multiple meanings. The dual functions of money have to be considered apart; otherwise, as Ruskin says of gold, they neutralize each other.

As his schema of the Crystal Palace and his acceptance of labor theory indicate, Ruskin actually pictured art subjected to the conditions and consequences of orthodox economy. However, he was understandably dissatisfied with the values that aesthetics under the economic discourse reflected. For labor, which ended in exhaustion and death, and exchange, which subjected worth to the market, ultimately diminished the transcendent meaning and the ethical effects of art, along with the importance of his position as Slade professor. With self-evident inscriptions of denominations or images that easily could be read as homonyms (Britannia as Britain, for example), money was severed from the complex mythical and even historical references which were the art historian's specialty. Advancing iconology, especially symbols that the public did not know, thus sustained the position of the cicerone.

Nonetheless, in *Val D'Arno* (1873), the studies at Oxford of medieval Italian history, Ruskin affirmed the economic source of civilizations and his syncretic view of the ideal and economic. In the fifth lecture, the same year he published his twenty-fifth *Fors* on the British florin and reproduced the *fiorino,* Ruskin presents civilization and its art in view of what earlier he has called the "material relations, governing spiritual ones" (23:13). The lecture primarily concerns the various mercantile wars of the period. Recounting the Guelphs' triumph over the Ghibellines in their continual struggles, he tells how the victors invaded their nearest neighbors, notably the Pisans and the Sienese. His attitude toward the trade wars vacillates. He writes sarcastically of the Florentines' "energetic promulgation of peace" and violent attempts to make "pacific mercantile states" of nearby towns (23:73, 70). Yet from his readings in Simonde de Sismondi and the Villanis' *Chronicle,* Ruskin infers that the Florentines invaded in "absolute good faith." With a "kindly jealousy of their neighbours, and in a true desire to . . . extend to them the privileges of their own new artisan government, the Trades of Florence have taken arms," he states (23:74). A twenty-four-carat gold florin commemorated their victory. It weighed an eighth of an ounce and bore an image of John the Baptist on one side and a fleur-de-lis on the other. Having a gold standard won the Florentines the privilege of free trade in Tunis, according to Sismondi (23:72). As participants in Tunisian trade, the coiners also could circulate signs of their origins and beliefs. In this way, the means of exchange became also a traveling exhibit of ideology. With this account, Ruskin shows that the monetary value of the coin affects not only the trading practices of the new city-state, but its higher values as well.

As his own manipulation of the tortoise-image suggests, Ruskin knew that beliefs and values engraved on money often occluded the historical conditions of the coining itself. Generalizing from Sismondi's account, he avers that any coin's value lies in its metal, other coins, or general produce and "varies . . . from instant to instant" (23:73). All pieces of money, though they merely contain "a given weight of a given metal" and cannot signify a perpetual value, are the efficient and final causes of societies. He defines the latter in mercantile rather than ideological terms. Peace between the Florentines and the Pisans in 1254 meant untaxed commerce between the towns, common weights and cloth measures, and the same alloy of money (23:73, 75). The gold florin established the value of a city-state's exchange, and men would fight to secure that value. If the opposers won, they would in their triumph make their own money. From Sismondi and the Villanis, Ruskin also learned that mercantile states were inaugurated with pillaging. As a result, the commemorative value of newly coined money is usually associated with violence. New coins are the first objects struck by new communities, and new communities themselves are formed by aggression, a coincidence uncovered long ago by Herodotus.[4] When the Pisans broke the trade pact, or peace, two years later, and the Florentines invaded and conquered them again, they cut down a pine tree by the Val di Serchio and struck their florins in its stump. A little tree appeared in the face of the coin. This image, so natural and benign in appearance, belies the spirit of its inception: it naturalizes the right to the land procured by force. Because as he told his university audience, "what is truly vital in the character which governs events, is always expressed by the art of the century" (20:279), Ruskin saw that the historical significance of the florin entailed a vital, often violent power illustrating the "arm" he had introduced as the source of value in his Inaugural lecture. It is, therefore, war, a species of labor, that makes trade as well as national art possible, even if its images disguise their inception.

In *Fors,* Ruskin's description of Sir John Hawkwood provides another example of the holistic economy conceived and sustained by actual and ideal labor, respectively. The victories of the English mercenary, who fought for the Pisans, Bolognese, and other Italian factions in the merchant wars, entailed violence and pillage. But Ruskin endows his invasions with the aesthetic (if not the moral) appeal of a chivalric code: "Theft could not, merely by that dignified form of government [monarchy], be made a holy manner of life; but it was made both dexterous and decorous. The pages of the English knights under Sir John Hawkwood spent nearly all their spare time in burnishing the knights' armour, and made it always so bright, that they were called 'The White Company'" (27:16).

Knights and peasants showed a high sense of honor, tested physically in their work, Ruskin continues, as though presenting laborers with suitable models for farming and industry, not class struggle. They paid loving attention to the beautiful objects of their profession, whether they were weapons, armor, wheelbarrows, or money. Further, they sensed the importance of rank in contrast to the amorphous middle and working classes of England and America toiling away amidst machines. The chivalric style, colorful and undomestic, is superior to the capitalistic brigandage of middle-class industrialists such as James Fisk, the financier and member of the Erie Railway "ring," whose mercantile pillage ended in his own assassination in 1872 (27:271–72). Although Ruskin cannot condone the "Divine right of theft" (27:17), he coldly approves of Sir John's methods because chivalry and war involved certain ritualistic elements that were missing from Fisk's speculations and investments. Whereas the modern mercantile warrior practices a factitious labor entailing the proliferation of money from itself, the medieval worker exercised a fundamentally domestic economy centered on his own body and its accoutrements. Ruskin's abhorrence, in theory, of interest sprang from the same impulse to make money the sign in a stable, finite system and goes back to Aristotle's distinction in *Politics* between unlimited money-getting *(chrematistikē)* and the disposition of wealth in household management *(oikonomikē)*.[5]

The medieval knight used his entire body to obtain control of land. Of course the body in labor could exhaust itself to death, but for this very reason it was an object of idolatry, its work circumscribed by ritual. Encased or surrounded by gold and finely wrought weapons, it engaged in "decorous" warfare for a particular good. Traditionally, Ruskin saw this good as land; its acquisition was the goal of mercantile warriors and the members of his Guild of St. George. In fact, the goods and coins of the guild confirm the place and role of money in Ruskin's economic model and follow to some extent the practices of the mercenaries in the Italian trade wars. (However, the guild was a pacific version of the model.) In founding the guild to purchase land for farming, homesteading, and preservation, Ruskin was saving England from the industrial depredations of government and industry.

The guild was Ruskin's contemporary version of these medieval economies, and thus it had its own money, whose double function and complex iconology Ruskin was designing. In *Fors* 58 (1875), he states that all coins and paper should be exchangeable at any time for part of the "National Store," his name for the repository of goods, in addition to land, which currency guarantees in a truly wealthy, or stable, society. Price and cost may fluctuate, but currency is always "a government receipt for goods received" (28:432). Ruskin wanted to forge his currency from metal, though in theory he had nothing against paper because it also was a sign of exchange which merchants issued against a consignment of commodities. (In 1833, Bank of England Notes became legal tender and by then, workers often were paid in them.)[6] However, because metal, with its double function, still signified wealth itself, and because St. George's was a nostalgic venture, Ruskin wanted coins to serve as the emblems of the guild and the culture that spawned it. He writes, in his catalogue of the coins of St. George's Museum at Meersbrook Park, Sheffield, that the size of the silver pence will be derived from the penny of William the Conqueror because that older coin was found by a fortuitously named Mr. Verity (30:268–69). The Verity penny thus would become the standard of the St. George pence.

Exchange among guild members would not be fraught with the perceptual opacity Ruskin sometimes evinced in his discussions of contemporary commercial transactions. For he inflated his tokens with a preexisting myth that sealed the gap between the economic and the ideal and fulfilled his desire for stability and a fixed signified. The interplay between image and legend, like a leitmotif, would tacitly mark every exchange of the guild's ducats with Ruskin's love for Rose La Touche. Further, the myth of an edenic land guarded by patriarchal property-holders would overarch the bit of the National Store the gold coin symbolized: "On one of [the ducat's] sides it will bear the figure of the archangel Michael; on the reverse, a branch of Alpine rose: above the rose-branch, the words 'Sit splendor';

above the Michael, 'Fiat voluntas'; under the rose-branch, 'sicut in coelo'; under the Michael 'et in terrâ' with the year of the coinage: and round the edge of the coin, 'Domini'" (28: 430–31).

Circulating emblem books, these ducats would inscribe every transaction with the blessing of God and work, for the parts of the legend come from the last verse of Psalm 90, which reads, "And let the beauty of the Lord our God be upon us: and establish thou the work of our hands upon us." St. George's coins were to be ideal examples of popular art, for they exalted economic value, asserted in every act of buying and selling, with society's important memories and myths. They were the possessions of beholders whose split perception had been healed, and they sanctified the daily commerce of those who exchanged money, especially because bearers of the guild's ducats would understand all the allusions. By purchasing goods, they affirmed Ruskin's devotion to Rose, the preindustrial landscape, and manual labor. And unlike the thirteenth-century florin, his ducats commemorated land and labor purchased or given, not conquered or compelled.

From his medieval studies, Ruskin realized that the genealogies of popular art were morally ambiguous, but he favored physical dominance over mercantile (and mass) exploitation and tried to distinguish the manufacturing prototype from the pre-Benthamite mercenary soldier who fought in the thirteenth-century Italian trade wars. Other suitable workers and defenders of the land such as Oliver Cromwell and Sir Roger de Coverley—the first with the temper of a "Huntingdonshire farmer" (27:272) and the latter a peaceable English squire— though not true mercenaries who epitomized Ricardian labor by endangering their lives for pay, did at least view money as a symbol of tangible commodities, labor and property. The real moral difference between capitalists such as Fisk and mercenaries such as Sir John Hawkwood lay in the absence and presence, respectively, of an outside referent for money. Ruskin condemned the view of money as valuable in itself and as self-referential. He thought it a form of idolatry and filled his late works with nasty asides about the Mammon-worshiping public. The definitions Ruskin himself used for currency eliminated self-referentiality and the threat of chrematistics. However, in stabilizing value, they further problematized his relationship with his audiences.

MONEY AS CURRENCY

Because money was a particular sort of commodity itself, it derived its aesthetic value from labor, or the *mythos* of its production. In this sense, paper or coins could signify the *mythoi* of a culture as they passed from one person to another. Circulating currency also had historical associations for Ruskin; the new florin was an example. And like popular art, it ideally signified something concrete and stable, though in reality its "meaning," the redeemed signified in the marketplace, often fluctuated. This instability in money's value and "meaning"—what it redeemed or signified—led Ruskin to form definitions of currency that ensured stable referents.

Writing as a political economist in *Munera Pulveris,* Ruskin follows the orthodox explanation of money's role in the marketplace. In the form of price, money indicates the amount of labor exchanged for something; in the form of cost, money represents the amount of labor required for the object's production (17:153). These, the chief elements of Ricardian labor theory as the public understood them, pervade all his writing. When addressing the laborers of Great Britain in *Fors,* Ruskin supplemented these ideas with definitions of his own which were to prove troublesome to his projected audience.

His alternative definitions arose in response to two popularized views from some relatively obscure pieces he had read. The first, a paper by T. J. Dunning entitled "On the Predatory Instinct of Man, considered in relation to the Science of Social Economy" (1860), calls man the "animal that exchanges" (28:102n.4; quoted in 28:159). It describes exchange as the civilized way of controlling aggressive forms of self-interest such as fraud and violence. Similarly, a "lesson" in *Household Science: Readings in Necessary Knowledge for Girls and Young Women* (1881) by Reverend J. P. Faunthorpe, defines money as the "medium of exchange" (29:553n.2). The second modern notion, drawn from various sources and succinctly stated by Edward Kellogg in *Labour and other Capital: The Rights of each Secured and the Wrongs of both Eradicated* (1849), is that "Money, the representation and measure of value, has also *the power to accumulate value by interest*. . . . This accumulative power is essential to the existence of money, for no one will exchange productive property for money that does not represent production" (28:144). Dunning's and Faunthorpe's description of human beings as selfish carnivores who exchange in lieu of stealing derives from the then well known model of Ricardo and Mill, who based their ideas on an "economic man" living to accumulate riches and satisfy his desires. Ruskin, of course, despised Dunning's model and founded his own political economy on humanity's altruistic motives. Despite his adherence to Ricardian labor theory, his whole economy lay outside the assumptions about human behavior of orthodox thinkers such as Nassau Senior, Smith, and Mill.[7] His objections sprang in part from misreadings of traditional theory. As John T. Fain points out, Ruskin seemed deliberately to construe Mill's descriptions of unproductive labor (any work that did not result in a consumable object) as insulting to the public (because such a category included all services), when the economist was trying simply to explain the conditions under which the productive power of the community could diminish.[8] Clearly Ruskin assumed that economists wrote as he often did—of what should be or, answering their wishes, could be.

One of Ruskin's main desires was for a stable economy in which money functioned like the biblical typologies his mother taught him as a boy: in the Old Testament, every sign was real and had a concrete counterpart in the New Testament. If money worked like a biblical sign, it meant something definite and procurable. His theoretical abhorrence of interest (though he actually lived on it) sprang from its violation of both this biblical parallel and Aristotle's prohibition of usury.[9] Contrary to Kellogg's belief, money should not signify its own production whether functioning as commodity or currency. Because it was coined to be exchanged, its *re*production as interest was unnatural, for then it functioned as a homogeneous likeness of the original. Therefore in 1880, with corroboration from Aristotle's

Politics, and in immediate response to Faunthorpe's notion, Ruskin redefined money to suit his desires rather than his observations. Ignoring its ability to multiply, he calls money an order for goods in a letter to Faunthorpe (29:554). In doing so, he not only prevents money from begetting itself and makes it a heterogeneous symbol, signifying something other than itself, but he guarantees an apprehensible signified. He also continues money's primitive role as a secular type or *symbolon;* this ring or clay token was divided in half and kept by each of the covenanters as evidence of their pact. [10] When a depositor went to collect his goods, he brought his half of the ring to the temple or bank to prove his identity. The sense of a coin as half a sign in Ruskin's writing is similar. Because it ensures its "anti-type," the redemption of goods is its half; without them, the coin as sign is incomplete and valueless.

In this light, Ruskin turns in *Fors* to an agrarian economy to ensure material signifieds, both land and labor. This reversion was necessary because he had accepted Malthusian and Ricardian assumptions about scarcity. In this way, he challenged Faunthorpe's definition of money as a medium of exchange from the nostalgic and overdetermined perspective of a Ricardian, Malthusian Physiocrat. He called money an order for goods to defy statements such as Kellogg's about its function as interest, but his definition is also compatible with the general drift of labor theory because, as he understood, basing the economy on production of goods made labor the source as well as the measure of exchange. In short, labor guaranteed what exchange could not: fixed meaning and value. Yet conceiving money as an order for goods emphasizes the consequences of Ricardian theory: for when labor is an expendable "good" figured in money, work means suffering and exhaustion. Convinced of this, Ruskin says in *Munera Pulveris* that work is not simply effort, but suffering in effort, but that the ideal political economy will spare work as much as possible (17:183). He championed labor that strengthened and ennobled the body, that glorified it while it was alive and forestalled its death. Factory work numbed and degraded the body in life; to oppose this sight, Ruskin created a cult of the body from the spectacle of the past. He looked backward, to the barons, knights, and squires whose original hold on the land was a sign of their physical power—exerted in suffering. That strength, now pacific and *passed,* would somehow help contemporary artisans and farmers retain what had become their legal and, more importantly, their moral right to the land.

Accordingly, in *Fors* 44, Ruskin defines money also as a "token of right" (28:135), giving the current money-holder an archaic lordship. Historical right exalts the suffering body that works itself 'til or to death; it deflects the fear of the present into bravado about the past. As a "token of right," money operates as a *symbolon,* a visible sign of a covenant from an earlier understanding possible in a hierarchical society that allows no movement between classes. As Paul L. Sawyer comments, Ruskin's conservative social model "assumes as immutable the present relationships of power in order to reform the present uses of power."[11] Sawyer is referring to passages Ruskin wrote in 1860 in *Unto This Last* in which he admits that what "is really desired, under the name of riches, is . . . power over men" (17:46). His examples of those who have earned the token of right reveal an allegiance to squirearchical, even aristocratic values (which obscure his own roots in the middle classes, as the son of a sherry merchant), and to inimitable models, such as Sir Roger de Coverley and Sir John Hawkwood. John Vernon argues that power became a signified of money only with the Industrial Revolution.[12] If this is so, Ruskin would be projecting a postagrarian metaphor on an agrarian past.

In conceiving money as an order for goods and a token of right, Ruskin healed the myopia that had divided economics from aesthetics and philosophy in many of his passages, such as the one on the oriflammes in his Inaugural lecture. His notions about ethical work and the ethical use of currency made labor and exchange expressions of higher values. But these were chauvinistic rather than spiritual. Giving money, as the guild members did, demonstrated nationalism through philanthropy; appropriating and cultivating land extended British culture through domestic and international imperialism. All these enacted an ideal centered on the body that, despite the inevitable end of labor, obscured the de-authenticated relations Ruskin saw in the contemporary use of money, which Marx called *Ver-*

dinglichung, or reification. Collecting coins provided another alternative to their multiplication and debasement through capitalistic investment, for hoarding ensured that money would still act in the market as a token or *symbolon.* Naturally, Ruskin felt that he needed to defend a practice that the public, even the Bible, condemned. He did so with his definition of money as an order for goods.

As he remarks throughout *Fors,* the unpardonably avaricious person desires money with no thought of changing it into goods. Usurers and speculators who make money from money threaten the stability of St. George's National Store because their money represents neither land nor labor. On the contrary, the properly avaricious person covets money as a good and in doing so has removed money from the marketplace. It is now an art object, like the coins of the guild and the tortoise tokens of Aegina. And money carries the echo of its referentiality in land or labor; at any time it may exchange for an existing good. Hoarded coins, kept from circulation, thus epitomize the proper double function of money. "The addition of coin to coin, and of cipher to cipher, is a quite proper pleasure of human life," Ruskin reasons in *Fors* 62 (28:518). Statements such as this disturbed some correspondents, for Ruskin's pleasure in accumulating ciphers sounded to them very much like the delight of the usurer and speculator. But by gathering, counting, and looking at money, he satisfied his aesthetic and historical interests while he undercut the primacy of exchange in the economies of Faunthorpe and Dunning.

Fors is filled with offhand remarks about the delights of hoarding coins. In Letter 24 (1872), he writes that a person can be "greedy of gold—in an instinctive, fleshly way" but not intellectually corrupt, and he describes the delight of "counting money, and laying it in visible heaps and rouleaux" (27:425). "For the miser," writes John Vernon, "money is time, and time piles up; time is what he hoards and stores, walling himself in against the future."[13] Together with pillage, stockpiling suggests retention and control, practices that Ruskin consistently chose over spending, which implies unleashed desire. In "Der Besenbinder von Rychiswyl" (1852) by Jeremias Gotthelf (the pseudonym of Albert Bitzius), which he began translating in

Fors 30 (1873) from Max Buchon's French version, Ruskin introduces readers to a paragon of misers. Hansli, a broom merchant,
makes and sells his own products by hand and has a fond,
proprietary feeling for nature, the supplier of all his materials.
(He calls his trees "master-brooms," names his willows, and
handles their twigs gently.) After learning the craft from his
landlord (in feudal style "the farmer they lodged with"
[27:549]), Hansli builds a cart to carry his brooms, in time
acquires a wife and a cow, and becomes the owner of his cottage.
The charm of the story for Ruskin lies in its sentimental account
of a peasant's daily tasks, as well as his Sabbath pleasures:

> On Sunday . . . he gave himself a personal treat. This . . .
> consisted in bringing out all his money, counting it, looking at
> it, and calculating how much it had increased, and how much it
> would yet increase, etc., etc. In that money there were some
> very pretty pieces,—above all, pretty white pieces. . . . Hansli
> was very strong in exchanges; he took small money willingly
> enough, but never kept it long; it seemed always to him that the
> wind got into it and carried it off too quickly. The new white
> pieces gave him an extreme pleasure,—above all, the fine dol-
> lars of Berne with the bear, and the superb Swiss of old time.
> When he had managed to catch one of these, it made him happy
> for many days. (27:632–33)

Hansli exploits money's dual role with no confusing or
unethical results. In fact, Ruskin uses Hansli to justify his own
love of collecting beautiful things. When he began publishing
his expenditures in *Fors,* he had to defend himself against claims
that he was violating the guild's principles by taking interest
and purchasing luxuries such as pictures and rings.[14] Thus
Ruskin agrees with the narrator that "Hansli was not avaricious
but economical" (27:632); his pastime is "perfectly natural and
legitimate . . . when the riches are very moderate" (27:633).
His joy over the bear-dollar resembles Ruskin's own over British
lion-shillings, except the Swiss peasant's coin is truly popular
art because Hansli has no idea what the bear represents.[15] Hansli's story and Ruskin's remarks about the joys of money resemble
descriptions of heraldic and mythic engravings on British,
Aegean, and Florentine coins; together, they compose an aes-

thetics of money that simultaneously depends on and ignores its circulation. Hoarding money (in "moderate" amounts) is "economical." The term is a moral one: Hansli's money does not multiply through interest as the capitalist's does; and when spent, it procures an implement. (Spending money, a dangerous act when not philanthropic, is naturalized and set in an animistic world with the clause, "the wind got into it and carried it off too quickly.") Finally, money's value never fluctuates. Hansli never works and saves only to discover that he has not enough for the goods he wants. In Gotthelf's idyll, money can function as a commodity and currency because the market is static and immutable, like the ideal value of the art object. It accommodates the childlike ambition of the peasant Hansli who desires goods as well as shiny things with pictures on them. But Hansli's primitive and charming economics illustrate what Marx described as modern fetishism. Everything in the story is a commodity. A wife counts as fixed capital; like a donkey or cart—archaic machinery—she eventually will lower the cost of production. Hansli takes pride in his work, and simultaneously work brings him more and more possessions. The story is propelled by the accumulation of goods toward a sudden deluge of money, an inheritance from a sister who was a rich man's wife disguised as a servant. This *deus ex machina* paradoxically ratifies all the peasant's values and identifies the essentially bourgeois character of the narrative, because it assimilates the broommaker into the monied "aristocracy," which is the aim of the "self-negating impulse" that identifies the middle-classes in general, remarks Michael McKeon.[16] It also links inheritance with land and labor, an intrinsic connection in labor theory from Locke to Mill; thus the right to private property exists because, and only as long as, the owner is in some sense a laborer.[17] The ending annoys Ruskin, who thinks the broom merchant should have remained a rustic rather than a rich, but still simple, man. Hansli's love of work attracts him because of the sort of preindustrial labor he liked to think it typified, but the willows and cottages and market days provide only an idyllic ambience. Hansli may live for his work, but the story lives in the wish for more things expressed by repeated exchanges, Sabbath prayer-play, and eventually a windfall. Because acquisition of objects is the fundamental motivation or base of the "economic man's" labor and narrative, the inheritance in effect signifies the wish of the writer and by projection, Hansli, to stop both desire, ambition, and work; these propel the plot. Ruskin's attraction to the story reveals the psychological basis of his own economics. The pastoral setting and evangelical ethics of work, like Dunning's notion of exchange, merely conceal the desire for power unleashed at the story's end.

I am not suggesting that the structure of "The Broom Merchant" is unique to the nineteenth century because of its growing, industrialized middle classes; after all, the miraculous appearance of riches is a stock ending of folk tales. I also am not imputing hidden motives to Ruskin's acquisitions for the Guild of St. George. Ruskin bought and accepted land to create a familial relationship between landlord and tenant, and to promote farming, preindustrial crafts, and other labor without machines. He considered the details of getting and spending important signs of character and attached his own accounts to *Fors* until 1878, when he sent them separately to members and made them purchasable annually to others.[18] I do think, however, that the iconographies of money in the Oxford lectures, the attack on the "meaning" of contemporary coins, the plans for the guild, and the use of Gotthelf's story were attempts to avoid viewing social relations organized around *Verdinglichung*. Collecting money for its look and feel (elevated into its iconography), working on and with the land, taking payment from the poor in kind (as Hansli does) all inflate money, Ruskin thought, into a bond between persons or nature. Even the trade wars involved societies that worked through human rather than objectified connections.

In summary, the story of Hansli illustrates the paradoxical source of money and the problematic of labor for Ruskin. It is earned by the work of the body on the land, yet it is then endowed by a birthright; through exchange and acquisition, it expresses the values of romantic humanism, but simultaneously it reifies all human relations.[19] Still, for Ruskin, money signified both labor and something that pre-existed labor, that had for him the appeal of social or temporal distance. He believed that in a healthy society, the manufacturer and artist are "developed states of the peasant" (27:260–61), but he also embodied the Christian virtues of this society in the *Spectator's* Sir Roger de Coverley, whose rank authorizes such virtues as signs of its dominance. It is thus from the *adopted* perspective of the landed gentry, rather than of the working, peasant, or middle classes, that Ruskin formed his notions of value. He acknowledged that by the rules of British rank, neither he nor the Yorkshire operative could ever become a gentleman, but he could simulate the condition of the lord through philanthropy (29:70). Ruskin often wrote contemptuously of the baron, describing him as a somewhat stupid, healthy guardian of the land—Arnold's barbarian—but like Arnold he admired the baronial style and its precedents in the chivalric code.

The *ethos* of the Guild of St. George reflects Ruskin's ideal but problematic definitions of money. Members will substitute altruism for pillage; philanthropists will replace mercenaries. Gift-giving, teaching, and understanding—the activities he prescribes in *Sesame and Lilies*—are privileges of comfortable little girls wealthy in time as well as money. One of their models is Largesse, from the *Romaunt of the Rose,* a figure of privilege whose exalted position lets her bestow. Ruskin copies these lines for the readers of *Fors,* for the pun, perhaps: "Si n'avoit elle joie de rien, / Fors quant elle povoit dire, 'tien'" (28:161).

Ruskin did not confine nobility to a certain social class, but he did tie its manifestations to money backed by property (essentially "old-labor"). As his feudal model in *Val D'Arno* illustrates, he was aware of how families historically got their land. P. D. Anthony notes his "clear understanding of the basis of ownership in power . . . as though he acknowledged that power was the basis of morality itself."[20] In *The Genealogy of Morals,* written in 1887, a few years after *Fors* ended, Friedrich Nietzsche concurs when he says, "The origin of the opposites *good* and *bad* is to be found in the pathos of nobility and distance, representing the dominant temper of a higher, ruling class."[21] For Ruskin and the allegorical Largesse, bestowing could replace stealing only through social distance signified by money, initially achieved by force and expressive still of that power. Charity was really for Ruskin the more distanced and visible act of "largesse," which was not simply circumscribed by such inordinate space, but caused by it. In *Fors* Ruskin stresses that virtue rather than inheritance brings true nobility and lordship, but he employs words freighted with class distinctions like "squire" and "lord," just as Gotthelf wrote his peasant Hansli into social supremacy and bourgeois wish-fulfillment.

In defense of Ruskin's aristocratic vision of modern labor, one might argue that he was stuck with linguistic and narrative repertories that did not completely suit his purposes; the era's language, as well as its narrative conventions, were the larger structures within which he had to create *mythoi*. But this sort of reasoning ignores not only his awareness of language's historical genesis but also the significance of his choice of accepted conventions. Ruskin exploited etymologies or created them when they served his purpose. For example, in *Munera Pulveris,* he brings philanthropy into his economic model by manipulating *charity*'s ties to money and labor. First he links the word with the French *cher;* both are adaptations from Latin *cāritāt-em*. The *caritas* of the Vulgate and the Old French *chierté,* or high price, were not always kept distinct in the English form, so the Christian use of the word was commonly linked to its popular meaning through the composite *cherité*. Ruskin is not this etymological; he traces connections through allusion. For example, he personifies the Greek notion of *charis* as the true wife of Vulcan, or Labour and the forerunner of Eleutheria or Liberality (17:226–28). When he goes on to connect these etymologies with the mythical Charis and Eleutheria, who symbolize, he says, benignity in government and freedom from corruption, he bases his patriarchal politics in the labor theory of value. *Charity* is the "dear" labor that passes, at great price, into privileged and highly visible benevolence.

In another passage in an early numbers of *Fors,* he calls himself a Communist, a word he probably picked up from Mill's *Principles* and the Parisian Communalists (27:115–16). Never seriously advocating public ownership of property, he links the term with cooperation and charity. His definition of *Communism* comes from Thessalonians and forges the link between labor, goods, and consumption: "It means that everybody must work in common, and do common or simple work for his dinner" (27:117). Coincidentally, a description of one of these communities appears in the disciples' reaffirmation of faith with the coming of the Holy Ghost (Acts 2:44): "And all that believed were together, and had all things in common." Although he does not refer to this passage, Ruskin does call St. George's a "world-wide monastery" (29:294) in *Fors* 84. By this time (1877), his desire to turn back history has assumed a definite spatial form: St. George's is communal but monastic like Cluny and Cîteaux in his later lecture, economically self-sufficient and apart from the unfruitful, industrial world. The guild shares the world's notions about labor as the source of value but erases contemporary contexts of scarcity and capitalism. Temporal and spatial distance from current troubles, as well as changes, does not mitigate the suffering of labor, but gives the worker more time.

Like the "token of right," the "order for goods" is regressive, in the sense that it reverts to a closed system somewhat like barter which encompasses all exchange and thereby heals the split between the ideal and the economic. The currency of usurers, capitalists and gamblers either dissipates or multiplies far beyond the amount of available goods, and Ruskin associated it with the chrematistical currency of words. When discussing the etymology of *charity,* he counsels that "the reader must not think that any care can be misspent in tracing the connexion and power of the words which we have to use. . . . Much education sums itself in making men economize their words, and understand them" (17:225). As we shall see in chapter six, this is an ironic statement in light of the profligate economy of *Fors*. In theory, however, Ruskin was trying to follow Aristotle and avoid chrematistics: to economize words or money, we must couple them with historical or material signifieds; we misspend when we open the household to unlimited symbolization. This happens in exchange as money accumulates interest and multiplies unchecked. It no longer represents the scantily stocked National Store. When money signifies itself endlessly, Ruskin detects mismanagement, a complete elision in a society's sign system. The natural model has vanished; money no longer has to name anything outside itself. Now it suggests a noumenal power and, appropriately, has its own term—Mammon worship (16:138; 20:234). The transparent signified that merely reflects the phenomenal is then inverted by a myopic people. As a result, money seems to manifest a godlike potential for infinite exchange. Ruskin found suitable images in literature for this baseless money. He uses Chaucer's Pardoner and Dante's lake of pitch to stress the evils of greed and peculation in *Fors* (27:312–13). He associates love of making money with the labyrinth-city, at the center of which lies the "bestial nature" that begets the "everlasting Pound" (27:510). In *St. Mark's Rest,* he suggests that the Venetians revive a custom that set lotteries and hangings on the same spot (24:221). In each case, he redirects tradition to support his wish that money always signify a debt, for death equals the absence of a commodity as the signified. But in a world of scarcity, the signified of money—goods and labor, the National Store—will vanish too, ending in this absence.

To avert this terrible and imminent void, Ruskin encased the laboring body in gold and distanced it in time and space. He advocated sharing and cooperation, or Communism, not only to exemplify charity but to ease the burden on the individual body. In *Fors* and the Oxford lectures, he described alternatives to alienating and exhausting work that glorified labor and emphasized the historical and aesthetic, rather than the exchange value, of labor's symbol, money. Because his economic model, in idealizing labor and producing belief from an economic base, was self-referential in inverting the Platonic hierarchy, Ruskin elevated labor and commerce into romantic and positivistic ideals with their own rituals and ethics about human conduct, and insisted on a fixed object of exchange. This utopian version of the model is appealing, but as a real solution to current monetary practices it was outmoded. Moreover, its apparent spirituality and virtue were transparently material and hence not essentially different from contemporary values. Hansli's bucolic work, Sir John Hawkwood's victories, the guild's re-greening of England, and the meaning of charity each create natural, even primitive affinities between people and land. But they were unsuccessful alternatives, for when philanthropy, broom-making, and medieval warfare are traced through their historical conditions, each is fundamentally an economic arrangement backed by the energy of the body that Ruskin identified as power in 1843 and tried to harness for ethical purposes in his late projects and lectures. In fact, he faced it as an aggressive and amoral force. "There is no great art possible to a nation but that which is based on battle," he writes in *The Crown of Wild Olive* (1866); war is "the foundation of all the high virtues and faculties of men" (18:460, 464). When he defined money as a token of right, he set value in military and baronial power metamorphosed into middle-class philanthropy and tried to freeze an obsolete social hierarchy. And his other definition of currency relied on a precapitalistic agrarian economy he knew had vanished.

Furthermore, money as an order for goods, his solution to currency as a chrematistical symbol, does not accommodate Ruskin's defense of hoarded gold, unless we consider the double function of money that he found so cumbersome. For hoarding did not just invalidate money's role as currency and imperil the altruistic purpose of the guild, it advanced objectified relations between persons, the very sort of fetishism Ruskin tried to avoid. Moreover, in his account of the thirteenth-century Florentine coin, he seems conscious that a nation's superstructure of values might rely on nothing more elevated than territoriality and physical contests. And comments in *Fors* and elsewhere, notably his description of the organist at the Crystal Palace, even his descriptions of Prout's drawings, show that the superstructure of values he wanted to see expressed in the use of money was simply a record of ever-changing transactions. Money's overdetermined position in Ruskin's economy confused the nonacademic public because his iconographies for it as art and currency often were recondite and outmoded. But they were familiarly ominous to those who understood that Ruskin was simply following the orthodox economic discourse, in which the ultimate value and meaning of money lay in the limits of human labor. He would face these limits when *Fors* entered the market as epistolary tender.

Circulating Value

Ruskin's major undertaking just before he began his tenure at Oxford was *The Queen of the Air,* three essays that connected mythology with natural phenomena. In part, the work reflected contemporary studies in myth and language by Max Müller, a colleague at the university, and the earlier moral approach of Carl Otfried Müller, who treated myth as a system of opposition.[1] *The Queen* also inherits over ten years of Ruskin's thought on political economy, beginning with two lectures of 1857, "The Political Economy of Art." As I have said, Ruskin actually had read little in orthodox economics, but ideas from the accepted discourse found their way easily into his writing, particularly into subjects that seemed unrelated, such as mythology. While writing about art and myth, he assumed a labor theory of value and an economy of scarcity even as the idea of exchange-value was changing economics and affecting his attitude toward interpretation and language in general.

The submerged presence of microeconomics—theories of production, value, and distribution—in Ruskin's readings of myth and the plastic arts has been overlooked by this century's critics for a good reason. The labor theory of value that still dominated the discourse in the sixties had nothing to do with art. As Ricardo himself said, the value of most art was a condition of scarcity, not labor; fine paintings were nonreproducible commodities.[2] Furthermore, *The Queen of the Air* does not even concern Ruskin's own political economy—that intersection of morality, aesthetics, and history. It is about myth, not money, or even the value of art. And although Ruskin combined an incipient form of his political economy and art when he discussed value in *The Stones of Venice,* he never ostensibly used economics to disclose meaning. This separation has led Ruskin's twentieth-century readers, who generally have viewed interpretation as a formalistic exercise, to separate the art from the social criticism whenever possible. The division is both natural and convenient; it was, as we have seen, encouraged by Ruskin himself after *Cornhill* and *Fraser's* had rejected his essays on political economy. Nonetheless, to explain the meaning of Athena and other beloved paintings and statues to a wider audience, Ruskin turned to exchange-value, even for supposedly nonreproducible commodities.

The Queen of the Air, three essays of 1869, provides evidence that Ruskin unwittingly extended economic principles to language and treated words the way contemporaries were using money, as transparent units of exchange. *The Queen* is an implicit acceptance of exchange-value, a concept Ruskin acknowledged as fact elsewhere. By admitting exchange or circulating value into his criticism, Ruskin could embrace many readings and many readers, particularly the unsophisticated minds who, through minimal education and technological developments in printing, had access to books and formed a potential audience for his own works. But their presence also provoked a kind of critical miserliness in which he withheld both object and meaning from those who devalued art with their ignorant perceptions. *The Queen* is a happy example of the liberating effects of exchange-value on hermeneutics, though it also exposes the reductive consequences of the new economics of meaning for the nineteenth-century reader.

HERMENEUTICS AND EXCHANGE-VALUE

As John T. Fain and P. D. Anthony have stressed, Ruskin entered the discourse of political economy in *Unto This Last* by ostracizing himself from its chief principles.[3] And as I have mentioned, he invalidated his arguments within the discourse by flaunting his ignorance of its important writings. In the Preface to his lectures at Manchester in 1857, he admits that he has read no works in the field but Adam Smith's *Wealth of Nations*. In 1860, in *Unto This Last*, he quotes from Mill's *Principles of Political Economy,* a book that he may never have read completely.[4] Instead, Ruskin culled his ideas from Livy, Xenophon, Horace, and Plato (17:xlix) and based political economy on moral tenets like magnanimity, largesse, and charity. Yet if he was, as Fain says, dissatisfied "with the narrow bounds of political economy as it was conceived by his . . . contemporaries," if "his conception of the science was sociological and ethical rather than strictly economic," he nonetheless supported his discussions of value with the tenets that had shaped and would change economics in the nineteenth century.[5]

Ostensibly, Ruskin objected to an economics of art because he believed in, and searched for a way to detect, inherent worth outside the marketplace. In matters of aesthetics, he had formalistic assumptions. However, he had trouble isolating internal from external or accidental qualities and, ironically, found the most explicit study of value in orthodox economics. It alone provided standards, and although it in effect explained away intrinsic value, it offered elements that Ruskin could treat as signifiers, all the while maintaining his belief in an absolute, inherent criterion. Committed to the idea of intrinsic value, he used quantifiable measures such as labor to estimate the value of work that already had some inherent worth.[6] In fact, Ruskin would never identify the source of value *before* labor. And although labor itself was not an intrinsic value, through habitual *objectification* Ruskin transferred the qualities of production to the object without at first seeing this as an alienating process.[7] In *The Seven Lamps of Architecture* and *The Stones of Venice,* he had stressed the beauty and worth of work done by hand, especially the hand of a sincere laborer striving for perfection, but he could only detect this earnest effort of the worker in the finished object. His own labor theory of value relied, therefore, on a projection that he insisted was an intrinsic quality of the object.

In the Manchester lectures of 1857, public desire further

upsets his quest for an intrinsic standard, for there Ruskin considers the effect of public perception on value. Within the market, price becomes the symbol of value, but the latter term has become more difficult to fix, even on an extrinsic standard like work. Ruskin comments that the price of a painting by a living artist can never represent the amount of labor invested in it. In the real marketplace, price also indicates the desire of the rich or the aspiring, the wish for gentility—the intangibles that somehow become associated with art or any commodity. To counter these invisible inflators, he ransacks political economy for a fixed standard of value. A "just price" for the object itself might be determined, he suggests in the spoken version of the lecture, by pricing paintings per square foot. The *Manchester Guardian* reported that Ruskin said this "seriously, and he meant it" (16:87n.2), though at first it seems more likely that the comment was an ironic solution derived from the utilitarian reliance on mathematics that characterized Mill's *Principles* and political economy in general. Yet the *Manchester Guardian* may have been correct, for, as I have shown, many of Ruskin's contemporaries had secularized labor theory into a quantitative standard, and Ruskin himself was still committed to fixed and intrinsic standards for judging the aesthetic properties of art. To maintain them in an age in which value hinged on changes in production and demand, he may have resorted to quantity, just as Edmund Burke unsuccessfully tried to depend on proportion to define beauty. Volume two of *Modern Painters* is essentially an argument with Burke's sensationism in which Ruskin tries to formulate innate properties of beauty, but in the process describes it as a phenomenon of perception. His use of economic principles places him in a similar dilemma: in defining intrinsic value, Ruskin ends up describing value-in-use or value in the eyes of a certain group of consumers.

Labor value was measurable and stable compared with market value. Twenty years after the Manchester lectures, Ruskin denounces in *Fors Clavigera* "what may specifically be called the Judasian heresy,—that the value of a thing is what it will fetch in the market: 'This ointment might have been sold for much,—this lake may be sold for much,—this England may be sold for much,—this Christ may be sold for—little; but yet, let us have what we can get'" (29:224–25). He thinks that a preposterous list of unexchangeables will invalidate circulating value for nonreproducible commodities. But this "heresy," of course, *is* one *because* it is committed. "I perceive it to be becoming daily more and more the aim of tradesmen," he observes in 1860, "to show . . . that commodities are made to be sold, and not to be consumed" (17:78). For Ruskin, market value subjected the commodity and labor to supply and demand, which economists were analyzing into "laws" that explained value and distribution; in a letter of 1873 he asserted to the editors of the *Scotsman* that no such laws existed (17:503). They conjured for him not only the utilitarian mania for statistics and mathematical equivalences but also the notion of an economy in which value fluctuated with the desires of consumers. Yet as he perpetuated the labor theory and the belief in inherent worth, Ruskin was including exchange in his formulation of value without ever abstracting the notion into a principle such as market value. In *Fors,* he describes how the laborer exchanges his work for that of another; their labor is objectified not in the thing alone, but in the mutual exchange of commodities such as kettles (28:159–60). Because Ruskin wanted to isolate pure value before exchange occurred, he would not acknowledge exchange-value in theory; in his economy, it was merely a "convenience" (28:160). Yet in practice he saw its importance in determining value, as his derisive comments on the organist in the Crystal Palace reveal. In acknowledging exchange as the basic expression of value, he advanced a working notion of an economy that, in the form of Jevons's marginal utility theory, would dominate microeconomics from the eighties to well into the twentieth century.

The Ruskinian economist J. A. Hobson notes that in the 1870s most economists did not know or understand the way heterodox ideas would change the classical explanation of value.[8] Yet a version of marginal utility steers the general argument in *The Queen of the Air.* Value at the margin fluctuates according to availability: if a thing is plentiful, its utility, satisfaction, or value—the same thing—diminish; if scarce, its value rises. This is especially true of art and other nonreproducible commodities; even Ricardo began his *Principles* by excepting them from his labor theory and attributing their value to scarcity. In *The Queen* the object of value is Athena or, rather, her various signifieds, and by extension, meaning itself. Ruskin proliferates both images and interpretations of Athena in these essays. He also recognizes the force of exchange-value—that the material and spiritual conditions of different readers and beholders will determine the meaning and value of this myth-product. In these two ways, he bases hermeneutics and value on the relative response to a flooded market of art—in museums, reproductions, pictures, books, and essays—from a heterogeneous audience. Hobson extends this instability to individual persons as well. "When we realize life in terms of values," he writes, "we shall realize how the source of value and the processes of relation differs {*sic*} not only in different persons but in the same person with the changes and chances of life. The philosophic demand for absolute values in truth, beauty, and goodness lose {*sic*} much of their authority and meaning when confronted with the actual concrete experiences of life."[9] Many of Ruskin's discussions of the effect and meaning of art begin and end in such actual incidents rather than in an absolute, abstract system.

Hermeneutics in *The Queen* is a constant process that reflects an economy whose source of value is shifting from production toward consumption. Just as in marginal utility theory price, the symbol of value, moved from its basis in labor to an intersection between supply and demand, in art the sign—verbal or visual—no longer derived its value simply from the producer's labor; its reception among a sundry group of readers both stimulated production and helped determine worth. Different groups of consumers naturally would understand the meaning of signs differently. Therefore, hermeneutics was subjected to value and the fluctuations of supply and demand. As I have discussed, Ruskin was not always willing to relinquish meaning to the marketplace; he often exhibited an autocratic and cryptic attitude toward the interpretation of language and images. When he did accept and try to influence the expanding audience and market, the meaning and value of art became subject to something like the laws of marginal utility.

Ruskin's growing interest in the effects of consumption,

especially demand, on value thus paralleled the shifting focus of economic studies, and it resulted not only from his awareness of different readerships, but from the effects of oversupply and scarcity. In his first Manchester lecture in July 1857, he concentrates on the production of commodities, including paintings, and raises the possibility of a surplus in the process. An ideal society will produce and use lasting materials, not those that guarantee demand through their "wholesome evanescence" (16:40). But durable work will result in an oversupply. At first Ruskin avoids the problem; intrinsic value, objectified here in the *production* of good art, should not be compromised by concerns about surplus. However, in the second Manchester lecture of 1857, he proposes to lower the prices of paintings partly to increase demand; then art will be available to more people, oversupply will cease to upset the economy, and each force will stabilize. This remedy assumes that the rate of production is consistent. It is based, moreover, on the orthodox notion that production and consumption are directly proportional, even though in the same lecture, Ruskin perceives a contrary movement between the two forces and offers another solution to oversupply. Having decried "the plague of cheap literature," he declares that "the dearest pictures are always the best bargains" (16:59, 78). Books should be difficult to buy; then they would be appreciated. He executes this idea some years later: when yellowbacks at railway bookstalls generally cost 3s.6d. or 2s., he fixed a guinea a volume as an acceptable price for his own series of reprinted works.[10] This price undoubtedly restricted his readership, as he intended, and it connected high prices with superior value and limited consumption. The conflict between Ruskin's proposals for cheaper painting and more expensive books reveals a more general ambivalence toward potential audiences. The plan for books prevails; therefore, the economy it illustrates—the one Ruskin practiced—must be the one he favored. It linked more money with more desire, with more sacrifice (of coin or saving-time) from the buyer, and with more labor-time from the producer, as well as with increased costs. As a result, value became tied to scarcity, as it had for rare wines, books, and pictures in Ricardo. Unlike Ricardo, Ruskin made scarcity a goal of production; eventually he created it through the limited issue and almost clandestine distribution of his books during the 1870s. In this practice, he incorporated the inverse relationship between supply and demand which he had introduced in the fifties. It would define value for the economists later in the century.

THE QUEEN OF THE AIR

Ruskin anticipated the marginal utility school in theory as well as practice by blurring intrinsic- and exchange-value in *Munera Pulveris*.[11] He brought his confusion over circulating and intrinsic value into hermeneutics, for by the time Ruskin wrote *The Queen of the Air,* he had lost a sense of the Absolute in other areas. Comparative mythology accommodated his skepticism about religion and language as well as his dawning awareness of the primacy of circulating value. The continuous changes in meaning in *The Queen* reflect not only Ruskin's own religious doubts but also his awareness that different readings by different sorts of people had destabilized both hermeneutics and value.

These ideas resemble a reading of conventional economics that had appeared two years before. Marx, in *Capital*, confronted the apparent paradox in the idea of an intrinsic value that was really an exchange-value "inseparably connected with . . . commodities."[12] He framed his economic theory with a conviction that all life is a process of constant transformation. This notion, culled from what John Kenneth Galbraith calls "the formidable, often appalling, aggregation of Hegel's thought," entered economics in the writings of Hegel's contemporary Georg Friedrich List. Dissenting from the orthodox school of Adam Smith, List envisioned a world of flux requiring continuous modification of economic "laws."[13] From this perspective, interpretation became what Marx called, in his "Critique of Hegelian Philosophy" in 1844, *"moments of motion,"* involving concepts that have "no validity in isolation, but dissolve and engender one another."[14]

Ruskin received these ideas diluted through popular discourse. They filtered into theories of mythology, for example. In

1877, several views of myth circulated which Henry Gay Hewlitt surveyed in *Cornhill:* they included a historical approach, which treated legends as exaggerated facts, and Max Müller's etymological theory, which handled myth as a "disease of language."[15] According to Müller, writers misread the metaphors and personifications of ancient dialects as evidence that primitive people believed in the deities. This was a linguistic refinement of the "poetic" theory George Grote presented in his *History of Greece* two decades earlier (1846), which suggested that ancient and modern writers fabricated metaphors to name the emotions they had projected onto actual objects. The etymological and poetic readings of myth correspond to Paul de Man's description of the first stage of conceptualization, a "wild, spontaneous" and often "wishful" metaphor, which Grote likewise attributed to distortions of fancy.[16] Müller, Grote, and the compiler Hewlitt all treat myth the way de Man treats language, as a continual act of *prosopopoeia*.

When Ruskin introduces the myths of Athena in *The Queen of the Air,* he deliberately avoids Müller's notion of misreading and embraces the poetic method that de Man says is innocent and inevitable. As in his reading of the Aeginian tortoise the next year, Ruskin suspends judgment of the correct or privileged meaning of the goddess because he wants to demonstrate her abiding currency in different centuries and cultures. He therefore grants Athena an inherent value through circulation. For instance, he connects her worship with Mariolatry and condones the religious practices of the rural poor, observing that the "common people's . . . idea of Athena was as clear as a good Roman Catholic peasant's idea of the Madonna" (19:347). Simultaneously, he views the goddess as a fiction. Never having existed, she is realized in a language of continuous substitution. He discerns her as the immanent form in birds which flutter about "like little winds" (19:360); he calls their plumage "the rubies of the clouds, that are not the price of Athena, but *are* Athena" (19:361). His most anagogic statement about her is one of his most famous: "Whenever you throw your window wide open in the morning, you let in Athena, as wisdom and fresh air at the same instant; and whenever you draw a pure, long, full breath of right heaven, you take Athena into your heart, through your blood . . . into the thoughts of your brain" (19:328–29).

The Queen of the Air is a complex string of linguistic sub-stitutions, and many have read it as a new version of Ruskin's fixed hermeneutics. George P. Landow observes that "natural myth serves the same polemical purpose as do Ruskin's theories of beauty [worked out in types in volume two of *Modern Paint-ers*], for both contribute to a kind of 'objectivity' in art and aesthetics. Both insure that human reactions, which are emo-tional and subjective, occur uniformly."[17] Raymond E. Fitch concludes that Athena is "the major symbol of the syncretic religious phase . . . through which [Ruskin] was passing."[18] Chains of images like "bird-cloud-air" that all lead to Athena support these statements. Yet to read *The Queen* summarily and find that everything means Athena—a conclusion with which Ruskin would agree—deflects attention from the continuous chain itself. When Ruskin says that clouds are *not* the price of Athena, but the goddess herself, he is trying to consolidate his hermeneutics into a single efficient exchange in an ideal econo-my; every object, like paper money, is documentary evidence of something greater and fixed—Athena. However, the visual chain that precedes this transfer of meaning cannot be erased. Because the bird "glows with air, in its flying, like a blown flame," then "rests upon the air, subdues it, surpasses it, out-races it;—*is* the air, conscious of itself, conquering itself, ruling itself" (19:360), no meaning supersedes the other unless we read these successive images as examples of Hegelian *Aufhebung*. In this sense, the bird supersedes but preserves air; it is air con-cretized. Both, in equally figural transformations, become Athena but retain their sensuous reality.

Arguably, "Athena" marks the ultimate significance in this chain not only because as the last term it closes the process but also because with the goddess's name the exchange becomes metaphorical. She is the second, absolute or metaphysical term, whereas the other signs are all material. But conceptualizing Athena as beyond her signifiers places Ruskin in a false position with the audiences whose readings he accommodates. For if myth can be read as a series of actual occurrences and an abstraction of natural phenomena, then Ruskin is annulling metaphysics only to reestablish them for either himself or the "common people" whose primitivistic conceptions of metaphor he wants to indulge (19:297–98).

The syncretic reading of Athena displays Ruskin's liberality toward reading and readerships, which is the real point of *The Queen of the Air,* but it challenges traditional interpretation because the real interest and color of hermeneutics lies in the series of images themselves rather than in their meaning. For example, "Athena Chalinitus," the first essay, traces what will be a frequent movement in the second essay, the "curious reversal or recoil of the meaning which attaches itself to nearly every great myth" (19:317). Ruskin connects the serpent with the seed's sprouting, corruption, and purification. For awhile, the serpentine form rivals the shapes of the air in number and power but winds its way toward the goddess. In "Athena Keramitis," the second essay, Ruskin comments that there is "scarcely a wreathed ornament, employed in Christian dress, or architecture, which cannot be traced back to the serpent's coil" (19:365). He espies the snakelike shape—a "running brook of horror"—everywhere on the ground and senses its presence, like the air's, in places where he cannot see it (19:362). It becomes the seed's sprouting and corruption, the "unconsuming and constant" fire, as well as the flame "consuming by excess" linked with Athena in the *Iliad,* Pentecost, and the parable of the ten virgins (19:364, 341). The snake has a number of offices: it is the spirit of horror and death, but also of agriculture and purification. It is the fellow-creature of Aesculapius and Hygieia. In addition, it is a "sacred earth-type in the temple of the Dew" erected also in homage of Athena as adoptive mother of Erichthonius, the "'tearer-up of the ground,'" the child of the "Lord of all labour," Hephaestus, and the earth (19:334). In his section on field herbage, Ruskin envisions the serpent's motion and venom when he sees the "passionless growth of the leaf out of the ground" (19:367). He remarks that the Draconidae, his name for non-cup flowers such as the snapdragon and foxglove, have the serpentine form; their leaves look "as if they had been touched by poison" (19:376). Concurrently, he reflects on an "Aesculapian as well as an evil serpentry among the Draconidae" and adds that "the fairest of them, the 'erba della Madonna' of Venice . . . descends from the ruins it delights in to the herbage at their feet" (19:377). The botanical family houses "herbs for healing,—all draconid in form," and sinuous evil with the Madonna who destroys it: all of the Draconidae—including the asphodels and lilies linked with Athena in legends—are "richest" "when crushed under the foot" (19:377). This interpretive move places all the images of the goddess in a dialectical continuum; Athena migrates from a virgin of constancy and guidance, a flame of both martial and evangelical energy, into an inimical form, the Gorgon, her "chief enemy slain," who turns living men to stone; his face decorates her armor (19:353).

However, Ruskin's readings of Athena are not truly dialectical: the serpent and, in another brilliant passage, Hermes (from Homer and Euripides [19:323–24]), reconcile merely at the original abstraction, Athena herself. The main signified in his retellings is always embodied in the exchange of images, but the series itself is never resolved into anything different. The recurring name "Athena" thus provides a distracting synthesis. It is the documentary evidence of the goddess—the images themselves—that really interest Ruskin. He even asserts in his discussion of the Draconidae that the "concurrence of circumstance is itself the supreme and inexplicable fact" to be confronted in the tangled correspondences of perception (19:377). Accordingly, he insists on the empirical origins of *mythoi*. "If the myth is about the sky, it must have been made by somebody who looked at the sky. If the myth is about justice and fortitude, it must have been made by some one who knew what it was to be just or patient" (19:301). All the complicated, contrary meanings of Athena have grown from both a literal story and a real person. She is both an autochthonous and metaphorical figure, accessible to naïve and sophisticated minds. A ubiquitous signified, she provides the fixed standard in Ruskin's interpretations. Everything means her, no matter how varied and seemingly different the signifiers. This leveled economy allows anyone to interpret. For religious, agnostic, figurative, or literal readers, she can be either term of the metaphor. The clouds are not only the *price* of Athena, but *Athena* herself.

In listing her different forms, Ruskin acts as a historian or a compiler, who describes what others have expressed. Consequently, he cannot articulate an intrinsic value for Athena apart from the myths and images of her that circulate. He tries to fix her meaning through anagogic symbolism, but if everything means Athena, everything means nothing. Like a commodity at the margin, the goddess has proliferated until she has no hermeneutical value. But this was not Ruskin's conclusion in 1869. I apply the principle of marginal utility to *The Queen* only because it exemplifies the devalued sign that he faced as an educator in the 1870s and 1880s. Only then did he perceive the results of freeing the sign from typological and other traditional exegeses. For when books, paintings, and sculpture became more visible and accessible, the people assumed the power to compose their own instant and perishable iconologies. The labor theory of value at least had allowed him to define value and meaning according to the perceived intentions of the writer or artist. But as Ruskin became more aware of the role of consumption and exchange in deciding value and less committed to inherent worth (and its false expressions as quantity or labor), both meaning and value became cheap to him as well.

ORDERS OF READING

In "Verona, and its Rivers," a lecture he gave in 1870, Ruskin declares that "even in deliberate symbolism, the question is always, as I have several times lately had to urge—not what a symbol meant first, or meant elsewhere—but what it means now, and means here" (19:437). His recent urgings had appeared in *The Queen of the Air,* in which he had observed about the Greeks that "to the mean person the myth always meant little; to the noble person, much" (19:299). This historical example helped distance him from the troubling fact that contemporary readers no longer shared a superstructure of beliefs and values. He continued to isolate himself from the troubling effects of disparate readings by retreating to theory and classification. In his "Preface" to Xenophon's *Economist* (1876), he describes how a myth can elicit four responses, each from someone with a particular set of values. His list is not objective, but hierarchical, based on the sincerity of one's belief. Thus, the first and worst reader treats the legend as fiction; the second views it with reserve and admires it as rhetoric. The third considers the myth a historical artifact, originally told by a credulous narrator but no longer plausible. The best reader does not claim superior knowledge. Instead, he or she "discovers and acknowledges . . . the tendency to self-deception, but with it also the capacity of divine instruction" (31:19). The difference between the third and fourth "order" of reader is hazy and rests largely on attitude. The highest reader wields no extralinguistic standard, even an empirical one, against the myth and, there-fore, does not assert its truth or falsity. He or she faces myth the way Ruskin treated the Bible—as if [it] *were* true" (10:xxxix). Because no reliable referent exists, he shifts his belief to the metaphor, which of course generates the ideal in his economic model.

In matters of religious faith, this seems like hedging, but Ruskin viewed himself as the best sort of reader, agnostic but sincere. In his essays on Athena, he places himself with some of the Greeks in the fourth order: "You might imagine that the employment of the artifice just referred to [in the third and fourth orders] implied utter unbelief in the persons contriving it; but it really meant only that the more worldly of them would play with a popular faith for their own purposes, as doubly-minded persons have often done since, all the while sincerely holding the same idea themselves in a more abstract form" (19:347–48).

As a "doubly-minded" reader, Ruskin "plays" with sym-bols of Greek and biblical myth in order to level down. His sincere belief in their abstract forms is untenable, however, for he has not only declared to his father that he will behave "as if" the Bible were true, but he has shown the conceptual world in flux in his treatment of Athena. Like the more worldly Greeks, Ruskin may have sincerely believed in the moral of the legends, but the forms of Athena signify too many various, even opposite concepts to compel belief in an Absolute. Later in this same essay, he remarks that "the purest forms of our own religion have always consisted in sacrificing less things to win greater." Using the Bible's monetary metaphor for promise, he continues, "The order, 'sell that thou hast,' is not given without the promise, 'thou shalt have treasure in heaven.'" The modern reader, for whom all value is unstable, hears the revised command, "'Sell that thou hast in the best market'" (19:350). The Greeks exchanged their labor for honor and rest, their myths for natural and moral explanations of the world. Old and New Testament figures sacrificed for salvation and read types as fulfillments of prophecies and covenants. The modern believer, though, can fix no permanent worth to forms of exchange because the significance of language as well as labor can change. In the above command, Ruskin is poking fun at the debased, shifting values of his age. He feels estranged from both the lower orders and language itself, which he regards as arbitrary metaphor, yet he must turn to the market—an array of forms in an arena of constant exchange—as the only existing ground of value, whether trade is in work or words.

This strategy, when practiced as actual description and interpretation, transformed Ruskin into a recorder of mass perceptions. His capitulation often was painful, and he never developed a constructive method of interpretation based on his implicit acceptance of exchange-value. Unstable value became especially vexing when he tried to assume or discuss appreciation of beauty or its effects. For instance, the tone of his description of one of his most cherished works, the tomb of Ilaria di Caretto in the Cathedral of S. Martino, ranges from cryptic reticence to diffused irony. His passages on this work show that while he tried to regulate the valuation of art and alter his readings for various audiences, he recognized a sort of market of response over which he had little control.

All his life, Ruskin loved the sculpture of the tomb of Ilaria di Caretto by Jacopo della Quercia lying in a recess of the cathedral at Lucca. He thought that it depicted the dead woman with great simplicity and no redundant illusionary effects. In a personal letter to his father in 1845, he declares that "the sculpture—as art—is in every way perfect: truth itself, but truth selected with inconceivable refinement of feeling." The cast of the drapery and fall of the hands are natural; "you expect every instant, nay rather you seem to see every instant, the last

sinking into death" (4:122n.1). The next year in volume two of
Modern Painters, Ruskin stresses the perfection of the tomb as
representation: "She is lying on a simple couch with a hound at
her feet; not on the side, but with the head laid straight and
simply on the hard pillow, in which . . . there is no effort at
deceptive imitation of pressure. It is understood as a pillow, but
not mistaken for one" (4:123).

Here, in public, Ruskin describes perception with the
"double mind" he later brings to metaphysics, by focusing on
effect. Yet to his father he had stressed the lifelike qualities of
the tomb: "You may stand beside it leaning on the pillow, and
watching the twilight fade off the sweet dead lips" (4:122n.1).
Now to readers of *Modern Painters*, Ilaria is no longer as close or
real. Her eyes and lips convey "something which is not death
nor sleep, but the pure image of both" (4:123). In considering
her effect on others, he treats her as a representation, and accordingly the impression she gives becomes more mediated—and
elusive.

As Ruskin makes her more and more a public image, she
begins to evade both detailed and comprehensive sight. In an
1874 lecture at Oxford on Quercia, he couches his observations
about the sarcophagus within the academic taxonomy he has
created during the term. Thus the monument is the finest
example of the mathematical school of art begun by Nicolo
Pisano. As opposed to the aesthetic (to which Ruskin says he
belongs), this school does not favor individual perception. It
places value in inherent and measurable qualities, like proportion. Mathematical work has a fixed truth, but it can evade the
human eye; frequently a sculpture is too large or elevated to be
encompassed by a beholder (23:218, 225). Obviously Ruskin
has not abandoned a belief that the material basis of value exists,
but he does not place himself in the mathematical school of
artists, mainly because in envisioning his or anyone else's response to a work of art, he privileges the actual, singular experience of seeing.

Thus, the mathematical qualities of Quercia's sarcophagus
and Ruskin's own aesthetic theory of seeing help make *Ilaria*
more inaccessible to the average viewer. In an impassioned
description of the sculpture four years later, Ruskin notes that

few see the statue because "it stands bare by the cathedral wall" (34:171). In the letter of 1845, he treats her as stone work but marvels at his proximity to what appears to be a dead woman. His Oxford audience, too, can get this close, but the scale and placement of the sculpture inhibit the illusion of life that struck Ruskin in his earlier viewing. Indeed, the sort of audience he imagines for *Ilaria* makes him withdraw her from popular view. To convey her effect, he describes a series of responses that all somehow miss the "truth" he first noted in his letter to his father. He tells his Oxford listeners that the effigy's lock of hair which "trembles loosely down upon the cheek with a perfect tenderness" lies unperceived. "You do not look at it—only at the face" (23:230). The "simple lady's hands" to which he devotes four or five lines likewise go unnoticed. "You don't think of saying, 'What pretty hands'; still less, 'How exquisitely they are cut'" (23:231). This neglect is, nonetheless, a normative response, Ruskin intimates, evidence of the mimetic rightness of the monument. The sarcophagus has an accuracy that distracts viewers from—while his comments emphasize—its artifice.

Other common ways of perceiving it reveal the religious beliefs, nationality, and class of beholders. In an extemporaneous part of his lecture, Ruskin compares three typical spectators standing before the tomb. The first, a burgess who puts his hat over the face of the figure, represents "English manufacture and liberal opinions"; he is "putting his English-made hat on the face" of the country's old art. The second is a group of Luccan peasants. One of the women kneels and kisses the statue's marble drapery. Ruskin's sympathies are with her; she is like the innocent mythmaker, and he uses her low standing in his hierarchy of readers to make an ironic point about modern belief: "The peasant is the slave of a miserable superstition, to be enlightened by the Bible Society if possible, but at all events to be taxed" (23:234). The taxer now approaches and gazes at the statue "with a sort of bird-like, chicken-like action," finding fault with the nose. "Money-takers of the country," they have neither interest in or respect for religious art and "rustle past the statues of the simple dead, their ancestresses, in the splendidest of gowns" (23:233–34). Ruskin still sees the beautifully chiseled hands, whereas the manufacturer, the peasant, and the new bourgeoisie do not. Of course, it is Ruskin's privilege as Slade Professor to claim special sight before his audience. Yet in a supposedly didactic speech, he dwells on the debased readings of the sarcophagus; he even creates from them allegories of popular response. He implies that they represent tastes that grow from a social formation he cannot change. Having acknowledged the impact on sight of individual desire, Ruskin realizes that the value and meaning of the tomb change with each passing spectator.

Ilaria is his favorite sculpture, and he never suggests that she is only the sum of popular views. He does state, though, in 1874 that her sculptor did not stoop to naturalized representation or trompe-l'oeil because "every fool would have gaped at it for its deception. . . . I must not have the mob coming here, he thinks" (23:231). Already the "mob" has destroyed the canopy and adjunct decoration of the tomb, perhaps in a pious fervor similar to that of the crowds in *Fra Lippo Lippi* who scratch out the figures of the torturing slaves in the fresco of Saint Laurence (23:221–22). Neither the monument's nor the fresco's viewers are appropriately double-minded. Even the sincere peasants kissing the chiseled drapery endanger the value of the sarcophagus because they cannot recognize illusion, feel emotion, and understand iconography at the same time.

Ruskin described *Ilaria* as both unseen and vulnerable to spectators' hands because at bottom he felt ambivalent about most public responses to her. The recess in which the tomb stands signified his withholding; the beauty of the sculpture was always beyond and prey to popular attention. His reading of *Ilaria* in 1874 developed from the aesthetic equivalent to the popular use of Gresham's Law, according to which bad money drives the good from circulation.[19] And the affinity between the value of money and art extended to meaning as well. Just as money "acquired its separate and distinctive personality" when it began circulating in paper without its equivalent metal base, in *The Queen,* the signifiers of Athena multiplied beyond any delimited meaning.[20]

In 1911 Georg Simmel linked the negative character of money—its ability to signify anything in modern economy—

to the fragmentary empiricism of contemporary perception, what Walter Pater had celebrated in his "Conclusion" to *The Renaissance*. To Simmel, empiricism "replaces the single visionary or rational idea with the highest possible number of observations; it substitutes their qualitative character by the quantity of assembled individual cases."[21] Similarly, to Ruskin excess of detail became the mettle of interpretation. He could always insist on conceptual meanings for everything he saw and fuse all signifiers into Athena, but this was transparent and unconvincing closure. For the proliferation of the sign, like paper money, devalued the meaning and made Athena a hermeneutical version of value at the margin: like money, she was the "expression, or symbol of the modern emphasis on the quantitative moment"; she was so plentiful, she in effect meant nothing in particular.[22] In *The Queen of the Air*, this impoverishment of interpretation only occurred when Ruskin insisted on making myth an enveloping and populistic set of symbols in order to display his own pluralism. However, he did not view the readings of *Ilaria* with tolerance as the procession of spectators glanced at her. She exemplified to him the way circulating value and the lower orders of reading invalidated the currency of stable or "true" meaning and appreciation. The fate of this beloved sculpture helped turn him against popular and multiple readings.

Leveling Down: Words Proposed and Practiced

The interpretive method Ruskin used with Greek myth and de Quercia's sarcophagus revealed the social implications of circulating value and marginal utility: the demands and tastes of a heterogeneous audience for books and the fine arts now began to guide meaning and determine value. As a writer famous for typological readings and moral iconologies, Ruskin no doubt felt uncomfortable with this populistic hermeneutics, and in passages such as those concerning *Ilaria di Caretto* he becomes alternately remote and ironic about meaning and value. During the last two productive decades of his life, his writings displayed the tension between his impulses to level up or level down. Nowhere is this more apparent than in his theories and use of language itself. His conception of words reflected both his religious agnosticism and current economic theory, and they paralleled his notion of money as an order for goods. Words represented a concrete rather than a metaphysical or abstract realm; they had no abstruse or hidden signifieds, and their power even could be aural rather than figurative. As a result, they needed little explanation, and readers could understand the meaning and appreciate the beauties of a text without needing a decoder like the critic. Ruskin spent part of the 1870s and 1880s promoting literal reading and materialistic language, but this democratic semiotics was not a complete new strategy in the 1870s. Long before he became concerned with new readers, Ruskin had a somewhat different but equally concrete notion of reading as a juxtaposition of syntactical units. He now modified this practice to a materialistic treatment of phrases and individual words to suit his later projects for leveling down. However, within the prevailing economic discourse, he could not sustain either a syntactical or linguistic focus during his thirteen-year correspondence to working men, *Fors Clavigera*. He withdrew in these letters from audiences whose demands forced him into a meaningless and valueless overproduction of misunderstood and unconsumable statements.

AURAL AND PRECRITICAL READING

No doubt Ruskin possessed exceptional visual and aural powers; with them, he read and created intricate symbolic languages in much art and literature. The belief that he was an extraordinary seer and reader began with his own assertions in volume one of *Modern Painters* that only a few use their intellectual and imaginative power at the moment of perception (3:96–97). But if Ruskin was one of the privileged few who could read art in this way, he was also one of the many who resisted both symbols and figurative readings. Throughout his career, he read various texts through iconologies, but he also fabricated stories from description and simultaneously "pictured" or "imagined" words. In the third volume of *Modern Painters* (1856), he began to insist on literal interpretations; he focused, that is, on the details of text, their physical settings, subjects, and social circumstances instead of their symbolic meaning. His hermeneutics thus rested on what Hans W. Frei, in his study of biblical narrative, has called the verbal or precritical sense of a text. [1] A verbal interpretation relies on the representative value of language: early typologists, for example, were verbal or literal readers because they assumed that the Bible described actual occurrences. Similarly, Ruskin often treated words as if they were true on the ordinary, denotative level. In verbal readings, then, meaning inheres in conventional signs and their syntactical arrangements. Precritical interpretation involves visual and aural elements rather than conceptual or abstract levels of language. This way of reading correlates with Ruskin's definition of money in the 1870s: thus as linguistic currency, words were an order for existing goods or visible signifieds. Moreover, they reflected contemporary doubts about Christian metaphysics, especially the historical truth of myth and the Bible. Matthew Arnold, for example, used, if not precritical language, then a concrete mimeticism in much of his poetry. David G. Riede observes that the "agnostic denial of the verifiable existence of anything beyond or above material nature, beyond or above the world of things, leads [Arnold] to a distrust of all words that cannot be referred back immediately to something 'concrete,' and ultimately to a distrust of a metaphysics of presence or being in language."[2] Ruskin learned the precritical method from his mother and adapted it for the concrete imaginations of unsophisticated readers. By the 1870s it became crucial to his readings and introductions of what he considered seminal texts for an expanding audience from the lower-middle and laboring classes.

The sensuous, demotic use of words in the 1870s was not merely a sign of his agnosticism or an adopted strategy; it was a habit developed from his own first lessons. In the first part of *Praeterita* (1885), he describes how he learned to read, as if to explain his remarkable visual and verbal power. His mother's method is crucial to any study of his criticism.[3] Ruskin first memorized entire sentences; he could "point with accuracy to every word in the page" (35:23). He did not assemble words by phonemes. Here is his testimonial to his mother's instruction: "My mother was both able to teach me, and resolved that I should learn, absolute accuracy of diction and precision of accent in prose; and made me know, as soon as I could speak plain . . . that accuracy of diction means accuracy of sensation, and precision of accent, precision of feeling" (35:121).

As a boy, Ruskin learned the Bible by heart in this manner, but he was aware that the aural was the imposed sense, the visual his preferred medium. Reading for him was a visual experience in which he grasped chunks of sentences instead of individual words. On the other hand, his mother structured his reading as an aural experience. She made him listen to each word and its accent within the sentence. In the passage above, Ruskin praises her method but evaluates it by visual standards, for a few pages later he observes that her "unquestioning evangelical faith in the literal truth of the Bible placed me, as soon as I could conceive or think, in the presence of an unseen world" (35:128). Eventually, he wields the aural method against his mother when he dramatizes his rejection of evangelical Christianity as an aural unconversion from the "cracked voice" of the Waldensian minister to the robust precision of a military band (35:495–96). Nonetheless, Ruskin retained the evangelical's ambitions after he began questioning the literal truth of the Bible: he read art and literature for a moral; he believed all art should reflect the glory of God, and he wanted it to reveal the divine and to perpetuate and inspire if not orthodox faith, then ethical conduct.[4]

Praeterita suggests that hearing was the sense Ruskin cultivated, sight the one he instinctively privileged. Reading, as well as writing about reading, was for him an experience as visual as viewing a painting or gazing at a water-spout. In volume one of *Modern Painters,* he demonstrated it through description. As a word painter, Ruskin could render detail and convey movement with active verbs, extensions of spatial images, and rapid visual associations that were simultaneously rendered into aural sensations through alliteration and rhythm.[5] He was, most acknowledge, a genius at transcribing the visual into linguistic "scenes" in which words vied with the reported images in affective power. George P. Landow has discussed how, in a description of Tintoretto's *Annunciation* (4:264–65), Ruskin extends spatial images into narratives, reading objects on the canvas from left to right and ending with a typological analysis.[6] Without invoking types, he approaches Tintoretto's *Massacre of the Innocents* in a similar way:

> The scene is the outer vestibule of a palace, the slippery marble floor is fearfully barred across by sanguine shadows . . . a huge flight of stairs . . . descends on the left; down this rush a crowd of women mixed with the murderers; the child in the arms of one has been seized by the limbs, *she hurls herself over the edge, and falls head downmost, dragging the child out of the grasp by her*

weight;—she will be dashed dead in a second;—close to us is the great struggle; a heap of the mothers entangled in one mortal writhe with each other and the swords, one of the murderers dashed down and crushed beneath them. . . . Far back . . . is a woman, sitting quiet . . . she looks down steadfastly on her dead child . . . and her hand is pressed softly upon her brow. (4:272–73)

In this passage, Ruskin visualizes the images in a painting that his audience might find difficult to understand and impossible even to see by extending the picture's space into a drama. The pictorial images are organized not only through description but also narrative. The clause "she will be dashed dead in a second" exemplifies Ruskin's way of interpreting visual images—developing stories from description.

The pictorial quality of Ruskin's descriptions, narratives, and analyses has nothing to do with the picturesque, though in the early nineteenth century the latter term commonly meant "in the manner of paintings," after Burke's usage. The *picturesque* denoted a style and had links with particular subjects that Ruskin thought unsuitable for art.[7] Nor does the *pictorial* as used here simply mean the extraordinary descriptive power of a Wordsworth or Ruskin (though he had described the poet in this way).[8] Rather, *pictorial* here refers to how we see—by focusing and framing; it is fundamental to all sight and representation, for any object viewed is pictured. Joel Snyder has written that the "object of depiction" is a "standardized, or characterized, or defined notion of vision itself"; thus "the relationship between characterizing what we see as pictorial and making pictures becomes a reciprocal one."[9] Similarly, W. J. T. Mitchell, in response to Joseph Frank's famous essay on spatial form in modern literature, has observed that the linear or temporal structure of hermeneutics, indeed any decoding, including iconology, is also spatial.[10] This means that even historical interpretations have a spatial pattern. Typology and hermenuetics, for example, entail a response to the whole even while they construct sequences. The pictorial sense Ruskin exhibited in his narratives and analyses involved juxtapositions or patterns of framed, focused space *within* a whole structure. His typological reading of the *Annunciation* and narrative of *The Massacre of the Innocents* are good examples, because in each Ruskin has a "spatial" sense of the entire story as he moves from left to right. He was no doubt caught in the hermeneutic circle, but this entrapment, as current theory has convinced us, is universal.

When I call his visual knowledge superior, I mean in part that Ruskin "spatialized" much more quickly than the normal observer or reader. One result is the densely allusive writing in *Fors.* Another is the attention to the syntagmatic effect of "scenes" in much of his literary criticism. In his first extended discussion of literary language in volume two of *Modern Painters* (1846), he frequently evaluates the pictorial qualities with, we would note today, an inattention to figures. For example, he presents what he considers a gem of contemplative imagination from *Hamlet:* "Here hung those lips that I have kissed. . . . Where be your gibes now . . . " (4:255). Here, the "essence of lip" relies on the emotion building from preceding scenes— Hamlet's memories of Yorick and happiness before his father died. The power of the image lies in the context, the plot. Similarly, more than a decade later in volume three of *Modern Painters,* Ruskin attributes the effectiveness of particular passages to juxtaposition rather than to the figural quality of verbal images. Casimir de la Vigne saves his ballad, "La Toilette de Constance," with just such a dramatic syntagm.[11] Ruskin notes that as the fire envelops the girl in the poem, the speaker cannot contain himself. Previously, he simply has narrated action, but for a moment he imagines flames that devour, "volupté," "sans pitié" (5:214); then he "retires into his pale and crystalline atmosphere of truth" (5:215). De la Vigne concludes by joining two scenes, that of the burned Constance and the grand ball where the young women dance until daybreak.

Appreciation for this sort of irony comes from a perception of words that is concrete and pictorial—or as I have said elsewhere, literal. Of course in the previous two examples, Ruskin is discussing effect, not meaning in the hermeneutical sense, but notably, he traces the force of these passages to nonverbal, spatial devices. The power of each segment depends on its place in the syntagm of other scenes. This pictorial conception of words, like Arnold's classicism, obscures the Romantic emphasis on individual perceptions or emotions. As David Riede comments, the grand style as Arnold conceived it "must emphasize plot rather than curious thought and feelings." The richness and profundity of language must be subordinated to "the architectonic whole in which action is presented."[12] The valorization of plot over symbol or thought results from Arnold's attempts to give the poet a suitable function in Victorian society. Ruskin's reasons for exploiting his habitual use of syntagm over symbol reflect a similar purpose and an awareness of a larger, less educated audience for literature.

The materialistic sense of language that underlies Ruskin's early typological and syntagmatic readings and that would develop into a mimetic conception of words also informs Ruskin's censure of metaphor. However, not until the mid-1850s did Ruskin detect what he called the pathetic fallacy, an overly subjective and arrogant substitution of writers playing God in an agnostic age. For in 1846, in volume two of *Modern Painters,* the essence of the poetic faculty, which he calls the contemplative imagination, is the formation of metaphor. It starts with an abstraction, perhaps culled from memory. Qualities associated with this indistinct conception emerge and coalesce. The imagination then strikes them "with the die of an image belonging to other matter"; as a result, they "pass current . . . in the peculiar conjunction and for the peculiar value desired" (4:291). To describe the imagination contemplative, Ruskin uses the implied metaphor of coining to show the arbitrary connection between the figure and its value. Like the coin, the metaphor means whatever is currently desired. Moreover, the metaphor and the coin are both realized or *struck* by an image or die that is "other"—naturally or logically unconnected to the original conception. Ruskin would continue to use money and metaphor as reciprocal figures to stress the arbitrary and teleological character of symbolization: one *begins* with an idea, then imposes a form; everything in between—the qualities metonymically related to the abstraction, the stamp of the foreign image—demonstrates the aleatory character of the verbal and monetary figure. In volume two of *Modern Painters,* he did not deride metaphor for this misrepresentation. Although it was only a perspective, it could mark "the thing represented with an

ideal character" (4:299). However, by 1856 in volume three of
Modern Painters, he found metaphor presumptuous because the
superstructure of shared beliefs on which literature relied for its
effect and meaning was vanishing. To compensate, he de-
manded that language be pictorial, that it yield conventional
images only.

By the fifties, then, Ruskin was reading modern literature
(from the eighteenth century and after) precritically—as an
objective imitation of visual impression. A few examples from
volumes two and three of *Modern Painters* illustrate this change.
In volume two (1846), he detects imagination in the lines from
"Lycidas" that contain adjectives or participles endowing
flowers with human qualities. The imagination produces "for-
saken" primroses and "pensive" cowslips, lines that project
emotion onto an object. Similarly, in *The Winter's Tale,* Perdita
pictures "frighted" flowers such as "pale primroses, / That die
unmarried." Ruskin praises the speaker's projection with a metaphor of his own. "Observe," he comments, "how the imagination in these last lines goes into the very inmost soul of every
flower" (4:255). In the same volume, he finds similes fanciful
because they keep images external rather than subjective, and
metaphors imaginative. Ten years later, however, he admires
similes because they control rather than project emotion, perhaps through the physical separation into two pictures of words
being compared. For example, in 1856 he mentions Dante's
"perfect" description of spirits falling from the banks of Acheron
("as dead leaves flutter from a bough" [from the *Inferno*]). In
contrast, William Shenstone's Jessy (from Elegy 26) violates
decorum when she has the flowers speak; in her sadness "something appears . . . to be in nature which is not" (5:206, 218,
219). But Ellen from *The Excursion* knowingly indulges in the
illusion of a plaintive bird and all the while distances herself
from the image, separating what she envisions from what is.

At times in his discussion Ruskin uses "pathetic fallacy" to
mark old-fashioned violations of decorum. For instance, he re-
jects Pope's "nimble" sail and "lagging" wind (in the translation
of the *Odyssey*) because they are attributes the speaker, Ulysses,
would not have invented while curious and impatient (5:207).
In this criticism, Ruskin employs the standard against which

Johnson measured Shakespeare—the normative in human nature. Yet Ruskin admires the way Homer in the *Iliad* reveals the
deaths of Castor and Pollux: "But them, already, the life-giving
earth possessed. . . . " This is "high poetical truth" for "the
earth is our mother still, fruitful, life-giving." The metaphor,
he claims here, is "pure fact" (5:212, 213). He means that
the epithet refers to a fact of nature, not to the emotions of the
speaker. Yet literally or visually, this sentence is not true; the
earth is no more our mother than Jessy's flowers speak.

The pathetic fallacy revived an eighteenth-century standard of naturalized decorum, but its ideological basis excused
certain nonliteral images such as the *Iliad*'s metaphor because it
represented the classical world's belief in "a definite spiritual
presence in material nature" (5:252). It conformed to the precritical standard because it described a fact that its readers
assumed. Ruskin's reading of the line resembles contemporary
poetic and metaphorical interpretations of myth and the Bible
in, for example, Grote's *History of Greece* and the Higher Criticism. But there is a crucial difference because Ruskin approached the text not in a metaphorical, but in a precritical,
way; he saw it as *embodying* history. This was a deliberately
primitivistic method, adopted out of nostalgia for a simpler past
of unquestioned faith in deities; it was used as a device to
capture the imaginations of a lower order of readers. The pathetic fallacy itself arose from Ruskin's awareness that not only
belief but also reading had transformed; projection operates
only in a god- or God-less age of changing values in which each
writer can stamp the external world with his or her individual
feelings. Ruskin realized this, and he may have used simple
and concrete transcriptions of ordinary sight either to reflect or
induce emotional restraint. His analysis of the lines in *Hamlet*
and "La Toilette de Constance," for instance, are pictorial and
formal rather than subjective or emotional; their truth lies in
their syntagmatic value or architectonics. Different pictures or
scenes are juxtaposed: the skull of Yorick with the remembered
man, the dead girl and the young dancers. By the fifties, then,
the pictorial standard became an alternative to the projective
metaphor.

After volume three of *Modern Painters,* Ruskin insisted

more and more on pictorial, literal, and formalistic interpretations as his conception of an "invisible" theological realm faded.
His tone, which became less effusive and more appropriately
objective, befitted his transcriptions of the material world. Always a collector of art and books, he began to perceive the way
painted manuscripts realized the visual properties of the letter.
Of his Saint Louis Psalter, he observes, "Half of its letters are
twisted snakes" and goes on to say that "there is rarely a piece of
monkish decorated writing in the world, that is not tainted
with some ill-meant vileness of grotesque" (19:365). In 1877,
he notes the visual absurdity of one of William Cowper's hymns.
The closing stanza in part reads:

> "Lord, we are few, but thou art near;
>
> . . .
>
> Oh, rend the heavens,—come quickly down . . .

Trinities and an omniscient God form part of the visual
impossibility of orthodox religion; it "never seems to occur to
[the singers] that if Christ is in the midst of them, there is no
occasion . . . for His rending the heavens to come down to
them" (31:115). Ruskin now was calling himself a Catholic, in
the unorthodox sense of the term (29:92). His specific beliefs are
not clear; he did not profess allegiance to Rome or to any other
church doctrines. It was, rather, the sensuous quality of
Catholic ritual and its association with the European peasantry
that attracted him. For now he often resisted elevating images
into metaphysical *noumena*. At the same time, he was concerned
with the social function of art for the expanding middle and
literate lower classes, and he tried to match primitive methods
with a primitive audience: *Fors,* addressed to the working men
of Great Britain, and various essays, anthologies, and prefaces
for or about late-nineteenth-century "peasants" introduced
readers to, in Ruskin's mind, the masterpieces of Western culture through the sensuous properties of words. The approach
anticipated what Terry Eagleton calls the trend toward
"healthy" literature in the first half of the twentieth century,
which rested on the naïve notion that words approach the condition of things. This sort of "pure mimesis" backed F. R. Leavis's
"essential Englishness," a notion of language that valued the

"robust vitality" of words and resulted in jingoistic celebrations of rural and populistic movements. [13] Ruskin's natural affinities for syntagmatic reading and his distrust of metaphor, along with his studies of money and need of a visible referent, culminated in a materialistic view of the word itself.

Just as the pictorial standard developed from typological readings to replace the religious or metaphysical referent of language with a concrete, political one, the aural method of reading he had learned from his mother and continued to use habitually became another populistic strategy by the last decades of his career. For instance, in *Fors,* Ruskin reread Scott by summarizing or inserting long excerpts from Lockhart's *Life* and some of the novels. Generally, he framed these segments with appreciative comments; sometimes he retold the biography. The retelling was considered neither derivative nor boring by many readers, partly because the technique was a staple of middle-class education (and probably appealed more to the middle than working-class readers of *Fors*). Richard Altick has written that, for middle-class children, studying English literature amounted to "cramming" and "spouting" selected passages. Many examinations, such as the one instituted in 1855 for the Indian Civil Service, tested a candidate's memory of particular facts as well as his ability "to parse and gloss." Students worked from a sort of canon of passages, like those in Vicesimus Knox's *Elegant Extracts: Or, Useful and Entertaining Pieces of Poetry, Selected for the Improvement of Young Persons* (1801). [14] Although the method had detractors such as Charles Kingsley, it suited the century's utilitarian and ornamental aims of education. Boys training for a profession could produce evidence of their reading—or in many cases, the reading itself, in total—which satisfied the middle-classes' desire for factual knowledge, because in spouting the student demonstrated that he had digested the text.

For Ruskin, the practice was inveterate; and though it stemmed from his first reading lessons, these in turn reflected the experiences of readers from similar backgrounds. His work up to and including *Praeterita* includes passages from writers he loved, particularly Scott and Carlyle, frequently with his own rephrases appended. Most likely, spouting was not perceived as a waste of time or space by the readers of *Fors* because it was a culturally acceptable way of teaching and learning. From our perspective, both cramming and spouting are governed by a metaphor of total physical consumption. They both represent the rights of possession—total mastery of words through repetition and appropriation. Simultaneously, they allow practitioners to avoid analysis, the probing of words through metaphors of penetration.

As I have mentioned before, Ruskin knew he could not educate the masses through iconology, for the religious symbols so familiar to him were not only unknown but also uninteresting to many new readers. He turned to the aural because of its initial connection with his mother; linked in his mind with learning to read, it became the medium of the primitivistic program he introduced in the 1870s with *Rock Honeycomb* (1877), volume two of his Shepherd's Library, and with the pendant *Elements of English Prosody* in 1880. In both of these projects, Ruskin concentrated on rhyme, meter, and musical accompaniment to catch the ear of an audience to whom the iconology of poetry had not appealed. He believed that music, like painting, was an "entirely popular" art (31:108). He also found a reason to call it moral: rhyme was Christian because, like the canticle, it made a ritual of sound (34:307–8). With the proper text, then, recitation could emulate religious chanting. The text he used in *Rock Honeycomb* was the 1823 Chiswick Press edition of Sir Philip Sidney's *Psalter,* which comprised metrical arrangements of the psalms. As opposed to more "genteel language," which diminished the force of the psalms with periphrasis, Sidney's psalms rendered the speech of the people. They included "any cowboy's or tinker's words" analogous to the colloquial tone of the Hebrew (31:116–17). Choosing the *Psalter* for the library thus was a populistic gesture toward the vast classes of artisans and laborers. Even the importance Ruskin gave to diction stressed the aural, for it evoked the dialect of a class or district that drew listeners through familiar sounds rather than through the meanings of specific sentences.

In his plan to introduce new readers to poetry, Ruskin was much more concerned with rhyme and rhythm than with symbol, but of course he did not ignore the imagistic property of words. By itself music was a formless and chaotic medium, as he noted in *The Queen of the Air;* with words, it intensified effect for the young and semiliterate. To a correspondent, Ruskin comments that "music gives emotions stronger than words only to persons who do not completely understand words" (31:111). Likewise, rhyme and meter convey feelings to "feebler and more impulsive dispositions" (31:130). He used sound to imitate and arouse those who had not mastered the meanings of words, abstract or symbolic. Aimed at a new audience, his primitivism favored the aural and pictorial over the conceptual power of language.

One might argue that starting in the sixties, the etymological approach that Ruskin probably derived from R. C. Trench's *On the Study of Words* (1851) rested on the hidden, cumulative, and historical meaning buried in language.[15] These hidden significances are never abstract, however, but historical; in some cases they are hearable in the root of each word. Ruskin's mining of *mercy* and *charity* in *Munera Pulveris* (1862) are good examples. And despite the now-famous formulations about imagination and the "symbolic grotesque," the critical method Ruskin used increasingly from 1856 on was narrative and nonfigurative.[16] His extensive use of allegory was based more on his narrative sense than on belief in a representational theory of language. The allegories of *The Bible of Amiens* (1884) were really stories pieced together from well-established iconologies, so Ruskin was still working at the literal level, stringing together verbal pictures. The symbolical meaning of certain sculpted figures on Saint Mark's, for example, was well established when, as exegete, Ruskin told his audience these stories. Moreover, *The Bible* addressed potential tourists who would be interested in the carvings on Saint Mark's, but this readership differed from the heterogeneous, newly literate one he envisioned for the *Bibliotheca Pastorum*.

Like allegory and religious symbol, precritical interpretation guaranteed a stable meaning, and its appeal at a time of intellectual questioning is, therefore, understandable. Nonetheless, Ruskin read and handled words with an ambivalence that George Levine argues characterizes the Victorians' attitude in general.[17] The "spirit" or power shaping all human sentiment could, Ruskin suggests in *The Queen of the Air,* elude language (19:351–52). Sometimes he ran out of words when describing visual effects, such as his first glimpse of the Black Forest rising into the Alps (35:113) or the power of the juxtaposed scenes in de la Vigne's poem. In the last two decades of his career, he often argued with correspondents over their diction. For example, he tells Frederic Harrison, who had written an essay on Positivism in the May 1876 issue of the *Contemporary Review,* "You continually say what you don't mean . . . because you have never been at the pains to learn language accurately" (29:569). Unable to control the use of words and, therefore, the spread of new ideas, and faced with the limits of language in his own criticism and description, Ruskin stayed on the relatively common ground of the visual and aural "surface." Forever his mother's pupil, he treated language as a repertory of words to be learned and rendered with semantic and phonetic accuracy.

In his early confidence, Ruskin set out to read in response to Edmund Burke, Archibald Alison, Dugald Stewart, and other eighteenth-century philosophers. Typology and metaphysics inform volume two of *Modern Painters,* but this work is an anomaly. With his growing agnosticism and loss of faith, his visual sense became less abstract. Nature's links with divine types still appear everywhere in his late writing, but in passages appropriated from the Bible often tacked on to the end of chapters, as in *Praeterita* when he spouts biblical passages as a nostalgic afterthought to preceding descriptions. From the fifties on, he remained on the surface of words. His most famous foray into literary criticism was an attack on the metaphor. His regard, especially in the years of Max Müller and Trench, for language as a great treasure-house to be used with precision probably grew from a conscious sense of metaphysical absence. But it also came of an intense love of the physical world that words almost palpably represented, a concern for new readers anchored in the material present, and an effort to develop a national language based on such materialism. This sort of fetishism dispensed with traditional iconology and made interpretation easy for readers whom the tradition intimidated. In theory, pictorial and precritical interpretation, as well as spouting and aural diction, would bring Ruskin closer to neophyte readers. But his dependence on language as a stable, autonomous system with guaranteed and obvious meaning estranged him from actual correspondents.

THE CURRENCY OF WORDS IN *FORS CLAVIGERA*

Fors Clavigera (1871–84), ninety-six letters to the laborers of Great Britain, with some of their correspondence appended, perhaps best exemplifies how this materialistic sense of language fit into the discourse of orthodox economics and prevented Ruskin from capturing a heterogeneous audience for his work. In *Fors,* Ruskin introduces his two definitions of money: as an order for goods and a token of right. *Fors* functioned like money too, first because Ruskin, like Goethe in *Faust* (1790), Emerson in "Nature" (1836), and Marx in quoting, among others, Shakespeare (1844), used economic language to express verbal exchange.[18] Adam Smith emphasized the parallel functions of money and language in an economy of production by translating from this statement of the Physiocrat Victor Riqueti Mirabeau:

> Trois grandes inventions principales ont fondé stablement les sociétés, indépendamment de tant d'autres, qui les ont ensuite dotées et décorées. Ces trois sont, 1° L'invention de l'écriture, qui seule donne à l'humanité le pouvoir de transmettre, sans altération, ses lois, ses pactes, ses annales et ses découvertes. 2° Celle de la monnaie, qui lie tous les rapports entre les sociétés policées. La troisième enfin, qui es due à notre âge, et dont nos neveux profiteront, est un dérivé des deux autres et les complette également en perfectionnant leur objet: c'est la découverte du Tableau économique, qui devennant désormais le truchement universel, embrasse, et accorde toute les portions ou quotités correlatives, qui doivent entrer dans tous les calculs généraux de l'ordre économique.[19]

Second, the parallel between money and *Fors* is more evident in light of Ruskin's growing precritical sense of words. Another order for goods, language operated as money in the regulated exchange Ruskin described in *Fors*. Ideally, the value of the letters joins the writer's labor with the reader's interpretation, which in effect is its intrinsic or use-value. In reality, however, the value of the letters demonstrated the consequences of labor theory and marginal utility, and the relationship between writer and reader operated under the law of diminishing returns. *Fors,* like currency, was a volatile product of the complex relationship between exhaustible production and a vampiric consumption.

Unlike Marx, who in *Capital* (1867) had linked continuous economic exchange with objectified human relations, Ruskin did not extend his version of commodity fetishism to language. Yet his relationship with the readers of *Fors* is similarly objectified.[20] As the author of the letters, Ruskin used language as a token of right. This means that *Fors* worked as a kind of artistic *largesse,* depending on the distantiated perspective of the writer. At the same time, the letters concerned Ruskin's efforts to restore romantic or human relations between persons. Like the function of money in Gotthelf's story of the broom merchant, *Fors* paradoxically referred to romantic, while exemplifying reified, relations. Generally, the attempts to idealize money by grounding its value in a philosophy of labor that emphasized the power of the body and included pillage, inheritance, and hoarding failed to convert readers because these ideas either emphasized the fatal effects of labor on the body or reverted to inapplicable pastoral and feudal economies. In addition, the fluctuating value of the letters distanced Ruskin from what Brian Maidment says was the "large alternative readership" which the subtitle of *Fors* implies and ultimately from the labor his audience forced him to continue.[21]

The process of distantiation worked in this way: when Ruskin proposed a National Store in *Fors* 1, he defined currency as a transferable acknowledgment of debt for existing goods. Because the cost of *Fors* to Ruskin was measured in labor, its value to readers was traceable to the work done by the writer and the limited time left to do more.

Ruskin's word on the market objectified the history of John Ruskin—the author of *Modern Painters,* the Slade Professor at Oxford, the aging sage who threatened silence and periodically went mad (27:353). And because all goods derived their value from their production, the currency of the guild—and of British society—was really a promise to give or acquire labor: Ruskin says so himself in *Unto This Last* (17:64). Likewise, as a plan for a company of landholders, *Fors* was precritical writing, an order for goods. It was also a promise that understanding of Ruskin's message would come with reading. The signified, which included not only the goals of St. George's but also the reformed conduct of business and use of money, was the equivalent of the guild's National Store; to read on, an audience had to believe that a practicable message really existed. Thus, when operating in an exchange for something else, *Fors,* like money, depended on the ability or intentions of the participants to fulfill the order, and its value diminished if as a commodity, it was not consumable.

Fors was supposed to be Ruskin's most precritical and practical work, and its power to effect deeds is shown in outside evidence of things done, according to Ruskin. In it, Ruskin's treatment of money as a bond between persons or a token of manual work—through the Guild of St. George and stories such as Gotthelf's "The Broom Merchant"—did propel a few troubled readers of *Fors* into new lives. John Guy, a carpenter, left his job in protest against the use of the steam engine, and Egbert Rydings, accountant and bookkeeper for the guild, helped organize an experiment in the manufacture of Laxey homespun. Nineteenth-century subscribers who waited for each letter, who wrote to their "Master," and who joined St. George's saw *Fors* as the bible and contract of the guild. Ruskin himself thought that *Fors* would become influential when people realized that he did what he said; for instance, he said he would not advertise and did not (27:353). Therefore, the use-value of *Fors* had its source in implicit promising.

In these letters, Ruskin proposed his company, reported its accounts, recorded its tenets, and quarreled with correspondents. *Fors* was often dramatic, if not performative. In other words, proposing his company did not set it up. St. George's was licensed by the Board of Trade in 1878, when its Articles of Association established it as a guild (30:8). These documents were the true operatives. They produced St. George's, and they are not part of *Fors,* though Ruskin did send out a draft of the articles in letter fifty-five with a list of intended revisions. I think it is important, if obvious, however, to say that St. George's would have had no members if Ruskin had not announced his plans in his letters.

In letter twelve, Ruskin announces that he has fulfilled an unexplicit promise he made in letter five by giving £7,000 Consols to his company. He then explains that English law prevents him from giving Consols directly to his audience and requires him instead to vest his gift in trustees. "These terms, and the arrangement of the whole matter, will become clearer to you as you read on with me, and cannot be clear at all, till you do;—here is the money, at any rate" (27:200). The sentences in these letters are merely constative. They do not give the money but record the giving. "Here is the money" is an ingeniously ambivalent clause, which for a second obscures the distinction between constative and performative. Read one way, it performs the linguistic gesture of giving, but read differently and in context, it simply describes the vague location of the already donated money. The second, contextual reading is the correct one; still, the words *represented* performatives to both Ruskin and his audience. Each treated the utterance signifying the deed as a social contract: some readers subsequently donated land of their own, and others joined the company.[22] Ruskin thought that fulfilling his first promise would make the condition of his next one acceptable. Having gained the readers' trust by describing fulfillment, he promised them a lucid vision of St. George's if they continued to read *Fors*.

The words of this implicit promise are vague, he admits later (28:427). In fact, the promised meaning of *Fors*, the philosophy behind St. George's, is deferred throughout the ninety-six letters. The infelicity of the utterances generally rests in Ruskin's shifting view of audience, an example of what J. L. Austin would label a "misapplication." Austin claims that for a contract to work, "the particular persons and circumstances in a given case must be appropriate for the invocation of the particular procedure invoked," but Ruskin successively excludes a suitable, even plausible audience.[23] Having been forced to repeat the tenets of St. George's because readers claim they cannot understand him, he says in letter thirty-six, "I write to the

labourers of England; but not of England in 1870–73"
(27:669). In particular, he is not writing to his enemies, the
disciples of Mill and Ricardo. But he is not writing to the poor,
either. To the clerk who complains that he can afford neither
Ruskin's books nor the time to walk in the country and develop
his taste for nature and art, Ruskin replies that he must improve
his situation before he can read (27:291). To others who grum-
ble about the price of *Fors* (in 1874, tenpence), he answers, "My
book is meant for no one who cannot reach it" (28:40). Those
who do read often are insulted and attacked: modern Christian
women are vacuous, "disgusting little savages" (28:567); correspondents who badger him for answers are unsympathetic and
should leave him alone (29:184); readers who do not answer him
are unfaithful and prompt him in 1872 to remove the salutations and signatures from succeeding letters ("You will probably
know whom they come from, and I don't in the least care whom
they go to" [27:417]). In 1880, Ruskin says he went mad two
years earlier because no one believed a word of his letters and
"nothing came" of his work (29:386). And before this, he bris-
tles and wonders at the constant complaint that he is obscure. In
Fors twenty-nine, an "inquisitive Republican acquaintance"
who has tried to clarify Ruskin's views writes, "You assume that
you understand me, and that I don't understand myself or you. I
fully admit that I don't understand you or myself, and I declare
that neither do you understand me" (27:543–44). This especially infelicitous utterance of 1873 typifies the response from
puzzled readers.

One of the more earnest was Stephen Rowland, who became interested in Ruskin's books when he observed that five
volumes fetched £38. "I was struck with the amount, and
thought that they must be worth reading." He had to visit six
booksellers before one would agree to get him more of Ruskin's
books. When he finally owned and read *Fors,* he admits, "It was
a tough job for me, on account of the number of words in it that
I had never met with before. . . . I was obliged to look at my
dictionaries pretty often: I think I have found out now the
meanings of all the *English* words in it." Rowland says that he
has received more "good and real knowledge from *Fors* than from
all the books put together" that he has ever read, but finds it

hard to use in his grocery-drapery-clothing business. "If I understand your teaching, I ought to keep hand-made goods *only*. . . . If I did this, I certainly should lose nearly all my trade; and as I have a family to support, I cannot do so" (29:415–16).

Ruskin prints Rowland's letter in *Fors* at a time when he has become comparatively understanding and compassionate. In letter eighty-five (1878), he announces that he will widen his audience (29:316). Letter eighty-six presents a self-critical Master ready for a fellowship with his readers. "It may partly account for the want of success of those writings [on political economy before 1875], that they pleaded for honesty without praise, and for charity without reward," he writes (29:335). Number eighty-nine, in which Rowland's letter appears, is the first one for workers, free to members of guilds and trade committees. Everything hitherto in *Fors* has addressed "your existing Masters, Pastors, and Princes" (29:400). The message, Ruskin reveals, has been purposely cloudy because of his "official position" as Slade Professor at Oxford, for the true issue has always been "the transference of power out of the hands of the upper classes . . . into yours" (29:400). By closing the gap between himself and his readers and facing the reality of class division, Ruskin became a helpful narrator, sympathetic with his alternative audience, but the alienating quality of the earlier *Fors* had already set its reputation and its value. For this reason, the new constructive and confessional tone of *Fors* could win over doubtful readers only at the expense of preceding letters, especially when Ruskin admitted that he had disguised his intentions and had in effect been writing for the last seven years in bad faith. Furthermore, Ruskin's pugnacious tone, equivocal sentences, and insistent descriptions of England's corruption and filth—the places where his readers lived—had made them equate the truth with the unpleasant and inaccessible. For readers such as the Republican acquaintance, *Fors* had worked through a kind of linguistic withholding—which someone like Stephen Rowland linked with prohibitive price.

Fors is filled with moving accounts from men and women such as Rowland who were struggling to fit word and deed. They fought the hindrances of money and word, and they eventually came to see these barriers as signifiers of the message itself. Their salutations to Ruskin—Dear Master, Reverend Sir, Honoured Sir—show how alluring they found the distance from themselves to writer and word. Further, the virtues their leader extolled in *Fors,* practiced by Gotthelf's Hansli and Sir John Hawkwood, were viewed from temporal or spatial, hence social, distance. Ruskin patterned St. George's after the White Company that fought the Italian trade wars, but he substituted altruism for pillage and philanthropists for mercenaries. Members would bestow money or property rather than steal it; but to do so—to do what Stephen Rowland could not afford to do— they had to be wealthy, in either time or money. In contrast, Ruskin's actual audience (before his confession in letter eighty-nine) and the working man's difficulty with *Fors* made it a series that already had incorporated the distance surrounding charitable action personified in Largesse.

The promise of the letters, then—that understanding of Ruskin's message would come to readers—was based on linguistic withholding in the guise of largesse. Ruskin thought that he and his readers had what Max Weber calls a status contract. Typical of preindustrial society, it depends largely on the close relationship of those involved and continues by an implicit and vague agreement about mutual obligations.[24] Cooperation and gift-giving, exemplary acts of the guild rehearsed in *Fors,* are status contracts: they involve an unspecified return in an unnamed amount of time. For prototypes of men who enter into these contracts based on trust rather than on written or monetary terms, Ruskin points to Abraham and Matthew, the latter because he is a merchant called from receipt of custom (24:344). More specifically, Abraham's covenant with God, the topic of letter sixty-five, illustrates the cryptic nature of promise and deferred fulfillment notable in *Fors.* Here, Ruskin observes that the "word" of the first line of Genesis 15 is in lower-case; therefore, Abraham is rightly skeptical of God's commands because they come to him in the form of the *rhema,* or mere words of sermons, rather than the *verbum,* or, as Ruskin explains, the *Logos* of John 1.1 (28:588–89). Abraham requires a covenant, which Ruskin sarcastically rewords for his audience in economic terms. Abraham is offered "exchangeable property"

(28:589) for his obedience. However, as Ruskin notes, "fair words butter no parsnips" (28:589): the rhetic act, with as Austin says, "a certain more or less definite 'sense' and a more or less definite 'reference,'" is formed in Genesis 15.5 in an analogy of innumerable stars to children ("So shall thy seed be"). Thus begins "the long chain of the will." Abraham must believe and obey; he must, in Nietzsche's words, "see distant things as though they were near at hand."[25]

Ruskin uses Genesis 15 to prove that promise is both prior and superior to short-term economic exchange. He thus confirms Nietzsche's definition of man as an "animal with the right to make promises," which nicely replaces T. J. Dunning's definition of man as the animal that exchanges.[26] God, after all, is the original cryptic promise-maker. Moreover, Ruskin notes that Israel never got the promised land of Canaan. "They got only the Mount of the Amorites; for the promise was only to be perfected on condition of their perfect obedience" (28:596). The seemingly eternal duration of the paternal contract between the Master and his readers, with superhuman demands for fidelity and obedience beyond understanding, thus was sanctified for Ruskin's disciples by its biblical precedent. Readers of the Bible and *Fors* knew how hard it was to continue to will what had been willed. For Ruskin's audience, the parallel sermon in letter sixty-five was telling. The writer had depicted himself as an agent of the Word, and used it as he did morals, to express his power over and distance from his readers. "The lordly right of bestowing names is such that one would almost be justified in seeing the origin of language itself as an expression of the rulers' power," observes Nietzsche.[27] But Ruskin was a lord of language who as yet did not understand what he himself said, and he became like the elided narrator of Genesis 15, a purveyor of *rhema*, or mere word. The actual Word of God, the Logos, was not available in the nineteenth-century marketplace, and a mere "printed thing" like the Bible would not procure understanding (especially because Ruskin no longer interpreted the Bible literally, despite his precritical strategies for reaching a wider audience [28:587]). The Logos, the supreme natural value, was beyond exchange and consumption, whereas the biblical and Ruskinian rhetic acts possessed value through the promise that understanding—the goods, to extend Ruskin's mercantile language—would come. Such a promise had to be renewed repeatedly through exchange in which words signified a claim to wealth or debt.

Fors lured readers on by its resemblance to the Logos even though Ruskin had devalued his word, like the sermon in Genesis, to *rhema*. As a result, during the exchange between writer and readers the letters fell in value. Subject to the Ricardian law of diminishing returns, they had, like much-tilled land, a decreasing yield, because they were a limited commodity based on a finite meaning. Their source was an aging, sick man at his productive limits. This sort of scarcity threatened both author and readers, as they demanded explanations for words they did not understand. Withholding meaning, even inadvertently, increased words. The cost of labor rose as the rate of profit fell, and *Fors* acquired the negligible value of a commodity at the margin. Even by the standards of orthodox economics, Ruskin felt estranged from his work and victimized by the productive process, for, according to Ricardo and his elaborators, demand for labor was nothing other than existing supply. This materialized desire, called Say's Law, is crucial to labor theory, because it throws all value into production. Ruskin never mentioned Say's Law, and his own political economy, with its stress on the ethical capacity for use, is an "indictment" of such a tenet, observes James Clark Sherburne.[28] Nonetheless, Ruskin thought of his dilemma in *Fors* in light of Say's Law. He was the overworked producer who had to accommodate increasing demand. He knew his mind was dissolving, and writing required more and more effort; according to doctors, overwork drove him mad (29:386). He thought, too, that materialized demand decreased the value of his word through proliferation and wore out his body and mind. In Aristotelian terms, *Fors* became a chrematistical text, proliferating itself. As a result, perhaps, the last letters, with their etchings of little girls and accounts from correspondents of sequestered orphanages and convents, are quiescent; Ruskin had reached the stasis of the exhausted worker. *Fors* had in fact translated the underconsumptionist fears of Smith and Malthus to publishing; underconsumption now operated within the new laws of marginal utility and diminishing returns. According to the orthodox economists earlier in the century, machinery would lead to overproduction and faulty distribution. Although not a machine, Ruskin's mind did function as circulating capital, and it generated a great number of words. But this very profusion of letters resulted from their failure to satisfy readers; they lacked value as fulfillments of promise in an inflated market.

To escape from the world of finite resources and the insistent questions of readers, Ruskin tried to fashion the letters as a restorative project for laborers of the past. Going back in time was in effect regreening land that now was waste and forestalling more devastation. And pockets of agrarian Britain—machineless, its people sheltered by benign patriarchal landlords—were proposed and achieved, on a tiny scale, by and through *Fors*. As of 1885, St. George's had fifty-seven members and more than thirty-five acres of land with some cottages (30:xxvi–xxviii).[29] The results were meager, but Ruskin, after all, was writing for an audience of whom he admittedly knew little (29:399). As John T. Fain comments, he understood nothing of the psychology of working men and treated them like children.[30] This social gap, in addition to the metaphorical and diffuse passages that puzzled all readers, made *Fors* an *objet d'art* for the middle and lower classes. Opaque yet portentous, it attracted readers by Ruskin's promise to start a new world and his call for their own pledge; it no doubt carried them by evidence of Ruskin's good faith, notably the tithe of £7000 Consols, the open accounts of the guild, and the master's own "*glass* pockets" (27:139). Through demonstrations such as these, Ruskin tried to form a status contract with his audience. The language of the letters, however, as well as their uncertain sense of audience, often kept the writer at a distance from them. Even the reputation Ruskin had by then as a great stylist and sage worked against his intention in *Fors*, because his prose had hitherto succeeded chiefly on an emotional, rhythmic level. Readers of Ruskin's proposal and diatribes in the letters were thrust into arm's-length negotiations with the Master for meaning, and the narrative of *Fors* was largely directed by the gap between the homogeneous, archaic community envisioned and the fragmented one addressed.

To a certain extent, Ruskin had this same audience, or the gap between audiences, in mind when he advanced his precritical method of interpretation for unsophisticated readers. Yet because he never actually composed a text entirely in this concrete language, it remained only a theoretical attempt to level down. The closest Ruskin ever came to practicing it consistently was in his publication of Sir Philip Sidney's *Psalter* and Francesca Alexander's stories, but, significantly, these were the work of others. The next two chapters will explore the tension between Ruskin and his audiences in essays and projects that illustrate his contrary efforts to meet and recoil from them. *Fors* also manifests this ambivalence, not only through its tone but also through its working definitions of money and charity. Even *fors*, which means the power of doing good work in 1871 (27:28), also indicates *force*, like the power of physical appropriation that won the patricians of England the privilege of benevolence. Only those with enough leisure and power are ready for practical conversion to the past. Like ideal money, then, *Fors* was a token of right and an order for goods. As we have seen, the former definition set value in baronial power imitated by middle-class philanthropy, while the latter kept money within the grid of "naïve mimeticism" because it always signified something existing and obtainable.[31] Just as money ordered goods whose price signified the cost of their production, the words of *Fors* betokened a meaning that reflected the efforts of the sage. Their value came from the labor of the aging John Ruskin; it was his failing hand that gave the ninety-six letters currency to nineteenth-century readers. But like interest, *Fors* multiplied itself rather than the object it signified. It thus had no currency for many readers, except as art—the unconsumable object in a consumer economy. The few who did donate land and change jobs as a result of reading the letters and joining the guild show that, to effect action, *Fors* required faith in the promise of the unreadable, or the unprocurable privilege of old money.

Fiction Fair and Foul and Ruskin's Late Literary Criticism

Ruskin wrote only one volume of sustained literary criticism, *Fiction Fair and Foul,* five papers published in the *Nineteenth Century* from June 1880 to October 1881. His other major contribution to the genre had appeared much earlier, in volume three of *Modern Painters* (1856), where he had attacked the solipsistic metaphors of modern poets from Pope to Tennyson. Between 1856, the year Ruskin formulated the "pathetic fallacy," and 1880, the year he denounced Wordsworth, he suffered through two mental attacks and an "unconversion" from evangelical Protestantism. Writing the Oxford lectures and *Fors Clavigera* with a number of other projects in mind as well as in progress, he was under physical and psychological strain and produced essays that often were discursive and fragmented. He himself noted a change in the circumstances of his work; in the final paragraph of *Fiction Fair and Foul,* he mentions the control he must summon to compose a coherent piece:

> I can only now write carefully of what bears on my immediate work: and must ask the reader's indulgence for the hasty throwing together of materials intended, before my illness last spring, to have been far more thoroughly handled. The friends who are fearful for my reputation as an "écrivain" will perhaps kindly

recollect that a sentence of *Modern Painters* was often written four or five times over in my own hand, and tried in every word for perhaps an hour—perhaps a forenoon—before it was passed for the printer. I rarely now fix my mind on a sentence, or a thought, for five minutes in the quiet of morning, but a telegram comes announcing that somebody or other will do themselves the pleasure of calling at eleven o'clock, and that there's two shillings to pay. (34:394)[1]

Ruskin begins by mentioning the serious threat to his work from within, but ends by describing a minor threat from without. An uninvited caller hardly constitutes a serious obstacle and may serve simply to distract both writer and reader from the uncomfortable confession of mental illness. Yet although Ruskin cannot seriously be blaming such vexations for his rushed and digressive writing, the intrusive note, the imminent visitor, the time, and the passing of money (for an unwanted message) illustrate the invasion of the "real" in *Fiction Fair and Foul*. In the forms of the telegram and money—two kinds of exchange—the economic real pervades not only these five essays but also the modern fiction he denounces in its pages, and it ultimately transforms, to Ruskin's acquiescence and scorn, all reading and writing.

As I have shown, although Ruskin often phrased his ideas about aesthetic value in economic terms, he did so with irony and generally resisted the encroachment of the market in the area of nonreproducible commodities. As the complaint above shows, evidence of the world—the petty, daily interruptions that in their insignificance are signs of reality in nineteenth-century realistic texts—also exerted a centrifugal pull on the hermetic text that Ruskin was trying to create.[2] In other words, noise and messages from the outside disrupted the unity and harmony that he tried to embody in his writing through uninterrupted thinking, and he encapsulated these annoyances in the exchange of words and money.

The idea of the text endangered by the outside in the form of exchange arises in part from his obsession with changes in the landscape and skyscape documented in *The Stormcloud of the Nineteenth Century* (1878). Similarly, in *Fiction Fair and Foul*,

Ruskin's objection to the real emerged with the appearance of the cityscape in literature, especially novels. The large concentration of people within constricted space, their hard and often violent lives, the social shifting of what probably seemed an amorphous bourgeoisie, and the blatant presence of money characterized an outside world that by the terms of his moral aesthetic was not representable. As a writer, Ruskin would not accept the details of the modern real, which intruded on his work; and, in the first essay of *Fiction Fair and Foul,* he voiced his resistance as a reader.

Because nineteenth-century cities had expanded through continuing population shifts, Ruskin recoiled from urban audiences as he shunned their physical surroundings.[3] However, by the last decades of the nineteenth century, when these areas held a mass reading public who bought popular novels, as well as periodicals, in the tens and hundreds of thousands, Ruskin had to face the city as an image of the collective form of response to literature.[4] Thus, in the third and fourth essays of *Fiction Fair and Foul,* he contributed to current revaluations of Wordsworth and Byron by examining the character of their popularity. This discussion is part of an extended commentary on readers and reading, popularity, and reputation which spanned much of Ruskin's writing at this time. It appeared, in submerged form, in *Fiction Fair and Foul,* the *Bibliotheca Pastorum,* and other essays and projects of the 1870s and 1880s. The importance of the attribute *popular* derived from the economic discourse; it described a continuous and prolonged production, distribution, and reception of commodities. In *Fiction Fair and Foul,* Ruskin confronted both the economic basis of value and the metropolitan consumers who responded to the urban referents of realism. It was the public's conferral of value that in effect interrupted Ruskin while he wrote and that, on a grander scale, infected these essays with many of the "real" elements he claimed had fouled fiction.

THE ECONOMIC MODEL AND FICTIONAL LANDSCAPES

In his late work as a literary critic, Ruskin rejected the contemporary cityscape as a suitable object of representation. Because reception and mimesis had been bound in intricate ways since Aristotle's *Poetics,* his attack of the city as a proper referent in his moral aesthetic established a conflict with city-readers, and they became the chief target in the first essay of *Fiction Fair and Foul.* In this section, I will explore the reasons why cities as objects of representation became less and less palatable for Ruskin as the century closed, and his problematical solution to them in the form of mythical provincial worlds and audiences.

The landscape was by the 1880s the fundamental referent of the moral aesthetic Ruskin had made famous in *Modern Painters.* As E. H. Gombrich has noted, most nineteenth-century writers and painters, from Wordsworth to the French Impressionists, announced that their work was true to nature and mirrored objective reality.[5] Ruskin's version of truth, selective representation on moral grounds often for didactic purposes, operated throughout the first three volumes of *Modern Painters.* It encompassed poetry and painting in the chapter "Of Received Opinions Touching the 'Grand Style,'" extending the province of realism beyond representative types to carefully chosen details (5:17–34). "Ruskin's program to fuse poetic idealism with scientific objectivity by means of the devoted intensity of the artist's realism—Fra Lippo Lippi's program, in short—was simply a restatement of the Romantic dilemma," writes W. F. Axton.[6] Strict evangelical training possibly restricted Ruskin's choice of subject a bit more than Fra Lippo Lippi's; obviously, not everyone had a soul that should be painted. Nevertheless, Axton's description applies to Ruskin's aesthetic, with this addition: in and after *Modern Painters,* Ruskin believed that art was public and depended for its effect on the joining of at least two imaginations, the artist's and the viewer's or reader's. This encounter between different eyes needed the stability of shared fact. Thus, as Elizabeth Deeds Ermarth argues, in a novel one reliable test of truth is a work's conformity to common perceptions of the outer world.[7] A viewer should judge a picture by asking, "Is it so? Is that the way a stone is shaped, the way a cloud is wreathed, the way a leaf is veined?" Ruskin himself asked (5:180). Beholders approach a painting or read a novel trusting that the work represents an outer world that both they and the artist see.

By the 1870s and 1880s, Ruskin realized that these ideas required a natural world that offered something worth imitating, and an audience who could both see and appreciate the same object. As he showed in the first essay of *Fiction Fair and Foul,* the representable world (within his aesthetic) was beyond the view of many. His antagonism toward the corruption of the outside was aimed at the human imagination via nature. It is "never space which is represented," observes Gombrich, about drawing, "but familiar things in situations."[8] Still assuming that art was true to nature, Ruskin attacked the circle of representation created by material conditions familiar to readers and writers: a writer who knew only the city—its violence, noise, and filth—could only represent that city. In turn, those who lived in such cities enjoyed reading about and looking at depictions of them. Because artists and readers must always begin with facts, modern realism had become a recording of police bulletins and the public's vulgar lives.

In a long footnote in the first essay, Ruskin explains that the "literature of the prison-house" or "Fiction mécroyante" (34:276–79) addresses readers who already have the diseases vaunted in the novels. They live in cities whose emblematic spaces are the prison, the morgue, and the asylum. (By juxtaposing "prison-house" and "mécroyante," Ruskin suggests that physical corruption [of the individual or social body] causes faithlessness, though he does not state so explicitly here; but he has already forged an enduring link between the two in *The Stones of Venice.*) Amidst physical bedlam, city-dwellers no longer believe in the dogmas of their religion. Whether it starts in the body or the mind, the plague then surfaces in art. The arabesques of Raphael and the *Contes Drôlatiques* of Balzac, Dickens's Miss Mowcher, the recurrent images of executions in Scott's *Fortunes of Nigel,* for example, are all evidence of brain disease in writers. Figures of "truncated and Hermes-like deformity," as well as of mutilation, are "sign manual[s] of the plague" (34:278–79). These indices then become the relational models for other artists intent on depicting reality; thus the "two frescoes in the colossal handbills which have lately decorated the streets of London (the baboon with the mirror, and the Maskelyne and Cooke decapitation [an advertisement for soap]) are the final English forms of Raphael's arabesque under this influence. . . . for the folly begets folly down, and down; and whatever Scott and Turner did wrong has thousands of imitators—their wisdom none will so much as hear, how much less follow!" (35:280).

Why does there not exist a conversely healthy modern literature based on the sound body and the pure air rendered in many relational models of Scott and Turner? Ruskin in effect answers this when he states that "evil and good are alike conditions of literal *vision:* and therefore also, inseparably connected with the state of the health" (34:280). Contemporary artists and audiences seek to repeat what they have seen and experienced. For nineteenth-century working- and middle-class readers, this is the "routine of counter or desk within doors," the natural world of pavement and arcade instead of ground and sky, of heat and cold rather than summer and winter (34:271). To escape from these surroundings, city-dwellers demand only a heightened form of the familiar—more noise, more violence, more dismemberment. Their imaginations are narrowly empirical: a commonly perceived reality conditions and limits their vision. Readers cannot respond to elements they have never seen. A Romantic writer such as George Sand, whose books are filled with "radiantly ideal" characters and landscapes "rich and true with the . . . life passed in glens of Norman granite and beside bays of Italian sea" (34:377–78), cannot be *seen* by readers. They demand what Ruskin calls Cockney literature—fiction about ordinary people "picked up from behind the counter and out of the gutter" (34:378) like themselves.

Thus, despite his reliance on relational models, Ruskin linked "Fiction mécroyante" (which includes Cockney literature and the "literature of the prison-house") to an urban aesthetic. He shared the sense of novelists such as Dickens that "modern life is city life."[9] From 1814, the year *Waverley* appeared, and 1880, the year the *Nineteenth Century* printed this first essay, the character of readerships must have been more and more conditioned by urban living, because two-thirds of the English lived in cities or factory towns by the 1880s, three-quarters of whom were working class. These people largely constituted what Richard Altick calls the "amorphous stratum between the old-

established middle class (merchants and bankers, large employ-
ers of labor, superior members of professions) and the working
class proper—the ranks of unskilled labor."[10] When Ruskin
judged current fiction against the depictions of nature and
character in novels such as *Waverley* and *Old Mortality,* he was
mourning the social realignment of these faceless readers and
the change in their material conditions that obscured the old
landscape as an object of sight and, subsequently, of popular
representation.

In reaction, he chose not to regard cities simply as despoiled country landscapes but, in theory, as giant villages. In
the appendix to his Oxford lectures of 1883 he writes, "All great
art . . . is *provincial,* showing its energy in the capital, but
educated, and chiefly productive, in its own country town"
(33:397). The lasting appeal of fairy tales provided an example
of the provincial power of cities. In his "Preface" to *German
Popular Stories* (1868), Ruskin observes that the walled village
and the "narrowness of social circumstances" restrain and calm
fantasies inspired by the woods beyond the town. In effect the
wall operates as a screen and window: it juxtaposes the super-
natural with the familiar while framing the countryside for the
domestic viewer. All the preternatural inhabitants of the woods
do not, therefore, affect the villagers' religious faith. Fairies
instead become playful illusions kept apart from religious dogma by the wall. Superstitions are imagined, but not lived.
Separated from the figures in the inhabitants' religious *mythoi,*
"the good spirit [of the woods] descends gradually from an angel
into a fairy, and the demon shrinks into a playful grotesque of
diminutive malevolence" (19:238). In other essays and lectures
he wrote around the same time, Ruskin called the city a nation's
cultural heart and imaginative core. Five cities—Athens,
Rome, Florence, Venice, and London—have furnished all the
world's great art, he states in his "Preface" to Xenophon's *Economist* (31:8). Repeating the list in his Oxford lecture of October
1884, he adds Paris, which in *Fiction Fair and Foul* is the "central
root" of "literature of the prison-house" (34:279). Clearly, he
must have blamed the proliferation of "Fiction mécroyante" on
the modern urban center, not on the city in general.

For Ruskin, the modern city was still the cultural heart of

the nation, but it did not have the protective transparency of the walled village; it stood apart from the country as a closed, impenetrable and seemingly inescapable labyrinth. The clerks who never saw the sky or sun and the "reckless crowding in cities" (34:276) were metonymic signs of the social changes that had transformed the look of contemporary London. In *Fiction Fair and Foul,* it is a Cockney hell, a maze of the middle and lower classes. When in the same essay he summarizes the plot of Balzac's *Père Goriot* and comments that the story could only occur in a large city, he is referring to amorphous social "crowding" that makes a marriage between a grocer's daughter and a man of rank possible. Because a "village grocer cannot make a large fortune" (34:269), the conception and plot of *Père Goriot* are fundamentally urban, Ruskin argues. This remark, along with his criticism of Cockney literature for portraying city drudges and criminals, reveals that he hated urban novels not only for the congestion, violence, and dirt they mirrored, but for the economic model they inscribed.

One of the chief elements of the novel that Ruskin deplored, but accepted, was the blatancy of money. It propelled the plot of contemporary novels such as *Père Goriot* and *The Mill on the Floss,* determining and forming the superstructure of values. This is why in *Fiction Fair and Foul* he turns the city upside down and visualizes it as a place of chaos ruled or disordered, as in Balzac's text, by the frenetic circulation of money. In his "Preface" to the *Economist,* Ruskin describes the Platonic ideal of the city as the index of a nation it crowns: "The Metropolis is properly the city in which the chief temple of the nation's God is built. . . . Thither the tribes go up, and under the shield, and in the loving presence, of their Deity, the men of highest power and truest honour are gathered to frame the laws, and direct the acts, of State" (31:9). In his addenda to "A Joy Forever" (1857), he describes what he sees: "Our large trading cities bear to me very nearly the aspect of monastic establishments in which the . . . worship of Mammon or Moloch is conducted with a tender reverence and an exact propriety; the merchant rising to his Mammon matins with the self-denial of an anchorite, and expiating the frivolities into which he may be beguiled in the course of the day by late attendance at Mammon vespers" (16:138).

Ruskin retains the metaphors of religious convention to indicate the passing of the metaphysical and the substitution of money as the object of worship. However, money or love of it cannot actually replace God, for it is a circulating rather than an ordering principle. An "incredible civilization" ruled by Mammon in effect is headless, and the images of that city therefore echo chaos and deformity (34:277).

Ruskin ends *Fiction Fair and Foul* in a display of his own vulnerability to the outside. The telegram, entailing an exchange of words and money, stops the essay and breaks the thread of Ruskin's thoughts. This conclusion gives symmetry to the whole series, which has begun with a similar encroachment. Ruskin's initial sentence runs, in part, "On the first . . . day of March, in this year, I walked through what was once a country lane" (34:265). After reciting the devastations of its cottages and roads, he speculates about the effect of such a sight on young eyes, then denounces contemporary fiction for its imitations of cities such as Paris and London and new suburbs such as this, called Croxted Lane.

Fiction Fair and Foul thus is flanked by descriptions of the real pressing first on the material and, finally, on the mental, landscape. For in the last paragraph of the series, the interruptions threaten both the progress and content of Ruskin's writing. This new real is aggressive and chaotic not only because it destroys the landscape that artists such as Turner, Copley Fielding, and J. D. Harding framed for his eyes, but also because it disrupts the order of the past which Ruskin has tried to preserve in his writing.

Philip Fisher has commented that, in denouncing the modern urban novel, Ruskin mistook technique for content.[11] This seems likely, especially when he alternates between criticism of despoiled nature and criticism of the inherited contagion from relational models like Raphael and the street posters. But Ruskin's apparent confusion was symptomatic of the Victorians' wavering belief in the primacy of the real over a growing awareness of the insularity of language. George Levine has stressed that naïve realism—"simple faith in the correspondence between word and thing"—never existed among Victorian novelists. He detects no consensus about or confidence in what the real actually was.[12] Ruskin often expressed the doubts of his era; he was aware, for example, that one could lose the "truth" of an abstraction in a word (19:352). Yet just as he tried to capture this naïveté with his precritical interpretations, he treated nature with equally affected innocence, as the place of truth which existed outside all representation. Ultimately, he valorized the extrareferential and asserted what Roger Ramsey has called a "non-fiction premise" in all of his writing.[13] Even though Ruskin often substantiated Gombrich's theory that realism refers to texts rather than to an unmediated outside, he finally blamed the corrupted state of mimesis on a physical world that provided the model and therefore marked the limits of representation.

In place of the referent of modern fiction, Ruskin offered a world and a readership without urban vices. His proposed library of great books, aptly called the *Bibliotheca Pastorum,* or "Shepherd's Library," celebrated the increasingly invisible landscape and untenable perspective he admired in the drawings of Allingham, Prout, and William Henry Hunt. The texts included were to provide model scenes for living; generally, they were a conservative lot, many of them part of the classical grind familiar to the sons of gentry and nobility. Writers to be represented included Hesiod, Virgil, Dante, and Chaucer. There were British and contemporary authors as well. Only three volumes were ever actually produced: a translation of Xenophon's *Economist* (1876), with a "Preface" by Ruskin, the first of a projected two-volume edition of Sir Philip Sidney's *Psalter* entitled *Rock Honeycomb* (1877), which I have discussed, *A Knight's Faith* (1885), Ruskin's collation of passages from *A Year on the Punjab Frontier, 1848–49* by Sir Herbert Edwardes of the First Bengal Fusiliers, and selections from Gotthelf.[14] Ruskin probably read Gotthelf's "Ulric the Farm Servant" in 1854 while touring Switzerland with his parents. Written in 1841, it is the only example of modern prose fiction in the Shepherd's Library, but like "The Broom Merchant," which Ruskin translated in *Fors,* it has more in common with the folk tale than the novel. "Ulric" is the story of a hard-working Swiss peasant who lives in a place without railroads, machines, or the kind of labor that came with them. Again, like "The Broom Merchant," Ulric would provide the "shepherds" using Ruskin's library with archaic models of household economy and exchange. As the name of the library suggests, Ruskin was not luring novel-readers from Balzac and Dickens. Instead, he sensed that a change in the referent automatically required a congruent change in audience, that representations of a preindustrial world invoked a preindustrial readership. The audience he envisioned was already part of this archaic landscape. Of course they actually were laborers such as the readers of *Fors*, but calling them "shepherds" was his way of summoning an audience who already shared his regressive fantasy.

The idiosyncratic contents of the *Bibliotheca* show that Ruskin chose books for their historical and social implications rather than for their literary value. His interest in what he called "domestic history" supports this. The editors of the Library Edition observe that he "cared little for the history of kings and conquests, though . . . he was a student of military history. He believed that the importance of political history was often exaggerated. . . . 'Write first,' he said, 'the history of your native village'" (32:xviii). To reestablish the pastoral landscape and life as the tenor of representation, he recounted and published the histories of erstwhile laborers, the peasants. He was a sort of nineteenth-century *annales* historian who adopted a sentimental perspective of the proletariat to defy the dominant Philistine empire of the vulgar and the useful—the whole capitalist economy. [15] At the same time, the selections insinuated the over-determined economic model he was trying to avoid. He was aware, for instance, that Gotthelf's idylls were the rural myths of urban capitalism. In his "Preface" to "Ulric the Farm Servant" (1885), he remarks that the story shows the "calculating and prosperous virtue of Protestant Switzerland" (32:343); Gotthelf captured "the Swiss character in the phase of change . . . when the noble customs of the past were still observed by the peasants of ancient . . . family, while the recent influences of trade and foreign travellers were gradually corrupting alike the lower peasantry and the city population" (33:345). Ruskin understood that, in Terry Eagleton's words, "rural society is rural capital-ism, permeated at every level by the forces and relations of capitalist production; it provides no alternative enclave to the dominant social mode." For this reason, the utopian passages in Ruskin's late work were compromised by a hostile and whimsi-cal tone because the rural, part of what Eagleton calls the "bour-geois ideology of pastoral," was alienated and envisioned "as an 'unreal' enclave."[16]

Ruskin's editions of *Roadside Songs of Tuscany,* a collection of Florentine ballads with pictures, and "The Story of Ida," both by Francesca Alexander, were contemporary examples of domes-tic history, and they also illustrate the way even Ruskin's nostalgic programs were implicated in the economic model. "The Story of Ida" is an account of a saintly girl's death from a broken heart. Described as a frail consumptive, Ida weakens from the story's first page; her faithless lover, who has children from another woman, resembles *Romola*'s Tito (though Ida would be the counterpart of Tessa). Ruskin recognized the con-ventional sentimentality of the tale, and he did not think he had discovered a great artist in Alexander. The drawings, he says, show no sense of light and shade (32:52), and "The Story of Ida" "concede[s] too much to the modern feeling of the British pub-lic that people who are quite good have nothing to do but to die" (32:256). Instead, he stresses the truthfulness of the small sto-ries that accompany *Roadside Songs.* Passed to Alexander by the peasant women among whom she lived, the tales have "historic candour" (32:54); they are a "careful record of providentially ordered Fact" (32:5). Her songs also convey actual facts, not sentiments or fancies (32:56). Alexander is what the poet and romance-writer should be, a "strict historian of days" (32:5).

Moreover, she wrote "The Story of Ida" to be read, not published. This information, which Ruskin supplies in his "Preface" to the first edition of the story, is disingenuous: it appears in a version of the book printed on "Whatman's hand-made paper . . . with the frontispiece pulled off on India paper" and priced at 6s. (Two thousand copies of a smaller edition sold for 3s. apiece [32:4].) These prices were not prohibitively high for cloth-bound volumes; by 1881, the average income of a lower-middle-class family was £110, and a working-class family who had made 20s. a week thirty years before now earned 32s. a week, or £83 annually.[17] Nevertheless, the transformation of Alexander's oral story into an attractive object and the conventionality of its contents insinuated a specific readership of collectors. And though buyers may have come from different social classes, their purchase of "The Story of Ida" in effect leveled them into a single stratum of consumers who had assimilated reading into their general mode of acquisition. Within this system, Ruskin was a distributor of Alexander's work, aware of his uncomfortable position as he confessed, "I have had a certain feeling of desecrating its [the story's] humility of affection, ever since I asked leave to publish it" (32:6).

In summary, Ruskin presented Francesca Alexander herself as a historian, not an artist, and her text as an inferior one in order to reclaim it from the circuit of representation. "That it was *not* written for publication will be felt after reading a few sentences" (32:6). Her literary inadequacies somehow divorce the text of domestic history from the fancy art book he produces. But in its desecrated form, "The Story of Ida" provides another example of the *Bibliotheca*'s metropolitan ruralism.[18] By not writing to be published, Francesca Alexander failed to satisfy the public demand for the repetition of urban experience heightened in violent and morbid images. Because she did not create a commodity, her story bypassed the circuit of exchange. "It is only by being exchanged that the products of labour acquire, as values, one uniform social status, distinct from their varied forms of existence as objects of utility," writes Marx.[19] In emphasizing the unsocial character of Alexander's work, Ruskin assumed Marx's theory of commodity fetishism without invoking Marx; he implicitly showed that, once exchanged, an article acquired a social character. Because Alexander expected no payment, either in money or in kind, but simply passed her story along, she enacted the role of scribe for a primitive community with an oral narrative tradition. Resurrecting for Ruskin the pastoral referent and the preindustrial economy, she avoided the mass audience that now conferred value on fiction.

"For Ruskin, as for the realist novelists everywhere, the quotidian, the merely human, must fill up the space of the sublime," observes George Levine.[20] Alexander's domestic histories and Ruskin's Shepherd's Library located images of simple domestic life in rural idylls. But these alternatives did not provide a domestic version of the sublime effect. In the realistic novel, according to Levine, the "peril" of the sublime is displaced to the human heart. In this light, the sensational novels of Dickens and Balzac, among others, offered the urban form of the sublime. Readers of a book such as *Bleak House,* tantalized by the "funereal excitement" of its violent deaths (34:274), were not interested in the humdrum realities of country life and could no longer recognize such an archaic referent as real; the novels they preferred debased the sublime effect of Scott's highland landscapes into the gross excitement of the streets. In "Fiction mécroyante," the sublime had been dislocated to the human body; this, with the proliferation of money, was the source of Ruskin's disgust with modern literature. But by leaving the sublime out of his favored literature, Ruskin failed to meet the demands of an audience of novel-readers for some form of excitement and escape. There were no realistic novels in his cadre of fiction, only Scott's work. Converts to Ruskin's library would have to wean themselves from all samples of what had become, in the last sixty years, the most popular and accessible mode of the novel, domestic realism. Those who did were an exclusive audience of conservative book collectors whose participation echoed general practices of prestigious consumption. Realizing these paradoxes, Ruskin hypothesized an unreceptive readership as he wrote the first essay.

This hostility toward his audience illustrates the antagonism between narrating writer and reader that typifies late-nineteenth-century realism, according to George Levine. Whereas, earlier in the century, readers had met sincere, commiserating narrators who encouraged expressions of sentiment, even passion, an audience now faced an indifferent or hostile persona who forced on them unpleasant details and who perhaps no longer echoed their values. The "later realists insisted . . . on an artistic integrity that alienated them from the traditional novel-reading audience. They imagined that the truth would be offensive to that audience, and found confirmation of their fictions precisely in their offensiveness."[21] Yet here Levine is speaking of the late century's "perfect inversion of mid-

Victorian conventions" by writers such as Emile Zola, George Moore, and George Gissing. Ruskin obviously was not part of this group, and he did not view the relationship between popular novelists, in their narratives, and readers in this way. He imagined that a modern audience liked having its face rubbed in what he called the "fimetic" heap of reality (34:269). There seemed to him a bond between the modern novelist and his or her audience based on a desire for sensation untrained by religious dogma. Whether nor not this was true—Levine suggests it was not—this perception alienated Ruskin from the mass reading public, because a work's wide circulation implicated its referent and its audience in the prison-house of urban sight.

ROMANTICS AND READERSHIPS

After castigating the modern urban novel, Ruskin turned his attention in the next essays of *Fiction Fair and Foul* to Wordsworth, Byron, and Scott. To some extent, he treated the first two as domestic historians. Just as *Roadside Songs of Tuscany* showed British peasants "the reality of the sweet soul of Catholic Italy" (32:xxii), poets had to depict the rural real credibly. Whereas Ruskin claimed to refocus history on the study of peasants, Wordsworth professed to make them, in the *Lyrical Ballads,* the subject of poetry. Yet it was not his attitude toward the rural poor that endeared him to Ruskin; Wordsworth's treatment of peasants became one of the objects of Ruskin's criticism in *Fiction Fair and Foul*. Like the novel of the modern city, Wordsworth, along with other Romantics, diverted and diffused Ruskin's aggression toward public reception of commodified texts.

Ruskin's attack of Wordsworth rings a jarring note in an opus that resonates with the poet's voice even after these essays appeared. The General Index of the Library Edition lists almost two pages, in fine print, of references to or quotations from his poems, especially *The Excursion*. For Ruskin, Wordsworth was essentially the great English poet of nature, and he often expressed Ruskin's own love of mountains and flowers. He is called, in volume one of *Modern Painters,* "the keenest-eyed of all modern poets for what is deep and essential in nature" (3:307). There, too, Ruskin uses passages from *The Excursion* as illustrations of both nature's effects and Turner's paintings. Wordsworth was to Ruskin the literary Turner, the verbal master of the sublime as well as of the picturesque, an exemplary artist whether working from relational models or from nature. In *Praeterita,* his last work, Ruskin is still weaving Wordsworth's lines into his own writing. He remembers walking around Avon and Kennilworth and, during a storm, finding shelter in a cottage filled with religious prints and family pictures. The two women who lived there, a mother and daughter, were peasants. Ruskin hears about the death of the mother's husband from hard labor in London, then leaves to walk past a churchyard filled with sheep and a rainbow that he says, "made my heart leap again" (35:431–32). This passage, from his diary of 1847, suits a largely nostalgic autobiography. For the poems that inform this scene—*The Ruined Cottage* and *Michael,* besides "My Heart Leaps Up"—refer to a landscape and a class *as* it vanishes. Michael, the dead woman of *The Ruined Cottage,* and the widow Ruskin meets are all *left,* realized in implicit relation to demographic and social shifts. In these poems, Wordsworth's pastoral, and Ruskin's use of it, concern the peripheral. To the writer of *Fiction Fair and Foul,* who sees Croxted Lane, the scene of his short walks, turn into a suburb; who resorts to reviving the pastoral world by publishing Alexander's stories and extolling the books of Scott, Wordsworth should remain the verbal counterpart of William Henry Hunt, a comforting reminder of mountains, flowers, and peasants which time and space are making invisible.

The assault on Wordsworth in *Fiction Fair and Foul* occurred within Ruskin's general war against reception. Like "Fiction mécroyante," Wordsworth's poetry absorbed the hostility Ruskin directed at the public, including his own readers. He still loved the poet's landscapes; he began his third essay with an epigraph from "Inscriptions, 1828." And his attack on urban perception in the first essay is indebted to similar, if cursory, remarks in the "Preface" to the second edition of the *Lyrical Ballads.* His quarrel was with Wordsworthians, and his assessment of the poet in the second and fourth essays in the August and November 1880 issues of the *Nineteenth Century* occurred in the context of the Wordsworth-Byron controversy provoked by Arnold's *Poems of Wordsworth, Chosen and Edited* (Golden Treasury Series [1879]). (Arnold's essay on Byron, which sparked the most furious exchanges of the debate, appeared in March 1881, after Ruskin had published four of the five installments of his series, and all of his comments on the poets.) Katherine Peek has summarized the arguments on each side.[22] However, Ruskin's part early in the debate discloses some telling ironies in his attitude toward readerships and reading in general.

The affectedly offhand detraction of Wordsworth begins toward the end of the second essay. There, Ruskin uses a passage from *The French Revolution* to measure the "results" of Wordsworth's poetry. In a rambling discussion of war chants, he correlates the singing of the "Marseillaise" with the advance of the French army on the Austrians, then compares the effect of English "songs," which generally are neither military nor religious. The British do have their "carnal orchestra," comprising Scott, Burns, and Byron, but no stirring religious poetry. Having rejected "Catholic Psalms as antiquated and unscientific" and "Puritan melodies" as "jar and twangle" (34:317), the nation vaunts only the quasi-religious innocence of the Lake School for its metaphysical poetry, headed by Wordsworth. Whereas Carlyle writes that "every heart [of Dumouriez's army] leaps up at the sound" of the "Marseillaise" (34:316), the British stir into pantheistic nationalism over mild forms of nature, like rainbows and lakes. The contrast, Ruskin implies, is not to the advantage of his countrymen and women. Domestic and refined, the Lake poets express the genteel views of a provincial people who no longer have the passion of religious conviction. As the head of this school, Wordsworth is an "aerial" rather than an "ethereal" poet (34:320); he speaks from Mount Skiddaw, not Parnassus, and his philosophy, "as pure as the tarns of [British] mountains," is "of corresponding depth" (which, Ruskin hastens to clarify in a footnote, is not "unfathomable" [34:318]).

In the opening passages of the fourth essay, Ruskin claims that committed Wordsworthians do not enact the lessons of their poet. He glances at the paltry response around Oxford to his project at Ferry Hinksey: his colleagues apparently would rather seek "the shades of our Rydalian laurels" than dig a road (34:349). The older Ruskin now assesses Wordsworth through things done, and the poet's often unprofound reflections have spawned a host of passive devotees who show allegiance to their master by becoming bucolic.

Carlyle had once referred to Wordsworth's peasants as "whining drivellers" and the poet as a man who, "if he had not fallen into poetry, would have done effectual work in the world."[23] Swinburne in 1865 had sneered at Wordsworth's didactic use of nature, and Byron had called the poet "unintelligible" in *Don Juan* (1.xc).[24] The more recent opinions of Wordsworth's detractors published in other periodicals during the debate of the 1880s largely coincided with Ruskin's, though many, such as W. E. Henley's and Alfred Austin's, appeared after *Fiction Fair and Foul*.[25] In most of these essays, Wordsworth is measured by one criterion: an ability to portray, hence arouse action. To such readers, poems like *The Excursion* and *The Prelude* seemed incessantly "talky," their author a man of little experience or passion. In judging Wordsworth's achievement by effect, specifically things produced, they became Byronists.

Ruskin belonged to the Wordsworth Society, and, in labeling the poet a practical failure, he contradicted the conservative program he had endorsed as a member. Established in 1880, the society intended to draw the poet from under the shadow of the popular Tennyson toward a mass reading public. As a member, Ruskin made his position very clear. In 1883, a letter from him appeared in the society's *Transactions* which defined the value of the poet in relation to an endangered ideology: "The grand function of the Society is to preserve, as far as possible, in England, the conditions of moral life which made Wordsworth himself possible; and which, if destroyed, would leave his verse vainer than the hymns of Orpheus. But on this political duty of Englishmen I have surely said and written enough."[26]

In Ruskin's eyes, the society should accomplish through historiography the conservative project he attempted, and so far had failed to fulfill, through purchasing land. In this light, the essays on Wordsworth and membership in a society honoring him are part of Ruskin's sustained attack of material and social transformations and the debased perception they engendered. Simultaneously, though, the goal Ruskin envisioned for the Wordsworth Society—thus his reason for joining—conflicted with the stand he took in the Wordsworth-Byron controversy. On one hand, he wanted to preserve the world that produced a Wordsworth; on the other hand, he criticized the poet for merely representing that world.

Ruskin further confused his position with contradictory remarks about the poet's treatment of rural subjects. He admitted that some of the poems represented the feelings and superstitions of British peasants, and he described a recent talk with a Cumberland woman whose literal sense of death replicated the little girl's in "We Are Seven" (34:319). Generally, however, he claimed that the poetics of "a new and only correct school" obscured the truth of the peasant and working classes (34:320). The pejorative "correct," may refer to form, though Ruskin's comments about the latter are cursory. His one example of bad iambics is the Thirty-Eighth Ecclesiastical Sonnet, and of inane rhyming, "The Idiot Boy." "Correct" suggests that Ruskin found Wordsworth's impressions of the pastoral world too disciplined by conventional rhyme and meter; the criticism is, at this point, unclear. Years earlier, in his "Preface" to *German Popular Stories* (1868), he had objected to the taming of Grimms' fairy tales to make their content and expression more didactic and genteel, respectively. Just as the modernized fairy legend concealed the material conditions of its genesis and its value, many of Wordsworth's pastoral poems denied the historical value of the subject, according to Ruskin. Diluted for drawing rooms, the idylls of Wordsworth exemplified the artful representations he condemned in his discussion of fairy tales.

Yet Ruskin did not generally dismiss the bourgeois-primitive; he detected the idyllic nature of Francesca Alexander's work but praised it anyway. His discussion of Wordsworth was marked by similar equivocations. For example, in the second essay Ruskin revealed contempt for the unadulterated pastoral: "Wordsworth is simply a Westmoreland peasant, with considerably less shrewdness than most border Englishmen or Scotsmen inherit; and no sense of humor: but gifted (in this

singularly) with vivid sense of natural beauty, and a pretty turn
for reflections, not always acute, but, as far as they reach, medicinal to the fever of the restless and corrupted life around him"
(34:318).

Here, Ruskin diminishes small praise with a long qualification between "reflection" and the understated compliment,
"medicinal." He derogates the talent for "reflection" with the
feminine adjective "pretty." Finally, he reduces Wordsworth to a
type—representative of many. All these pejoratives are associated with the passive, isolationist poetry of the Lake School, as
opposed to the inspiriting song of the French Revolution. But
Ruskin does not deride Wordsworth's poetry only for its lack of
perlocutionary effect, even though he seems to demean the Lake
School by juxtaposing its ideological role with the revolutionary
function of the Marseillaise. For he also calls Wordsworth a
"Westmoreland peasant"—in fact, worse than a peasant, because he has less shrewdness and no sense of humor. If Ruskin
were merely damning Wordsworth for sentimentalizing rural
subjects or for creating genteel versions of the primitive, he
presumably would not use "Westmoreland peasant" as an insult.
Ruskin chose these words because he was aware, and approved
of, an acknowledged distance between the poet and the peasantry he depicted. With "Westmoreland peasant," he strikes a
metaphor for dulled perception and the improper appropriation
of the vision of another class. A few paragraphs after this, his
point becomes clearer. Wordsworth should have told "what he
knew of his own villages and people" from the position of "a
country gentleman" (34:320)—such as Hunt. The separation
between the laboring and middle classes, which Ruskin seems
to regret when he mentions the pallid work of the Lake poets,
becomes fundamental in his most pointed criticism of Wordsworth. The shiftiness of his argument may prevent him from
discussing the faults of the poetry in any detail. He could easily
have shown that the attempt to develop a poetics from primitive
vision culminated in a work (the *Lyrical Ballads*) that mimicked
the social rift between literary convention and the republican
subject matter. Coleridge had, decades before in the *Biographia
Literaria*. Ruskin did not explore the inadequation of content
and form in the ballads or any other of Wordsworth's poems. He

only claimed, in passing, that the overly primitive poetics of "The Idiot Boy" disclosed the false position of the gentleman poet.

Passages such as these reveal an ambivalence about the social formation that produced a Wordsworth. In general, Ruskin professed to endorse the spiritual alliance of gentry, aristocrat, and laborer against the bourgeoisie, especially in *Fors* and in his praise of Alexander's work, but his specific charges against writers and insensate readers throughout *Fiction Fair and Foul* frequently betray a sense of unalterable class distinction behind all aesthetics. This is why he was concerned with mimesis and degenerate images of the city in the first essay, for they indicate the physical and social conditions of the audience they interpellate. Thus Wordsworth correctly based his fiction on the rural landscape, but from the wrong perspective. Clearly, Ruskin required the sort of distance from a subject that he associated with the squirearchy; for this reason, history became the privileged form of writing in these essays on fiction. For this reason, too, Byron, whom many still saw as the enemy of British middle-class propriety, emerged as the paragon of proletarian and aristocratic ethics.

In a central but dense passage in the fourth essay, Ruskin condemns Wordsworth most strongly for his violation of social distance through the abuse of historical fact. The contested version of history comes from one of the *Ecclesiastical Sonnets* ("Scene in Venice," 1.38). Retelling Sismondi's version of the truce between Frederick Barbarossa and Pope Alexander III in 1177, the critic invalidates the poet's image of the Venetian crowds "invoking a vindictive ban / From outraged nature." To counter this description of the people at the ceremony of reconciliation, Ruskin uses a line from *Childe Harold* (4.12) which juxtaposes the same scene with the Austrians' seizure of Venice in 1798. It reads simply, "An Emperor tramples where an Emperor knelt." The kneeling emperor, Frederick Barbarossa, abjured the anti-Pope, acknowledged Alexander as the Pontiff, and thereby ended the seventeen-year schism of the Roman Empire. According to one surviving record, when Frederick reached the throne before the church of Saint Mark the Evangelist, he "threw off the red cloak he was wearing, and prostrated himself before the Pope, and kissed first his feet and then his knees."[27] Describing this incident in his Thirty-Eighth Ecclesiastical Sonnet, Wordsworth writes that the pope placed one foot on the neck of the prostrate Barbarossa—an apocryphal detail; but the image serves Wordsworth's commentary; to him the truce was a humiliation for "Caesar's Successor."[28] The victorious pope is a villain: "Black Demons [are] hovering o'er his mitred head," and the crowd turns away from this imperious display in sorrow and scorn.

This account does not capture the immediate effect of the truce: Barbarossa stayed in Venice for eight weeks more; princes and merchants flocked to the city; Venetians profited from the long celebration and secured from Frederick assurances of safe conduct and exemption from imperial tolls in all parts of the empire.[29] Ruskin does not mention these circumstances, but I do to clarify his vehement but unsupported assertion that the Thirty-Eighth Ecclesiastical Sonnet gives "innocent readers" false information. The poet has created a "dogmatic sonnet" from "every idea that comes into his own head" with "no shadow of doubt" (34:360). His solipsism is both individual and national, for Wordsworth has written a Protestant version of the fall of Venice. Barbarossa seems "Caesar's Successor" from an Anglocentric perspective, whereas Sismondi's history presents him as, Ruskin says, the "blight of Italy"—"Bandiera della Morte" (34:359). Truth to nature—the "nature" of human emotions perceived by the artist—thus involves a political perspective. It seems less apparent when Wordsworth (or Ruskin) is looking at a flower or a leaf. But in descriptions of history, Wordsworth must hold to authoritative texts, here the particular histories; he must exhibit an emotional and temporal distance from his subject, a respect for historical fact. Thus the same "real" incident that Wordsworth distorted becomes the touchstone of Byron's "honest and open heart" (34:361). Byron understands Catholicism and its history; therefore, he can depict the situation accurately, whereas Wordsworth is "for ever incapable of conceiving either a Catholic's feeling, or a careful historian's hesitation" (34:360). Ruskin adjusts the angle of history, and, as a result, "Catholic" becomes synonymous with "peasant," just as his whole move toward primitive Catholicism became part of a spiritual alliance toward the laborer and away from the middle classes.

Ruskin allowed Wordsworth no poetic license because he detected the ideological implications of formal qualities, whereas formerly he had separated poetry from history. When, in the third volume of *Modern Painters* (1856), Ruskin compared the two, he showed that poetry included false details. "Generally speaking, poetry runs into finer and more delicate details than prose; but the details are not poetical because they are more delicate, but because they are employed to bring out an affecting result," he elaborates (5:30). The importance of reception, signaled in the words "affecting result," helps explain the severity with which Ruskin treated a poetic violation of history later. He perceived that the Thirty-Eighth Ecclesiastical Sonnet became dogmatic when it reached "innocent readers" as a metonymy of the revered Wordsworth. Because "affecting result[s]" inflated false social perspective into the dogma of a revered poet whom readers misconstrued, Ruskin had to correct the public's view.

To some extent, Ruskin also used Byron to reveal mass impercipience but, in the process, betrayed a kinship with the very readership he insulted. The defense of Byron in the third essay, which precedes the section on Wordsworth's dogmatism in the fourth one, is on one level another indirect thrust at an Evangelical Protestant readership. Cast as disapproving moralists, readers have accused Byron of blasphemy because he has disturbed their comfortable view of prevenient grace. In a highly allusive passage, Ruskin uses an allusion to the "Thanksgiving Ode" in *Don Juan* (viii.9) to remark that the "death of the innocent in battle carnage" is not God's "'instrument for working out a pure intent,' as Mr. Wordsworth puts it; but Man's instrument for working out an impure one, as Byron would have you know" (34:328, 326). Whereas Wordsworth connects the material world and his perception of it with a transcendent realm, divine or ideal, and a transcending insight, Byron (in *The Island* and *Don Juan* especially, which Ruskin quotes most often in this essay) ranges over the phenomenal; his sight is of the world, even worldly: "So that, for instance, while Mr. Wordsworth, on a visit to town . . . could walk . . . on Westminster Bridge, remarking how the city now did like a garment wear the beauty of the morning; Byron . . . contemplated only the garment which the beauty of the morning had by that time received for wear from the city" (34:342).

Byron answers Wordsworth's "irrepressible religious rapture" with a bitter view of "the mighty cockney heart" beneath the roofs of the great city (34:342). Like the fiction Ruskin criticized in his first essay, Byron's poetry has the taint of the city. But unlike Dickens, Wilkie Collins, and Balzac, Byron is the "truest, the sternest, Seer of the Nineteenth Century" (34:397); "modern London (and Venice) are answerable for the state of their drains, not Byron" (34:341). The fimetic reality of his poetry—the "escape of gas," the "evening flavour of Covent Garden" (34:341)—indicates that "with deeper than Evangelical humility," Byron recognized "what is sordid in . . . civilization" (34:342).

Ruskin's praise of Byron was timely, if belated; it occurred almost a decade after other writers, such as Karl Elze, John Morley, and Edward Dowden, rallied to defend the poet from Harriet Beecher Stowe's sensational article "The True Story of Lady Byron's Married Life" (1869).[30] The details of this controversy are well known, but I will repeat a few to show how Ruskin's part in it continued the attack on public reading and perception begun in the first essay of *Fiction Fair and Foul*. First of all, Byron's reputation grew as the revolutionary spirit on the Continent rose. From the 1850s on, the Byronic hero attracted those who favored British intervention in European struggles such as Italy's, and though plenty of adverse criticism—by Walter Bagehot and Edward John Trelawny, for instance—still appeared, the poetry answered the need of many liberals for an antagonist of British comfort and provinciality.[31] Second, Stowe's focus on Byron's private life undoubtedly aroused much moral opprobrium, but it simultaneously stirred many who already were tired of middle-class righteousness. Moreover, it prompted enormous coverage of the scandal and a great rise in the sale of Byron's poems, both in England and America. An article in the 9 October issue of the *Athenaeum* notes that "Lord Byron's complete works for nine pence are selling at the bookstalls like herrings in a plentiful season . . . another consequence of the detestable scandal."[32]

In defense of the poet, Ruskin never mentioned the specific arguments, then ten years old, for and against Byron as a moral model, but championed the poet for political and social reasons. He did so, however, as he derided Wordsworth—through the screen of form, admiring the concentration of the poet's lines, for example, and quoting stanzas from *Don Juan* (iii.85–86) that resemble his own prose in these essays, with their nests of embedded allusions (34:329). Next to Wordsworth's effusive and artificial language, Byron's is demotic, argues Ruskin. It has a natural syntax, a simple diction, and a command of passion. He likes Byron's economy—the "utmost spiritual contents" and "quantity of contained thought in briefest words" (34:336–37). The aphoristic lines in *Don Juan* and viciously funny attacks on others are of course practices carried from the eighteenth-century wits and just as self-consciously constructed as are Wordsworth's canny repetitions in "Tintern Abbey." However, whereas the poets in "Tintern Abbey" and "Composed upon Westminster Bridge" hesitate, confess, exclaim—in short, exude sincerity—the narrator of *Don Juan* controls his panoramic spectacle of death, adultery, and cannibalism from an ironic distance effected by the frame of ottava rima. As a result, he creates the illusion of his own restraint. The wildly digressive "content" of *Don Juan* is crammed into a pre-formed container of meter and rhyme, and the morbidity and violence that excite readers of contemporary fiction and offend Ruskin here become hermetically sealed—harmless conversation. The position of the conversationalist, like the views of the country gentleman, marks privileged vision for Ruskin because both perspectives frame, therefore distance, content.

By calling Byron's stance natural and, in contrast, Wordsworth's "correct" or conventional, Ruskin subsumes complex social issues involving the conditions of writing and reception under his Romantic aesthetics. Byron now conforms to truth-to-nature; Wordsworth does not. In this judgment, Ruskin maneuvers himself into a position similar to the compromised perspective that produced the derogatory "Westmoreland peasant" from the compiler of the *Bibliotheca Pastorum*. As Byron's apologist, he envisions an audience of disgusted evangelicals who cannot appreciate a man less orthodox in his theology, but "certainly more reverent" than they (34:328). Clearly, these are not the readers of "Fiction mécroyante." Because the character of the hypothesized audience changes from the first essay to the second to the fourth ones, Ruskin's conception of them is less definite than we might have first assumed. Now, as in his initial criticism of Wordsworth, Ruskin confronts the bourgeois moralizers, the leaders of an isolationist nation that had not joined with France and Sardinia against Austria in 1859, or with France on behalf of Poland in 1863 and, according to Ruskin's latest allusion, that had watched Eugene Louis Napoleon die in the Zulu Campaign of 1879 (34:360).[33] In all of these causes, Ruskin had sided against the Tories and the policy of nonintervention. In a lecture delivered at the Royal Military Academy, Woolwich, in 1865, he declared that "we English have, as a knightly nation, lost our spurs" and calls the country's passivity selfish, cruel, and dastardly (18:480). No wonder that during these wars of liberation on the Continent Ruskin embraced Byron, a poet whom for a time in the fifties he thought corrupting and sentimental.[34]

Many admirers of Byron's politics traditionally had comprised the young and downtrodden—in William Ruddick's words, "struggling working class self-educators."[35] In his *The Condition of the Working Class in England* (1844), Friedrich Engels had noted that "Byron attracts [the workers'] sympathy by his sensuous fire and by the virulence of his satire against the existing social order. The middle classes, on the other hand, have on their shelves only ruthlessly expurgated 'family' editions of these writers."[36] To Ruskin, then, Byron represented the man of action, the revolutionary. But this did not mean, of course, that Ruskin had "gone over" to the laboring classes. Rather, as Byron's admirer—and Wordsworth's detractor—he had already accepted the paradox of the aristocratic poet who finds public acceptance by presenting himself as an outcast. By the 1880s, this had been a popular motif of poetry for years; to use it, Ruskin invoked the labor theory of value to portray himself as the isolated martyr to a literary cause even though he was part of a large group of Byronites, including Charles Kingsley, George Meredith, Alfred Austin, and, most importantly, a large reading public who followed the sensational accounts of the Stowe controversy.[37] There was a wave of sympathy for Byron in these years. A passage from Mark Rutherford's *The Revolution in Tanner's Lane* (1887) depicts a young craftsman in 1810 absorbed in the passionate parts of *Corsair*. As William Ruddick observes, "His poems brought to the surface . . . many of the concealed urges and pressures of the age."[38]

In the role of apologist, Ruskin was responding to an image of Byron that the poet or his audience had perpetuated. According to Philip Martin, Byron's success with certain readers lay in their illusion that "a wealth of worldly experience, or at least a huge capacity for worldly experience, provided him with the essential qualifications of a great poet."[39] Like many others, Ruskin bought this image; he never indicates in *Fiction Fair and Foul* that Byron's reputation has been rising among critics for the last ten years, but gives the impression that he alone must defend the poet from a "selfishly comfortable" and "piously sentimental public" who have no conception of moral frankness or morbid love of beauty, qualities he shares (34:344). Four years earlier, the *Art Journal* mentioned the "national indifference" to Byron. A committee planning to erect a statue of the poet in Green Park, presumably "to extend knowledge of [Byron's poems] among the humbler classes," raised only £3000 and received no proposals from top-ranked sculptors. Advancing Byron was still an invidious project, for he "inculcated evil."[40]

In trying to explain *Don Juan*'s and Byron's appeal for Ruskin, I want, ironically, to demonstrate the insufficiency of any explanation that does not involve the way the commodified Byron fit into the relationship between critic and audience in *Fiction Fair and Foul*. Ruskin did not see the narrator of *Don Juan* as a leveler of value or as a voluble character represented in the act of leveling. Reading Byron closed a temporal distance for him: his father had loved *Don Juan* and read it aloud to the family when John was a boy. (In *Praeterita*, the earliest memories of hearing Byron lead Ruskin to remember his first sampling of wine and the theater [35:141–42].) Ruskin's continued love of Byron entailed a nostalgia for those childhood readings, as well as a rejection of evangelical strictures against such literature. For in reading Byron now in his own essay, Ruskin defies the Protestant audience, the lovers of Wordsworth, and reenacts those evening performances of Byron which still seem anomalous and recalcitrant for an evangelical family. The defense of Byron thus maintained Ruskin's disaffection from the common middle-class reader in these essays.

In a similar but more complex way, Ruskin revalued Wordsworth to denigrate the "popular national prejudices" that had made his words authoritative (34:350). He detected the drawing-room quality of Wordsworth's concern with the humble classes—a humanity, Michael Friedman notes—that disguised social inequities and ratified established social structures.[41] And although Ruskin himself treated revolution as a spectator, supporting British involvement on the Continent while his own England was to remain undefiled by military or social struggle, he separated his appreciation of Wordsworth from genteel misperception. He could not, as with Byron, simply ostracize himself as a revolutionary sympathizer—a strategy that stemmed from regressive desire and marked him as a consumer of the Byronic image. Instead, he attacked the commodified Wordsworth, the poet as he had become his admirers, and made him a casualty of reading in general.

POPULARITY AND READING

The fate of the Romantic writer in the late-nineteenth-century market is well illustrated by the Wordsworth Society. Its purpose and methods were sometimes at odds. Members wanted to rescue Wordsworth from the sentimental cult that had kept him from a larger audience. To popularize him, they published volumes of his poetry every year from 1882 to 1886. They did not, however, issue the cheap reprints that would really have broadened his readership.[42] In addition, as Peek relates, the society itself had a cultish tendency to present Wordsworth as a personality; members such as founder William Knight stressed not only their personal acquaintance with the poet but also his meditative depth, "transcendental" view of subject, and private life.[43] In dispelling the image of the poet as a provincial, ill-read lover of nature, one that a coterie had created, they reasserted an older view of Wordsworth as a philosopher—ironically one that Arnold, the society's president in 1883, had challenged in his 1879 "Preface" to the selected poems.

In this context, then, the poet whom Ruskin devalued was the commodified Wordsworth, the one constituted in the readers' market most recently by the "Golden Treasury" anthology. Arnold wanted Wordsworth to be known as a nature poet rather than a philosopher. Like other members of the Wordsworth Society, Arnold felt that the poet owed his faulty reputation to a small but fanatical audience that had made the poet seem too abstruse for a general readership. In his famous "Preface" to the edition, Arnold states, "If we are to get Wordsworth recognised by the public and by the world, we must recommend him not in the spirit of a clique, but in the spirit of disinterested lovers of poetry."[44] To make Wordsworth more accessible, Arnold selected short pieces characterized by what he at one time called *simplicité,* a natural, as opposed to an artificial, simplicity.[45] "Michael" and "Lucy Gray" have *simplicité,* but some of Ruskin's favorites, such as *The Excursion* and "Ode: Intimations of Immortality," do not; Arnold writes that the latter has "no real solidity" and that the first is "abstract verbiage."[46] In his anthology, he intends to clear away those poems "obstructing" Wordsworth's best work. These remarks show that Arnold's reasons for freeing Wordsworth from Wordsworthians differed from Ruskin's. Arnold wished to broaden the poet's audience by rearranging a body of work which presented more immediate emotions and sensations ("His poetry is the reality, his philosophy . . . the illusion").[47] Ruskin, on the contrary, liked the so-called philosophical poems; when he calls the poet a "Westmoreland peasant," he adds, "Water to parched lips may be better than Samian wine, but do not let us therefore confuse the qualities of wine and water" (34:318–19).[48] Because he thought that Wordsworth's poetry had the transparency of water, that it showed the perception of a common peasant, Ruskin attacked the former poet laureate for precisely what Arnold praised. Within the polemics of *Fiction Fair and Foul, simplicité* became the vulnerable spot of Wordsworth's aesthetic. Readers loved him because, like the novelists of the city, he recycled a heightened form of the familiar which was the bourgeois pastoral, the same vision of the alienated rural that propelled *Fors*.

Because Ruskin disagreed with the reasoning behind Arnold's "Preface" and selections, he may have besieged certain poems in *Fiction Fair and Foul* in retaliation: Arnold said he liked the *Ecclesiastical Sonnets* and the "Thanksgiving Ode," and parts of both receive special denunciation in Ruskin's essays. More specifically, at the beginning of his discussion of Wordsworth in the second essay, Ruskin dismisses Arnold's endeavor, saying that although he has read the anthology with "sincere interest," "a great poet's work never needs arrangement by other hands" (34:318). He forgets his own edition of Sidney's *Psalter*, revealing, perhaps, a muted dislike for Arnold himself, who had "much disappointed" him at their meeting in 1877 (25:xxi). These, however, are minor animosities beside Ruskin's hostility toward the separation of poetry from its systematically didactic function, which Arnold advanced through his popular anthology. If, as Arnold claimed, showing readers how to live and giving them joy through description and emotion were Wordsworth's claims to greatness, the poetry was indeed shallow by Ruskin's standards. Without a stated philosophy, the poetry might be instantly consumable by an unthinking public.

Colin Campbell has defined modern, middle-class consumption, which developed in the nineteenth century, as a search for pleasure, the crucial commodity in an affluent society. Linking modern consumption with day-dreaming, he writes, "The essential activity of consumption is thus not the actual selection, purchase or use of products, but the imaginative pleasure-seeking to which the product image lends itself, 'real' consumption being largely a resultant of this 'mentalistic' hedonism."[49] Ruskin viewed Wordsworth's readers this way, and Arnold's edition of the dreamy nature poems only confirmed his opinion. Yet contained in this criticism of Wordsworth anthologized and read was another Wordsworth for Ruskin. He was the deeply reflective writer whose poems did not yield meaning to the common, careless reader taking them up for pleasure. At the end of his 1881 essay, Arnold still thought that Byron's poetry would "give pleasure more easily" than Wordsworth's.[50] Ruskin agreed, as early as 1843. Some great artists, like Walter Scott and the painter David Wilkie, reach a wide audience because they touched "passions which all feel" and express "truths which all can recognize." Wordsworth does not have this breadth: "Neither their intrinsic excellence, nor the authority of those who can judge of it, will ever make the poems of Wordsworth or George Herbert popular, in the sense in which Scott and Byron are popular, because it is to the vulgar a labour instead of a pleasure to read them" (3:82).

In the same passage, Ruskin broaches the problem of misdirected acclaim and interpretation. The "commonplace and feeble" of great artists such as Shakespeare, he comments, often are taken as the chief excellences of their work (3:82). Years later, Ruskin still distrusts popular reception and accuses Wordsworth's disciples of not reading enough and of missing the essence of the poems (34:348–49). But Ruskin never states exactly what the poet's true message is, though he avers, "I know, more vitally by far than they, what *is* in Wordsworth, and what is not"; there is in his ideas "a beauty and rightness" (34:349). Ruskin only tells us that these virtues have not resulted in any sort of large-scale *praxis,* because the love of Wordsworth has generally meant a love of physical and imaginative isolation—of the alienated rural.[51] For this reason, his "vivid sense of natural beauty" can be debased by the "pretty turn," a mark of a genteel and distantiated perspective that Ruskin both derides and affirms in the second essay (34:318). On the other hand, he reads Byron with no ambivalence because the poet disdains middle-class pretensions. In siding with Byron, Ruskin again postulated a hostile, misunderstanding public, but he did not counter with an extralinguistic truth in the poet's work. Rather, he defended a Byron whose truth was too plain for readers, whose offensive life was a text more familiar to many than his poetry. "That he confessed—in some sort, even proclaimed defiantly . . . the naughtiness of his life" brought him into the arena of later writers who confronted readers with the "real" (34:361). In his criticism of Wordsworth and defense of Byron, Ruskin maintained a gap between writer and reader; he distrusted the poet reembodied for consumption.

As a writer himself, he most likely was identifying with

the sense of dispossession from one's work that occurs when an audience reads in various unexpected ways. This happened during *Fors,* as I have discussed. And as Brian Maidment argues, Ruskin could not control the impact of his work on Victorian thought after 1878.[52] He was suspicious of wide popularity, but of course did not see himself as part of the misreading populace. Instead, he readily accepted the invitation to identify with Byron, which Philip Martin convincingly argues was implicit in the poetry; in the third essay, Ruskin points out his own Byronic qualities, including sarcasm, morbidity, and sorrow (34:344).

Thus far, I have said little about Scott, who is the subject of much of the second and fifth essays in *Fiction Fair and Foul.* Ruskin also identified with him as a writer and revealed more of his attitude toward popularity in his account of Scott's career. He saw the novelist as a victim of commodification on a grand scale. Quoting from Lockhart's biography in the first essay, he refers to a promise in the form of a contract with Constable & Co. that compelled Scott to "fill" projected volumes:

> Before *The Fortunes of Nigel* issued from the press Scott had exchanged instruments and received his bookseller's bills for no less than four "works of fiction," not one of them otherwise described in the deeds of agreement, to be produced in unbroken succession, *each of them to fill up at least three volumes, but with proper saving clauses as to increase of copy money in case any of them should run to four;* and within two years all this anticipation had been wiped off by *Peveril of the Peak, Quentin Durward, St. Ronan's Well,* and *Redgauntlet.* (34:292)

Perhaps Ruskin italicized these words with his own promised essays and books for the *Bibliotheca Pastorum* in mind. In 1832 Scott died: "mercilessly demanded brain toil" killed him, declares Ruskin (34:276). Writing this in June 1880, he himself was recovering from a nervous collapse brought about from overwork, according to his doctors. He denied this in the February issue of *Fors,* blaming his illness on an unreceptive audience (29:386). The two may be related, for the success of both men impelled them into various forms of written contract to produce more. Overwork may occur under the aegis of a contract drawn as a result of an audience's confusion or misreading, as in *Fors*. There is no hint, though, in *Fiction Fair and Foul* that Wordsworth, Byron, or Scott kept producing because they felt misunderstood; but Ruskin's discussions of each writer made misreading an alloy of popularity. When Ruskin set literary value against popular acceptance, as he did in different ways with the three Romantics, he opposed the aesthetic kernel of their work with a notion of them as social or, more precisely, commodified entities constituted by the dissemination and reception of their writing.

"Misreading" itself may be an inaccurate word, for Ruskin, like Arnold, sometimes implied that the public did not read Wordsworth or Byron at all. Disciples and detractors construed the poets as composites of touchstone-phrases from their most widely known works and published details of their lives. When Ruskin asserted that the truth of Byron and Wordsworth had eluded the public, he was deploring the spurious currency of reputation which could replace reading entirely. Likewise, it could make an artist such as Scott or an editor such as Arnold supply what the public wanted, which in effect was what it had misread. This then accounts for the decline of Scott's novels during the contract with Constable; written for the trade, they regurgitated the commonplace and feeble of former works— what the public had mistaken for the kernel. But Ruskin never supported these claims with statements about the truth of Scott; and as I have shown, he was unable to articulate the truth in his own essays in *Fors*. In reading Wordsworth, the public missed a lack of profundity, or missed the profound (Ruskin's opinion varies); and this absence was recycled in Arnold's *Golden Treasury*. Similarly, the popular absorption with the immoral, even Satanic, Byron overshadowed his great descriptive and "foretelling power" (34:329). Yet neither Wordsworth's truth nor Byron's Catholic sympathies did get much attention because Ruskin focused instead on the divergence between reception and truth. His approach in *Fiction Fair and Foul* only confirmed the prevalence of the public value he attacked; he had no other value with which to replace the popular one, no other "Wordsworth" or "Byron" to assert. They simply were "other" than the public thought them, which said only that the public was wrong, that it could not rightly see. It said too that in the careers of Scott, Byron, Wordsworth, and Ruskin—the popular writers—the commodified artist reflected demand, which, Ruskin observed in his November 1883 lecture at Oxford, was always limitless.[53] If popularity equalled demand, then the relationship between writer-supplier and reader merely illustrated Say's Law, part of the dismal science of orthodox political economy.

Finally, Ruskin's revaluations suggested that demand could create content, but that the truth was not marketable. In the November lecture, entitled "The Hill-Side," Ruskin tells students that wisdom transcends exchange. He is referring to the purpose of art and learning. Education should not be parleyed, like a continuing wager, into a living, and skills acquired at Oxford are not a source of income. "Buy the Truth and sell it not," he commands, using Proverbs xxiii.23 (33:391). The truth must transcend exchange. As the possible pun suggests, one must use or live through the truth by removing it from circulation. But how can one buy the truth if it is not sellable; if, according to Ruskin, it does not circulate as linguistic currency?

The answer, of course, is that the truth does circulate, but in a disguised, objectified form invisible to the public. It does not really become usable as truth until it leaves the circuit of exchange. Ruskin declares to his listeners that wisdom—the truth—"is to be costly to you—of labour and patience; and you are never to sell it, but to guard, and to give" (33:391). This sublated truth has a parallel in hoarded money. Gotthelf's Hansli, as Ruskin related in *Fors,* receives coins for his labor which he converts to signs in a problematic aesthetic: the coins have become beautiful, hence unexchangeable objects of the peasant's scopophilia, "used" or consumed by his gaze. At the same time, they are signifiers of a wealth that is impervious to labor, hence exchange. Hansli's fetishized coins preserve their materiality and significance as wealth while they transcend without negating the labor and class system through which they have circulated.

Because language and money are parallel systems of exchange, the truth, the object of Ruskin's scopophilia, can be obtained through the "current coin" of metaphor (5:216). Locked into words, truth is indeed buyable but not saleable.

Within the shelter of language, it can be transferred; it simply cannot be expressed. Once it leaves linguistic exchange as truth it becomes unspendable, like Hansli's coins. In *Fiction Fair and Foul,* Ruskin hoarded truth as something transmittable by but beyond language. Thus the truth of Wordsworth eluded popular readers, but it evaded Ruskin's grasp as well. What he preserved, like the Oxford education and Hansli's coins, was the name itself. By asserting but not explaining his knowledge of Wordsworth, Ruskin simply stopped exchanging.

For Ruskin, ideally the reader had a scopophiliac relation to truth. The possessor gathered but distanced the object through sight; the gaze sustained power and desire. At the same time, the value of the object never changed because it never entered circulation. It was a regressive and miserly aesthetic. Ruskin, who loved the story of Hansli and stressed that Francesca Alexander never composed to publish, naturally feared popularity because it entailed frenetic exchange. One of his alternatives besides withholding words was to adopt an authoritarian detachment and write from a privileged perspective. Thus, Wordsworth should have written as a country gentleman outside the "frame" of representation, and Scott ruined himself by letting demand produce content, but Byron rightly remained distant from and seemingly unconcerned with both his subjects and the public.

Ruskin ended the fifth essay of *Fiction Fair and Foul* with remarks about the messenger, message, and payment to show, perhaps, how the two parallel forms of exchange—transactions of money and language—could thwart the pursuit of truth through reading and writing. As I have said, Ruskin believed he alone could read correctly, and he supported this assertion by setting truth beyond language and public exchange. However, he enacted his own susceptibility to intrusions of the real by stopping his essay at the moment of interruption and payment. Exchange, a sign of the real, had won. In view of this final victory, the Romantic writers Ruskin discussed mediate another concern altogether, as does his attack on the modern novel in the first essay.

Belief in the ultimate power of the real to alter, even stop, writing beget a view of reading that preserved it from the reality of audience. It is evident not only in the cryptic assertions about the truth of a text but also in the urbane elitism of one of Ruskin's most famous readers. Marcel Proust observes in "Sur la lecture" (1906) that books bespeak places, not themselves; if there is a truth or beauty beyond language, as Ruskin believed and Proust in this essay suggests, "it remains hidden to the masses." "Distinction and nobility [of literary men] consist[s] . . . in a kind of freemasonry of customs, and in an inheritance of traditions."[54] As an example, he notes that a book by Anatole France "implies a multitude of erudite ideas, contains perpetual allusions which common people do not notice, and which, aside from its other beauties, account for its incomparable nobility."[55] Ruskin endorsed this secret society of meaning when, in *Fiction Fair and Foul,* he attacked the spurious truth coined and exchanged by the public but withheld his own transcendent meaning from readers. In doing so, he replaced the idea of reading as conversation in the "company of the noble," his definition in "Of Kings' Treasuries" (1865 [18:59]), with reading as reception from authoritarian narrator to uncomprehending audience. Literature, Proust confirms, communicates in hieroglyph because the common mind "does not know how to separate from books the substance that might make it stronger."[56] But like the Victorian lovers of Wordsworth whom Ruskin mocked, Proust's "literary man" can only tell you what he has read; a subtle spouter, he has developed a "fetishistic respect for books": "Smiling, the literary man invokes in honor of a certain name the fact that it is found in Villehardouin or in Boccaccio, in favor of a given custom that it is described in Virgil."[57]

In short, Ruskin depicted reading as a conversation in 1865 when instructing boys; but fifteen years later, when, addressing and referring to both mass audiences and coteries, he turned reading into purely passive reception, as his treatment of popularity in *Fiction Fair and Foul* and his correspondence in *Fors* both show. For both Ruskin of the 1880s and Proust, reading fundamentally was the consuming of a "foreign substance, a source of death."[58] Writers, correspondingly, addressed books themselves rather than audiences. For Ruskin of 1865, books impart wisdom if we read them correctly; but for Proust we "feel quite truly that our wisdom begins where that of the author ends, and we would like to have him give us answers, when all he can do is give us desires."[59] In the essays on fiction, Ruskin enacted his regressive desire for the landscapes of his childhood. He further showed that, as a reader of modern fiction, he had transferred truth to place—London and Paris. This is why he began the first essay deploring the modern look of Croxted Lane and ended the fifth essay describing a disruptive message from the outside.

Ruskin's ideas about reading had to change because he remained committed to a material view of language and a conception of the novel as "photographic evidence" of reality even as he watched the social and physical "outside" become unrepresentable within his moral aesthetic (34:277). He still believed in the Romantic mode of representation which Axton calls "Fra Lippo Lippi's program"; Naomi Schor describes it similarly (in arguing for a feminine aesthetic), as "sublimating—in the sense of elevating—the humble or prosaic detail."[60] Ruskin objected to the detailed reality depicted by novelists because its ingredients, unleavened by any orthodox superstructure of religious belief, remained in their "brute and unsublimated materiality."[61] As I have observed, he knew that domesticating the sublime produced a frightening sensationalism; "Fiction mécroyante" brimmed with unsublimated details that emphasized modern reality as urban. Simultaneously, the city was the social center of capitalism. The jump in *Fiction Fair and Foul* from "literature of the prison-house" to reviews of the Romantics suggests that Ruskin connected the growth of the city with a degenerate, collective response to texts, for he focused on the transformation of the poets into commodities either by their own collusion with publishers, by editorial reconstruction, or by mass misreading. The essays strike angrily at the middle-class audience, which included Matthew Arnold; but despite his criticism of affected rusticity, Ruskin showed himself a willing consumer of the image of the isolate circulated by Byron as well as Wordsworth, and even assumed that persona in order to claim authority for his readings. Ruskin was never ready to see himself with contemporary readers "as being made by what makes the book."[62] *Fiction Fair and Foul* was his last public fight against the cultural shifts that had changed the landscape and the mass reading public, but its final passage capitulated to a reality that he had long since accepted. For at least a decade before writing these essays, he had behaved as if the real were, in Norman Bryson's words, not "a transcendent and immutable given, but . . . a production brought about by human activity working within specific cultural constraints."[63] His efforts to control production and distribution disclose how well he could maneuver within a system he claimed to despise.

Hoarding and Spending:
Ruskin's Experiments

The Oxford lectures, *Fiction Fair and Foul,* and other essays of the
1870s and 1880s all depict the fine arts and literature as commodities whose value changes in the eyes of each viewer or
reader. The idea that circulating or exchange-value applied to
art objects often appalled Ruskin, and he tried to rescue articles
from the market by claiming for them an intrinsic worth. Yet
withholding the essence of a sarcophagus or a poet did not confer
on them an expressible worth or meaning. In *The Queen of the
Air,* Ruskin accepted multiple meaning without sensing that
the value of a pluralistic symbol could fall in consequence, as it
did when the populace read *Ilaria di Caretto* and Wordsworth's
poems. Books, sculpture, paintings, and even the British florin
lost what he believed were their true meaning and worth in the
eyes of a mass audience.

When, with an expanded, undefined readership in mind,
Ruskin devised his own ways of producing and distributing art,
he wanted somehow to retain the worth of an object throughout
its exchange. He could maintain control by relying on labor as
the source and magnitude of value; yet resorting to orthodox
economics was not satisfactory, for, like Marx, Ruskin had
grasped that work did not completely account for value. "Who-
ever directly satisfies his wants with the produce of his own

labour, creates, indeed, use-values, but not commodities,"
Marx states in *Capital:* "In order to produce the latter, he must
not only produce use-values, but use-values for others, social
use-values."[1] As a lecturer, writer, and organizer of a museum,
Ruskin was transferring things to others for their use, and his
focus on production and distribution in his years as Slade Professor tacitly acknowledged Marx's principle that, in society,
exchange-value is the only form in which the worth of an object
emerges. This silent admission explains the miserly streak in
Ruskin's schemes, for he continued to withhold in various ways
precisely because he realized that terms of transfer such as cost
and price constituted the only manifest value of his treasures
among an uncultivated and amorphous audience.

As I have shown, hoarding for Ruskin became a real and
metaphorical solution to circulating value. He turned to Hansli's collecting just as he saved the meaning of Wordsworth's
poems and de Quercia's sculpture. But when he published books
and designed a museum, Ruskin had to decide how to spend and
still keep his objects from the corrupting circuit of sight. As a
purveyor of meaning, he already was flooding the market with
the unconsumable words of *Fors Clavigera,* and the meaning and
value of his message were in jeopardy. As a businessman and
educator, he could not repeat this experience, and he looked for
ways to regulate the process from production to consumption.
"The miser was a throwback to an older, perhaps more primitive
bourgeois world, the spendthrift the product of a newer, urban
one," writes John Vernon.[2] In his publishing experiments, his
plans for a museum, and his other educational projects during
the 1870s and 1880s, Ruskin used profligate as well as retentive
methods to produce and distribute literature and drawings for
consumption. But his spending of art for a modern audience
disclosed the fears and heart of a miser who wanted to hoard not
simply meaning and value, but time.

WITHHOLDING AND SPENDING—PUBLISHING

When in the 1870s he was issuing his most popular books and
writing new ones, Ruskin was almost morbidly aware of over-

production and its consequences. He had two cautionary examples, Scott and Dickens. Writing had ruined the former, lecturing the latter. Asked in 1874 by the Glasgow Athenaeum Committee to give a speech, Ruskin refused and cited the "miserable death of poor Dickens" (in 1870) as evidence that the public's demand for performances rather than instruction debilitated speakers. According to Forster in the *Life of Charles Dickens*, the novelist's readings in St. James's Hall produced "disastrous excitement," which led to his death four months later (34: 517n. 1). John Bayley has remarked of Dickens, "The secret side that had originally produced the London horrors . . . could be driven further into the darkness by more and more spectacular public success."[3] Likewise, Scott, as Ruskin often mentioned, wore himself out fulfilling his contract with Constable, writing book after book "for the trade," producing work such as *Peveril of the Peak* which was "slovenly" and "diffuse" (34:292). In Ruskin's mind, audiences such as the readers he attacked in *Fiction Fair and Foul* were uninformed, passive, and in search of excitement; their "pestiferous demand" resulted in inferior and life-threatening work (34:517).

Thinking of these men and his own exhausting labor in the 1870s, Ruskin revised his notion of writing; from an act of associative, penetrative, or contemplative imagination, it became a Grub-Street mode of drudgery. In giving Constable four novels, Scott was providing an anticipated product; he was filling up a preestablished form, the three-decker. Constable even had a provision for imaginative overrun; the contract contained a saving clause in case any of the novels should spill into four volumes. Of course every genre is in some sense an already shaped space to be filled and sometimes remolded. But Ruskin did not see Scott laboring within literary convention. His comments about both novelists indicate that the genre itself was a convention of the market rather than of literature and that writers themselves viewed their labor as production rather than creation. When in a letter of 1873 to the *Pall Mall Gazette* Ruskin called Turner "a good labourer," he deliberately subsumed art under the Ricardian theory of value (17:555). Arguably, he may have been using labor as a metaphor or analogy of the imagination; but in the 1870s the figure of production obscured all the traditional images of artistic imagination. The writer was a social entity constituted by the dissemination and reception of his or her work.

Convinced by the 1880s that an artist who worked for the public was at the mercy of its "vile demand" (34:276), a demand that exhausted and eventually killed him, Ruskin was careful to set the terms of sale for his own books. When he started his own small publishing business, the nineteenth-century economic discourse which, according to Say's Law, still assumed that demand could not exceed supply, was implicit in the venture. His goals were clear: by seizing the means of production for himself and controlling distribution, he could regulate the number and look of his books, their cost, price, and ultimately eligible buyers. In particular, he could keep the public at bay and still write. His experiment in bookselling was an effort to control not only production, then, but also consumption.

Long before, in "The Nature of Gothic," Ruskin had shown how labor and its products manifested the values of a society; similarly, in "Of Kings' Treasuries," he had made well-printed and well-bound books part of his moral aesthetic. Such volumes were "healthy," Ruskin said, and they suggested to an audience familiar with *The Stones of Venice* or *The Seven Lamps of Architecture* his doctrine of sincere labor within an ethical economy. As readers must have known, however, health was a prerogative of wealth: for instance, the pricing scheme he introduced in 1872 enforced the theoretical connection Ruskin had made between wealth, labor, and healthy books: "I intend the price asked for them [the books of his new Revised Series] to be half a guinea for those without plates, and a guinea for the illustrated volumes. . . . I do not care that anybody should read my books who grudges me a doctor's fee per volume" (27:257n.1).

Using the guinea, Ruskin portrays himself as a professional laborer, specifically a healer who makes and prescribes healthy books. The guinea further suggests that his advice and medicine are for the financially comfortable; it is only their diseases that he can understand and treat. At a time when a shilling Shakespeare existed, along with an illustrated Byron for 7d., Ruskin's books, which addressed an audience with comparable interests, were expensive. Indeed, their price rose in 1874 to 18s. for a plain volume, and £1,7s.6d. for an illustrated one (18:11).[4]

In pricing, Ruskin again had Scott's work as a cautionary precedent. Just after the Napoleonic Wars, when printers were the highest paid skilled workers in London, and when paper was scarce and production slow, some of Scott's novels appeared in luxurious and costly formats.[5] *The Lay of the Last Minstrel* (1805), for instance, was 25s. *Waverley* (1814) sold at 21s., a high price even at this time, when the average book cost 15s. or 18s. These sumptuous volumes and their staggering prices (a set of *Ivanhoe* at 30s. in 1820) induced some firms to start runs of moderately priced literature.[6] In 1829, Cadell's "Author's Edition of the Waverley Novels" appeared in five-shilling volumes. As the copyrights of Scott's novels expired, cheaper and cheaper versions of them appeared. Complete novels became available at 6d. This was a common price for books in the late 1860s and after; still, new hardcovers, which cost 10s.6d. a volume, were much too expensive for the average reader.[7] Even though at midcentury the average price of a single volume had fallen to 7s.2 1/2 d. from 12s.1d. in 1828, ordinary working people still could not afford to buy one. For the iron founder and the mill-worker, "book-buying capacity was still to be reckoned in pennies, not shillings," according to Richard Altick.[8]

In this light, 18s. in the 1870s for hardcover volumes of Ruskin's Revised Series must have seemed exorbitant to anyone outside an affluent group of purchasers. Ironically, the price of these reissues limited their sale to a small audience even though their production had resulted in part from the popularity of some of Ruskin's earlier works. Along with the luxurious dark-blue calf, Ruskin's prices recalled the days of the lavish novels of Scott, of paper shortages and slow production. In effect Ruskin was reviving the market of scarcity in publishing even as lower manufacturing costs and expiring copyrights were allowing publishers to turn out reams of inexpensive paperbacks.[9]

Not interested in making affordable volumes, Ruskin also scorned the circulating libraries. He may have regarded Mudie's as a competitor because he shared with it the audience of middle-class women. Although its subscriptions had begun to decrease during the last quarter of the century, Mudie's was still influential enough to dictate the format and price of the novels. Three-deckers for sale at 31s.6d forced most people to borrow rather than buy. The situation caused Matthew Arnold, in the *Fortnightly Review* (1880), to call for a well made three-shilling book and an end to the libraries' monopoly. [10] Ruskin, however, did not dislike the lending libraries for keeping prices artificially high. He opposed borrowing in general. In addition to advising young girls in 1873 never to borrow books (27:646), he discouraged his readers from purchasing inexpensive reprints and yellowbacks (available at railway bookstalls). "Have not you Shakespeare, cheap? and the Bible, now-a-days for nothing?" he responded to someone who complained in 1884 about the price of his books. "What good do they do you?" (34:576). In Ruskin's economy, only the scarce and inaccessible had value.

These statements about price and borrowing alter his stated definition of value. In *Munera Pulveris,* intrinsic worth meant use-value to Ruskin. He regarded the power of a sheaf of wheat to nourish the body and of a flower to sustain the heart as examples (17:153). In business practice, however, Ruskin linked worth with scarcity, which he signified by price. In the law of marginal utility, scarcity is expressed through exchange: in a famine, for example, a bag of moldy potatoes will fetch a high price or almost anything else as barter, whereas in normal circumstances it will be unexchangeable. [11] Everything Ruskin had come to treasure by the 1870s—the sky, the countryside, buildings, paintings—was disappearing. In his praise and lament for what was vanishing, he inadvertently confirmed the importance of exchange.

This emphasis on exchange-value, traceable in theory to the economies of scarcity envisioned in Malthus and Smith, resulted from the abundant market within which Ruskin was publishing. Amidst the glut of reprints, a shilling Shakespeare, whether strong or shoddy, had little value. By the law of marginal utility, it set the standard for the market. Ruskin refused to define value in terms of supply and demand, but, as his remarks about other writers disclose, he realized that demand affected production. Indeed, his performance in *Fors* reveals that he conflated supply with demand and made the latter a material force. In practice, Ruskin phrased marginal utility as a natural development of labor theory and used it to explain his plan for a balanced circulation of commodities. Thus, books that had been hard to write had to be hard to get. In 1887 he wrote, "If I thought it good for you to have my books cheap, you should have them cheap or for nothing, but please remember the profits told you [£4000 in 1886] are made by a man of sixty-eight after a hard life's work—just as he is dying" (34:610n.1). If, as Say's Law describes, demand is in essence production, limiting the number of volumes issued and signifying this scarcity with a high price would control public desire, which was for him the most frightening element of marginal utility economics.

When Ruskin wrote in *Fors,* "I don't want any poor people to read . . . my large books, nor anybody else's, till they are rich enough . . . to pay for good printing and binding," he was turning back to the postwar conditions of scarcity under which Scott's books sold so well (27:276–77). Reserving his work for those who could afford to buy a "healthy" book was one way of controlling reception. Of course Ruskin never said that material wealth disposed people to read or understand his writing. He surely knew what one of his more voluble correspondents from Glasgow told him: "The wealthy classes who could afford to buy books at 10s.6d. a volume, as a rule . . . don't drive themselves insane by much reading of any kind" (27:289). But Ruskin did believe that his true audience—those, in other words, who could execute his ideas—must come from the classes to whom the English rural landscape, the great cities of the Continent and their museums—all the objects in his contemporary iconology—were available either through ownership or leisure time. "Even the oracular Mr. Grant Duff says that they [the poor] are all to be rich first, and only next to be intelligent," Ruskin comments in *Fors* (27:277). This is a facetious distortion of a speech advocating nonintervention made by Duff, the undersecretary of state for India; and although Ruskin's flippancy exemplifies the gratuitous antagonism of the early letters of *Fors,* he has made similar statements quite seriously.[12]

Along with high prices, Ruskin's refusal to use bookstalls and other accessible outlets "point[s] to the extremely circumscribed and largely wealthy readership which *Fors* obtained," writes Brian Maidment.[13] Readers frequently complained that Ruskin's works in general were hard to find, and even Carlyle told Emerson that they were inaccessible (27:lxxxii). A notice in each volume instructed readers to request copies from George Allen, Sunnyside, Orpington, Kent; they then would come carriage paid anywhere in the United Kingdom. Orders could also be placed through booksellers for a slightly higher charge, readers were told. Because after 1874 Ruskin no longer notified the press about new volumes, this method of announcement really offered books to existing readers. Except through word-of-mouth, the only way to get Allen's address was already to have a book by Ruskin. He intended the purchase of each volume to cost effort; in this way he ensured a receptive if small audience. No doubt some Jude Fawleys existed who, though intimidated by the assertive act of buying a book that had never in a sense asked to be read, ordered one anyway. [14] Stephen Rowland and John Guy do seem to be real-life Judes.

Buying was not the only way to get one of Ruskin's books. Interested persons could have visited one of the sixty-three free town libraries that possessed some of the volumes. [15] Of these, forty-two libraries owned *The Stones of Venice,* thirty-six owned *The Queen of the Air* and *Modern Painters,* and thirty-four owned *Fors.* Many of these could circulate, though the Liverpool and Manchester holdings, the largest in the country, were for reference use only. (Circulating volumes were held by the branch libraries at Manchester.) But, as I have mentioned, even patrons curious enough to take advantage of these holdings may have been discouraged by Ruskin's command in *Sesame and Lilies,* one of the more plentiful volumes, never to read borrowed books. Circulation devalued them in Ruskin's economy of scarcity. Indeed, emphasis on the book as a commodity and physical sign of health strongly favored ownership. An audience of borrowers who confronted this stricture in *Sesame* and elsewhere may have had to think of themselves, in some way, as owners. Certainly they had to aspire to ownership. In other words, they had to be socially ambitious and disaffected from their class.

The borrowers who read Ruskin's prohibitions may not have felt rejected, for a public may expect this kind of explicit attack if it perceives the writer as an Old Testament–style prophet who rails against existing circumstances. This is probable if it considers the author a sage and if, as George P. Landow has argued, sage-writing itself is a genre with specific "rules by which one reads [and] interprets."[16] In this case, borrowers who regarded Ruskin as their master and sage would not be offended because they expected an estrangement between themselves and the writer. And as I have just suggested, they may even have viewed their own borrowing as part of the deplorable social conditions they were trying to escape. That borrowers and the provincial, modest classes from which they came were part of the audience for Ruskin's writing is probable, not simply from statistics of holdings. Ruskin seems aware that he is addressing them; they explain not only the presence of his prohibition on borrowing but also its confrontational tone.

In summary, the scarcity of Ruskin's books encouraged both a select audience and a huge, aspiring one. Like the price of paintings which, Ruskin noted in his Manchester lectures, signified the wish for gentility, inaccessibility both limited and expanded his readership by stimulating the desire for a text whose exchange-value signalled social motivation. Naïve readers such as Stephen Rowland in *Fors* who separated intellectual from social ambition discovered an inseverable link between the two in Ruskin's work.

His audience now circumscribed by the connotations of class in the word *guinea* and the stigma attached to borrowing, Ruskin addressed a prosperous and, as he knew, small readership through his means of production as well. Making books became a preindustrial craft. E. T. Cook, one of the most enthusiastic of his employees and readers, described the business of producing and selling his Master's books in 1890 as a cottage industry (30:359–60). Ruskin's goal was to eliminate the middleman by turning the bookseller into an artisan. Under this plan, the potential reader would buy directly from the true makers of the book, who had effaced the division between writer, binder, and seller.[17] Price would reflect the cost of labor. No portion would pay the costs of a distributor; postage was figured simply as part of the natural price of labor. Because the scheme reduced the number of workers, it simplified selling into a closer exchange between the maker and the purchaser, who offered the symbolic, *true* price for a good. Novels were coming out faster than people could read them, but under this system Ruskin's books never deluged the market.

Ruskin's solution to the flooded market of cheap books, the gilt-edged volumes in purple calf produced in a garden outhouse at Kent, actually illustrates a modern phenomenon, what N. N. Feltes has called the "commodity book."[18] Prevalent through midcentury, it was foremost a physical thing that granted its owner a prestige the yellowback never had. (The latter was a "commodity-text" which came, says Feltes, from "the new capitalist mode of production, produced in struggle by the new 'professional' author within the new structures of control over the publishing process").[19] Ruskin became manufacturer and seller in order, he says in the first issue of *Fors,* "to retain complete command over [the books'] mode of publication" (27:11n.1). To do so, he set the price of each letter at 7p. (in 1874, 10p.) and announced the amount of his profits in letter six of *Fors* (27:100). He had individual purchasers and booksellers buy directly from Allen and allowed no abatement to anyone. This arrangement displeased the booksellers, and in 1882, when the sale of his books had become his main source of income, Ruskin gave retailers a fixed but small discount (27:lxxxiii–v).

Under this system, Ruskin could stabilize the value of his product and, he thought, guarantee a select audience. He further ensured a comparatively limited readership by refusing to advertise. In letter twenty-one of *Fors,* he states, "You ought to read books, as you take medicine, by advice, and not advertisement" (27:353). Again, the medical analogy in which Ruskin as doctor charges a professional fee for well-made books giving readers ethical health exalts his labor into spiritual healing. To make art a substitute for religion, one first had to differentiate it from a commodity, even if that commodity was a doctor's prescription. Thus Ruskin stopped sending advance copies of *Fors* to the press in 1874. "The public has a very long nose and scents out what it wants, sooner or later," he reasoned (27:lxxxv). Advertising, like underselling, would attract buyers who might not otherwise be interested, and this kind of demand would devalue his work. By withholding all notice of his writing, he created an audience of converts who purchased books at some effort and expense.

As Ruskin and Cook described it, their publishing venture, tucked in the hills of Kent, operated outside contemporary terms of trade. Thus it exemplified Ruskin's effort to withhold his words from competitive retailing and the huge audience it was reaching. But despite its retrograde character, the experiment was commercially successful and made Ruskin money.[20] It anticipated a method known as the net-book system, which would revolutionize the book trade by the turn of the century. Ironically, as a pioneer of net-book pricing, Ruskin became "a great tradesman" in the eyes of some precisely because his strategy accomplished what it appeared not to do (27:lxxxv n.3).

First, it reached a large, previously uncharted audience. This is apparent in the marketing strategy of more organized companies that adopted the system later. In 1890, for example, the publishing firm of Frederick Macmillan began a policy that curtailed underselling by trading only to booksellers who agreed not to lower the established or net price. Unlike Ruskin's original plan, Macmillan's allowed a small discount to booksellers. According to Altick, Macmillan's first tried the scheme on select volumes costing over 6s.[21] The first one announced was Alfred Marshall's *Principles of Economics*. Because its author was a professor at Cambridge, the firm expected an instant status for the book; on publication, it would enter the corpus of literature on economics. (Coincidentally, this book developed Jevons's principle of marginal utility.)[22] The *Principles* sold well and characterized the sort of text that publishers began to price under the net system. According to Feltes, net books, usually on erudite topics, appeared in expensive formats, or bore what he calls a "reputation-value."[23] Ruskin's volumes, issued twenty years earlier, satisfied all these conditions; they were, moreover, commodity-books. Although perhaps not all abstruse, they appealed to a group of readers interested in aesthetic and social criticism, had a physical form that emphasized their "thing-ness" and sold largely on the reputation-value of their author. Ruskin's first net book was a reissue, the very popular *Sesame and Lilies*. Likewise, *The Seven Lamps of Architecture* and *The Stones of*

Venice were relatively famous works by the time they became net books in the 1870s and 1880s.

Although to some extent the high price of Ruskin's books assumed a specific socioeconomic position for their buyers, the reputation-value of the author attracted many purchasers who did not belong but aspired to this select group. Ironically, then, by netting his costly, rare books, Ruskin began a practice that, in the hands of others two decades later, would beckon to a much larger, less-known audience than the one he wanted to attract. An initially select readership became an amorphous one when books sold by reputation rather than price. The confusion about audience in *Fors* and the Oxford lectures, his ambivalence toward those who wanted to read but could not buy, along with the frequent attempts to exclude them, all show that a good part of his readership lay outside the socioeconomic boundaries Ruskin set with high prices. When he decided not to advertise and to trust instead the public's "long nose," he hoped for an audience who had access and means, in time and money, to the artificial and natural surroundings he loved. But this strategy often lured those who had neither. The production and distribution of Ruskin's writing thus drew different readers in opposing ways: the cottage-industry manufacture of commodity books attracted a select group, whereas the net-book system promoted the reputation-value that would open his texts to a less identifiable readership. To complicate matters, Ruskin named representative readers for some of his work: *Fors* went to the laborers of Great Britain, and *Of Time and Tide* went to a particular worker, the cork-cutter Thomas Dixon, even though many of Ruskin's remarks did not address these persons in any practical way. The audience of these works remained heterogeneous and unspecified.

The net-book system was a modern success (to Ruskin's followers) because it not only inscribed a vast and varied readership but also secured control of production for the capitalist publisher. The idyllic style in which Ruskin published and traded obscured the capitalistic structure of his enterprise, but he took command of his entire business, acting like a guildmaster and refusing to advertise for the same reason Macmillan established similar terms twenty years later: he wanted to control production, and this desire implicates him in a modern struggle. It also includes him in the nineteenth-century reaction to a combination of labor theory, industrialization, and class consciousness. Ruskin's business was a nostalgic, centralized, patriarchal version of the labor theory of value in which even demand was a controllable factor of production. Under this scheme, he could create his own audience through the reputation of his goods.

By conceiving of demand as production, Ruskin enacted Say's Law, and he was not alone in this practice, for net-book pricing, with its focus on manufacture and supply rather than demand, assumed the principles of Say. In addressing a larger, unknown audience through the writer's reputation, the system "denied the dictatorship of the consumer," comments Feltes, "insisting instead on the control of the capitalist publisher."[24] That Malthus's ideas of scarcity and underconsumption were precluded by Say's Law made it attractive both to entrepreneurs such as Ruskin, who never invoked it explicitly, but built his publishing business on its assumptions. The conflation of supply and demand provided an illusion of control for producers. It seemed to prevent underconsumption and oversupply, even though in *Fors* it actually explains Ruskin's prolonged and exhausting labor as the necessary result of demand.

But Malthusian fears remained. Invectives against the industrial transformation of the land, sea, and sky increased after *The Queen of the Air;* in essence they were Ruskin's jeremiads about scarcity. As I have mentioned, the Guild of St. George was based on the fear that arable pasture and woodlands were vanishing. And in earlier chapters I have noted how Ruskin skirted problems of demand and oversupply: in his Manchester lectures on political economy, for example, his practical suggestions about the value and price of art illustrate concerns about scarcity and diminishing returns. As a writer, Ruskin justly feared the consequences of increased production and oversupply, for they resulted in both an unreceptive public and a lower intrinsic value for his word. Scott and Wordsworth were alarming examples of de- and in some instances mis-valuation. In view of these precedents and the overall Malthusian climate of his political economy of art, the scarcity of Ruskin's books—at least the public impression of scarcity—combined with high prices to prevent overproduction and attract the long-nosed readers whose veiled identities *Fors* and the Oxford lectures supposedly registered. Thus, the net-book system did control consumption, but eventually it lured a larger audience through its valorizing of reputation. In the nineties, Ruskin's works would become much more popular on the mass market when their publisher, George Allen, combined net-book pricing with wider distribution by moving his manufacture from Kent to London.[25]

WITHHOLDING—RUSKIN'S MUSEUM

The experiment in publishing restricted but eventually en-larged Ruskin's readership; conversely, the museum at Walkley, Sheffield, beckoned but distanced the local audience it surveyed from a suburban hill. Following Ruskin's ideas in *The Stones of Venice* and the "Preface" to the *Economist,* the collection was arranged to instruct observers in the history of great cities through artifacts, to teach the principles of art through master-pieces, and to preserve memorials of vanishing places through drawings of landscapes and buildings. Yet everything about this tiny museum signaled an ambivalence toward its ostensible audience, the lower-middle and laboring classes of industrial cities such as Sheffield.

Ruskin's museum began in a small stone cottage that over-looked the Valley of the Don and the Rivelin. The prospect, according to Ruskin and other visitors such as E. T. Cook, was lovely and instructional: the climb to the museum from Shef-field to Walkley signified the same sort of effort Ruskin de-manded with the pricing and publishing of his books.[26] De-scribing the view in the *Art Journal,* William C. Ward observed that nearby mills had polluted the Rivelin, and jerry-built homes spotted the hillsides. But even these elements were sym-bolic to Ruskin.[27] The view from the museum showed visitors the place from where they came: having walked the steep road, they could look down and frame the blighted land from the perspective of high culture; having seen the remnants of great cities, they could objectively see Sheffield.

Such a vista could stimulate reform, but neither Ruskin nor his critics ever considered the site a catalyst for better building and sanitation. They were concerned, rather, with the dynamics between Walkley and its unlikely audience. The *Magazine of Art* hinted at this dilemma in 1878: "Sheffield is the centre of trade tragedies, the home of trades-union terrorism, the birthplace and inglenook of Broadheadism. It is from the corrupt thraldom of such social heathenism that the religion of Ruskin would deliver us."[28]

The irony of the location, the *Magazine* implies, will not prompt visitors to make instructive comparisons; it simply will negate the collection's effect. In the *Art Journal*, William C. Ward broaches this dilemma without sarcasm. The museum is, "as Mr. Ruskin admits, a place of education for advanced students, not of elementary instruction for beginners." If this is so, the problem of audience becomes trenchant: "But among the class of people living in the vicinity, composed almost entirely of workers in the Sheffield forges, with a sprinkling of small shopkeepers, how many advanced students of Fine Art and geology—examples of which subjects form the bulk of the collection—are likely to be found?"[29]

In the same year (1882), in his "General Statement Explaining the Nature and Purposes of St. George's Guild" (30:51), Ruskin justifies his choice of Sheffield as the site. The city is a center of ironwork, a useful art that the British have mastered. At the same time, it lies in beautiful country, and its inhabitants, like those of all Yorkshire, have Old English virtues of honesty and piety. His explanation is sentimental and myopic. In characterizing the people of Sheffield as the simple persons whom he wanted the ideal museum to attract, he did not mention the city's history of political and religious dissent in the days of the Chartists or, Robert Hewison points out, its enduring communitarian spirit, qualities that made the location suitable in light of the cottage production Ruskin was advocating.[30] But although the history of these agitations is elided in this particular text, it informs his choice and display of objects at Sheffield, as well as his general ideas about exhibition.

Walkley's intended audience—the one inscribed in the location and collection itself—is delineated in Ruskin's essay on the formation and function of a museum, which appeared in the *Art Journal* in 1880, four years after the cottage at Walkley opened. In it, he remarks that any collection of art and artifacts should provide examples of "perfect order and perfect elegance, in the true sense of that test word, to the disorderly and rude populace" (34:247). The ideal order of an exemplary collection contrasts with the "confused museum of objects" at the South Kensington School (19:223). Ruskin had complained about the exhibits there for years. Many of the things on display lacked printed labels; good and inferior works stood together under no evident principle of arrangement. As a result, the workman or student wandered through a "Cretan labyrinth" (34:249) and absorbed high culture "by chance" (19:223). Most likely Ruskin was thinking of South Kensington when he declared in 1882 that Walkley exhibited a limited number of objects, all with "intelligible description" (30:54). South Kensington may have provided the explicit contrast—the bad museum that bewildered the worker. But the implicit contrast, as the quotation from the *Art Journal* shows, is with the audience: it is their disorder that the collection will correct. If, then, Ruskin were aware of the Sheffield radicals, he designed his museum to transform them. The visitor was to leave the stone cottage with the impression of "elegance," "stateliness, durability, and comfort" (34:249)—everything, Ruskin stressed, "in its *own* place" (34:247).

Comfort was an especially important feature of the ideal museum because Ruskin envisioned his audience as "gentlemen and gentlewomen, manservants and maidservants" (34:252), the latter by now euphemisms for the lower orders in an industrial, capitalistic society. They had to be clean and comfortable before they could look at art, he commented in 1867 (19:215). But when he discussed the museum, "comfort" did not simply mean shelter and heat to Ruskin; it evoked the snugness of the provincial hearthside celebrated in Dickens and Patmore. In his plans, for instance, Ruskin wanted to hang larger paintings mainly because covered walls made rooms warm and cheerful (30:55). The museum would not be a haven for the idle and cold; an entrance fee would discourage them (34:250). But a cozy interior would offer what Peter Gay, in his discussion of middle-class family homes, calls "subtle erotic inducements."[31] In essence, Walkley would exhibit the "sensuality of material artifacts and conditions" (in, Gay adds, "unexpected places") with which Ruskin had associated the Continental tours—hence, museum-going—of his childhood.[32] Walkley would also suggest to visitors the attributes of the proper bourgeois home.

When he insists on the museum's elegance, Ruskin means correct taste, grace, and refinement; the word has a slight taint of lower-middle-class pretension about it. In an elegant museum, every visitor must sign his or her name and pay a fee, preferably a silver groat (34:250). Because this coin, originally equal to fourpence, had not circulated since 1662, Ruskin may have meant to suggest it merely as a gratuity; no doubt it was a whimsical choice of a word and part of the archaic trappings of all his aesthetic and social experiments in the 1870s and 1880s. In addition, he declares, an elegant museum has a tearoom that serves no meat. This (perhaps) affected repulsion of the carnal refines the sensuality latent in Ruskin's notion of comfort and, moreover, in the actual clutter of Walkley. According to the *Sheffield Daily Telegraph,* the one-room cottage "cribbed, cabined and confined" the "costly treasures." The curator, Henry Swan, and his family also lived there (it is unclear how).[33] In reality, the gallery with drawings crowded on the walls and objects stacked in corners may have been just as bewildering as the South Kensington museum.

The plans for Walkley, rather than the jumble it became, reveal much about Ruskin's didactic techniques and the audience he envisioned. Ever since *The Stones of Venice,* he had treated buildings, the fine arts, and books as repositories of cultural values. Their features were symptomatic of external qualities like intention, labor, and belief. In devising instructional programs for late-nineteenth-century "peasants," he tried to elicit these qualities through various signals, here physical arrangements. Those who walked through the room at Sheffield would see the aesthetic products of the world's greatest cities. Beauty was an alloy of culture, and Walkley would show an accumulation of objects that were chiefly ideological. The exhibition of a few objects to illustrate, in Arnoldian fashion, the best that the world had produced, thus was to introduce visitors to high culture. Clearly Ruskin wanted them to feel privileged and elevated. Students should see the collection of an elite group: a "small body of men" from "among the upper and educated classes of England" should assemble a teaching museum, he remarks in an essay of 1867 (19:223). The editors of the Library Edition acknowledge that the museum represents Ruskin's "labour in collecting" (30:liv). When Ruskin first proposed the museum, someone scoffed that "the greatest curiosity he could exhibit would be—himself."[34] Yet he intended to do more than illustrate the labor theory of value; he would show people memorials of cities and things that had disappeared through decay and restoration. The casts of sculptures from the Ducal Palace are good examples of this sort of commemorative work. In addition, he would teach art through masterpieces. These also were tokens of scarcity—vanished cultures—because, apart from Burne-Jones, Turner, and Ruskin himself, most of the artists represented were not modern. In general, the pieces shown typified the work done by old masters in an alien past, so the collection ultimately taught visitors to value traditions and landscapes that their lives had ignored or disrupted. If the museum had its intended effect, people would leave thinking of the best in the world as gone, the way of life Walkley extolled now unavailable. No doubt some did derive pleasure from the individual objects displayed and failed to discern the referential value of the whole collection. Clearly, however, Ruskin's printed ideas about the function of the museum emphasized the temporal and social distance of observers from the traditions represented.

In 1878, the *Magazine of Art* recounted a humorous instance of the gap between Ruskin's aesthetic and the interpretive skill of his audience. A gentleman farmer bought *Notes on the Construction of Sheepfolds* "just before lambing season under the delusion that it was a book on bucolic architecture."[35] Like the titles of his books, the gallery at Walkley depended for readability on the iconologies it supposedly taught. It presented a cohesive history of art only if one already knew and valued the iconography of each object. Otherwise, the collection signified John Ruskin collecting, a meaning that relied on reputation-value rather than on the intrinsic or even syntagmatic value of the pieces. Ruskin's name—perhaps, by this time, his notoriety—would be the main draw for the Sheffield audience. This is especially so because almost every work of art at Walkley was a copy. Through reproductions, an audience might see what it could never afford to buy or visit. For this reason, the museum even included copies of paintings and drawings from the National Gallery and the British Museum. To the provincial art lover who might never get even to these places, Walkley was a digest of western European culture, truly a poor man's museum, and with its congested space, a public sample of the bourgeois home's décor of prints. Unlike those who attended exhibitions at the Royal Academy or the Grosvenor, the persons who trod up the hill to Walkley probably did not hope or care to see an original Carpaccio or Veronese. The desire for originality was limited to the prosperous classes; it spurred them to make grand tours, to start collections and, by the 1830s, it helped create a market for Old Master fakes.[36] In establishing a museum of copies, Ruskin did not envision an audience who had the money or knowledge to care for what the middle-class museum-goer, then and today, often regards as essential to the worth of an object.[37]

An original is, of course, the artistic expression of scarcity. The reproductions at Walkley conveyed scarcity through the geographic and social distance of the lower classes from the elite's choice of great western European culture, available only in facsimiles in Sheffield. The value even of the reproductions, moreover, depended on the mortality of the laboring body. For besides collecting, Ruskin directed a small industry of copying. The Carpaccios and Botticellis were executed by one of his journeymen, Charles Fairfax Murray. The drawings of decaying or soon-to-be restored Venetian architecture and frescoes were done by Angelo Alesandri. T. M. Rooke made studies of the mosaics at Ravenna and Chartres, as well as the eastern dome of Saint Mark's. It took another copyist, J. W. Bunney, six hundred days to draw the west front of the cathedral. William Ward reproduced Turners. Although Ruskin was particular about these copies, he viewed their executors as artisans and employees, and their work for the museum was meant to be transparently representational. He assumed that Bunney's drawing of Saint Mark's would direct the beholder's attention to the condition of the façade rather than to the journeyman's skill; similarly, Ward's Turners showed spectators what the great artist's work basically looked like. Of Arthur Burgess, who went with him to Verona in 1869 and later did the woodcuts that illustrated many of the Slade lectures, Ruskin recalls, "He drew the mouldings of the Scala Tombs as never architecture had been drawn before—he collated and corrected my measurements; he climbed where I could not." The drawings that eventually appeared in *Ariadne Florentina* and *Aratra Pentelici* were "unequalled, whether in precision of facsimile, or the legitimate use of the various methods of wood engraving. . . . he never put name or initial to his work, trusting to my occasional acknowledgment of the relations between us,—heaven knows—not given grudgingly, but carelessly and insufficiently."[38] Ruskin, however, does not linger over this negligence. He does not link Burgess's illness at Verona from "overstrain" to exploitation; instead, he identifies with the engraver as a worker. "In writing so much as this implies of my own epitaph with my friend's, I am thankful to say securely for both of us, that we did what we could thoroughly, and that all we did together will remain trustworthy and useful—uncontradicted, and unbettered, till it is forgotten."[39] Earlier, in this elegy, Ruskin notes that Burgess always worked "perhaps too wisely foreseeing that it could come to nothing."[40] Burgess's anonymity, for which Ruskin is responsible, becomes in this essay the fate of every laborer, including his employer's.

Perhaps only those who had read this article or knew about Ruskin's journeymen would see Walkley as the product of men who had exhausted themselves in labor. Certainly, they did not consider Ruskin as the profiting overseer, because he always styled himself as a laborer working within an economy of scarcity. The simple connection some like Cook and Wedderburn did make—that the museum represented the labor of collecting and that drawing itself was work—prepared them to notice that each piece conveyed something of its own production. Certain objects were meant to display technique: the sculpture Ruskin planned to put in the museum would demonstrate the process of chiseling, for example. This focus suggests that Walkley also was supposed to be a center for aspiring artists, a teaching museum. And in reality, Ruskin's conception of audience was ambiguous enough to include sundry groups, such as Sheffield operatives and art students. The idea of a museum for all classes is attractive, if naïve; and the collection at Walkley exhibited the progressive exclusion also operating throughout *Fors* and *Fiction Fair and Foul*.

For instance, in addition to the Eyton Collection of ornithological plates, a copy of Bewick's *Birds,* and a pencil drawing of a lion by Landseer—all favorites of Ruskin—Walkley possessed some etchings and woodcuts of John Leech (30:245). His "character-drawings" and satirical cartoons represented some of the few renderings of the human form in the museum. They were also some of the few samples of modern work. That the human body in contemporary setting appeared mainly in "political skits" (30:245–46), really social drawings (Leech's forte) is telling in light of Ruskin's envisioned audience, the Sheffield "peasants." For Leech depicted life at the traversed border between the prosperous trading classes and the squirearchy. He counted himself as rustic English and, according to June Rose, flaunted his "John Bull" qualities. "Give me a good day's hunting and some good claret and I'm quite satisfied," he once stated in the company of his associates at *Punch*.[41] Accordingly, as his cartoons show, he distrusted all foreigners, including the Irish and the Jews; in midcentury he focused much of Britain's xenophobia on Disraeli. Ruskin said he collected Leech's work for the pencil technique, but in doing so he revealed his sympathy with the lifestyle satirized.

The "Mr. Briggs" series exhibited was a Pickwickian look at country sport ("The Pleasures of Horse-keeping," "The Pleasures of Hunting" [30:247–48]). The stiff Englishman was frequently a target of gentle humor, and the jokes themselves entailed particulars of dinner parties, dances, riding, the rifle corps, and round bowling. All were portrayed as thoroughly English pastimes. At Walkley, though, they presumably were to be seen by men and women from another England. Although encouraged to examine them for exemplary drawing, viewers could hardly ignore the sort of world they represented, especially because, in Ruskin's announced intentions, the museum was foremost a repository of culture rather than an exhibition of technique. To inhabitants of Sheffield, such drawings were a spectacle of a life modeled on the tastes of the landed classes.

One of Leech's *Punch* drawings, *A Cool Request,* illustrates the way the museum might have excluded viewers.[42] In this cartoon, a gentleman stands in front of a shop selling photographic chemicals. Next to the store window hangs a display of stereoscopic slides "for the millions." It directs the viewer to "look steadily with both eyes" and admonishes, "Boys keep your hands off." Of course, a little boy stands below the display and hails the stiff gent, "I say, sir—heave us up to have a look at them pictures!" Here, the haughty Englishman is the ostensible object of fun but partly because of the anxiety the situation evokes. For the boy is an urchin: both his language and his dress tell this to readers of *Punch.* Like other members of the underclass, he is kept by physical conditions from the advantageous view afforded by modern improvements and inventions. And his desire to see—basically to widen his prospects—is perceived as a threat. In looking, he will contaminate. Under a congenial laugh at boys lurks the self-conscious fears of an ambitious and vulnerable middle class.

Coincidentally, Leech himself was driven by a desire to inhabit the social group he loved to draw. His life had the appurtenances of a country squire. All but his closest friends thought he was rich, but he was often pressed for money. The son of a bankrupted proprietor of a coffeehouse, he was noted for his gentlemanly bearing, but it was cultivated and fortified by his flippant attitude toward the poor. In his lithographs of 1841, for example, collected in *The Children of the Mobility Drawn from Nature,* London waifs show off mock coats of arms and invented pedigrees. Leech intended them to parody the upper-middle-class interest in nobility, and in general he used images of distress, like a ragamuffin warming his behind before an outdoor fire, to focus on manners. At least one critic lashed out at him for slighting the poor, but most like Thackeray thought his cartoons endearing and innocuous.[43] There was little chance of giving offense; the poor, after all, would probably never see them.

If Leech's cartoons were not obviously insulting to Sheffield operatives, Percival Leigh's *The Comic English Grammar* and *The Comic Latin Grammar* were. Ruskin displayed them because they contained Leech's drawings, which look like schoolboy caricatures of teachers, bullies, and adults. The text interpellates a public-school audience through inside jokes similar to those in Leech's other drawings. These include the presumedly inherent humor of Cockney pronunciation. Common targets of Leigh's adolescent mockery are incorrect grammar and dialect. *The Comic English Grammar* ends with an "Address to Young Students," which assumes the linguistic and social norms of the aspiring gentleman: "In the course of your reading . . . you will be frequently brought into contact with hackney-coachmen, cabmen, lackeys, turnkeys, thieves, lawyers' clerks, medical students . . . who are all very amusing people when properly viewed, as the monkeys and such like animals at the Zoological Gardens are."[44] Readers are advised to avoid slang and call things by their proper names in order to separate themselves from their inferiors. "Observe, when your tailor comes to measure you, the way in which he wears his hair; and should your own style . . . unfortunately resemble his, be sure to alter it immediately."[45]

Leech's work provided some of the few samples of modern English art at Walkley. Because Ruskin had begun his career ostensibly in defense of "modern painters," the paucity of contemporary British pieces seems odd. His lecture of 1867, "On the Present State of Modern Art," explains this under-representation. There, Ruskin hinges the difference between nineteenth-century, or modern, painting and previous work on the depiction of poverty. The poor are picturesque in premodern art; they are, in other words, exploited for the aesthetic effects of physical distress. Modern art, on the other hand, makes poverty its *subject*. Here, Ruskin may have in mind the work of social realists such as Herkomer. His point remains unelaborated, though he observes that poverty is "tenderly watched" by the artist in modern art (19:198). To watch tenderly may require the social and emotional distance Ruskin missed in Wordsworth and saw in Byron. When his discussion moves to popular taste, he becomes clearer. The public prefers excitement over conception, and narrative painting, a popular genre, offers much of the former and little of the latter. In domestic subjects beholders see their own lives represented. Because the situation portrayed is familiar, they tend to continue the painted story outside the frame. On the contrary, noble art, which concerns heroic subjects, does not portray a familiar situation, and those drawn to it may see human beings "as they lived and moved and suffered," but not as reflections of themselves (19:206). For such painting inspires and instructs rather than simulates.

In the first part of the essay, Ruskin is reiterating his complaint against the picturesque from *Modern Painters*.[46] His famous and enduring dislike of its subject matter (rather than technique) also underlies his assault on much modern art. Now focusing on narrative painting, he has simply changed terms and leveled his criticism of the picturesque at the dramatic. In using narrative painting as an example of modern, dramatic art, Ruskin confuses poverty, the original crux of his comparison, with the domestic—two intersecting but by no means conflatable subjects. This carelessness suggests that Ruskin perceived the middle, lower, and underclasses as genre subjects all opposed to the heroic, which he continued to advance as material for the noblest art.

Ruskin himself liked much narrative painting, but his reservations about the drama of the domestic imply that in his ideal aesthetic, noble art inspired its viewers to imitate, not to identify. It created this distance by presenting a subject that observers would recognize as already detached from their daily lives. In this light, genre painting of subjects *ideally* inferior to viewers should be "tenderly watched" by those whose distance from such lives afforded the luxury of tenderness. Indeed, by criticizing viewers' identification with dramatic painting, Ruskin is proscribing certain subjects and certain beholders. The "compassionateness" of modern art is "warping it away from its own proper sources of power," he declares (19:198). If one of the characteristics of modern art is compassion with the poor, the audience addressed must have shared the poverty represented. The result of such engagement between treatment and reception is a dramatic art based on a social referent that Walkley was designed to exclude.

As this argument suggests, Ruskin's prohibitions and ex-
clusions went beyond the poor and the Cockney. When in his
lecture of 1867 he asserts that dramatic elements are vulgar
because vulgar people enjoy them (rather than perfect form or
character) (19:204), he cannot simply mean the vulgar underclass. The abiding popularity of narrative painting, the "the-
atrical" genre, is a good example of the way taste crossed class
boundaries. According to Dianne Sachko Macleod, in the last
quarter-century, when "the new patriciate in the art world was
comprised of the painters, critics, and collectors of the Aesthetic
movement," the "more entrenched members of the middle
class" wanted not only "an inspirational message in art" but also
paintings that told stories.[47] A taste for the "familiar, the sentimental, and the pathetic," which had been prevalent early in the
century, likewise had not declined among the audience who
were buying reprints. The wealthy were also collecting narrative painting. In the 1890s, George McCullogh, who had made
his money in Australian gold and silver mines, amassed a number of paintings "noteworthy for storytelling rather than aesthetics," says Macleod.[48] The *Art Journal* sneered at his purchases, but they typified the judgment of a huge population
who had little in common but their ignorance of the vanguard in
the art world. They were part of Ruskin's audience, and their
consumption of art—their purchase of narrative paintings and
prints, their visits to galleries and museums—was, as he knew,
redefining its value. In these ways, the system that commodified
a single painting through exhibition and reproduction was expanding an audience and thereby changing the ways to see and
discuss art.

As the author of *Modern Painters* and the Slade lecturer,
Ruskin upheld what he had defined as the great European tradition, and speeches such as those he gave in his first tenure at
Oxford, along with projects such as his museum, attempted to
educate public taste. However, within his texts, groups such as
the Sheffield operatives stayed on the doorstep of Ruskin's
quaint house of Culture. They carried invitations, but they
never felt welcome. In practice, Ruskin spoke to a nation of
Leonard Basts, the fictional character in *Howards End* who es-
pouses an aesthetic that ultimately dismisses him. As Feltes

comments, Bast belongs to a vague group, "gentlefolk perhaps, or those obliged to pretend they are gentlefolk, or those who are neither, but merely 'unknown.'"[49] For these, Ruskin had to make culture both accessible and remote. Of course, as an admirer of Landseer and some narrative painting, he himself was part of the entrenched class Macleod describes, and his lack of interest in the Aesthetes as well as the Impressionists, his eclectic preferences—for Dürer, Beatrice Webb, and Burne-Jones—make his cultural program look today as conservative and prosaic as the audience he imagines. The son of a sherry merchant, reared as an evangelical Christian, now a Slade Professor who could, however, never be a gentleman, Ruskin elevated his status through a retrograde standard of "noble" art while projecting his ambiguous social position and mobility onto an inferior group. Like him, they had to reconceive themselves in order to become his ideal public, the "gentlewomen" and "maidservants" whose archaic epithets kept their lineage vague. The education of these aspirants thus meant repeated social definition through aesthetics. In particular, it entailed a continual process of detecting and, if they remained adherents, deflecting rejection.

SPENDING: RUSKIN AND DISTRIBUTION

The prohibitive prices of Ruskin's books, their scarcity, and the exhibitions of high culture in the museum at Walkley simultaneously invited and excluded an amorphous and potentially vast audience. A composite group, it emerges in Ruskin's writings as a dreamlike combination of peasant, industrial laborer, artisan, squire, and scholar. Perhaps because Ruskin could never visualize this mix of history and class, he both approached and retreated from readers during the 1870s and 1880s. Withholding, exemplified in his cottage publishing industry, his elimination of the middleman, and his choice of objects for the museum, makes him a miser of goods and time. His actions betray a repulsion from those he meant to reach and a nostalgia for a past of social hierarchy and equivalency of monetary, material, and spiritual signs.

As a hoarder of time and meaning, Ruskin was naturally suspicious of public taste and efforts to gratify it. He feared its effect on the value of the object. For this reason, he recommended that provincial museums permit visitors to handle only inferior things; he warned against a travelling exhibit of the British Museum's Turner collection, preferring that a Standard Series, composed of copies, be available in provinces throughout the country. In a letter to the *Times,* he declares, "If you *must* make them [Turner's paintings] educational to the public, hang Titian's Bacchus up for a vintner's sign, and give Henry VI.'s Psalter for a spelling-book to the Bluecoat School; but, at least . . . do not send them about in caravans to every annual Bartholomew Fair" (19:230). When a Turner or a Leech went for public view to a provincial town, it became a social object, according to Ruskin. In economic terms, its use-value, which he measured by its creator's labor but which materialized only through consumption, became an exchange-value when shown to others: they traded their money or time to absorb the touchstones of culture sent to them.

Ruskin advocated hoarding artwork to protect it from public contamination, and the carelessness with which he disseminated his own possessions realized a miser's nightmare of spending. Cook and Wedderburn describe the unstable stock of his library: "Often when he had exhausted a particular use of [books], he cleared them out—either selling them, through a dealer, or, more frequently, giving them away. With books, as with everything else that he possessed, he was a lavish giver; and mention has already been made of books, often of great value, presented by him to Oxford, Sheffield, and Whitelands College" (34:697). When acting so, Ruskin was not the fetishist of Walkley or *Sesame and Lilies.* Rather, he was a consumer of books: after he read them, he gave them away, generally to school museums (where, ironically, they became hoarded objects, protected in locked display cases). Although he did keep some volumes from what his editors called "permanent affection," he treated most as "auxiliary tools," note the editors (34:698, 697). Sometimes he ruined books to disperse or display their pages. The Saint Louis Psalter, revered in his diary of 1854 as "the greatest treasure I have yet obtained in all my life," eventually went in separate pages to Oxford, the Bodleian Library, and Charles Eliot Norton (12:lxix–xx). Cook and Wedderburn relate that Ruskin "annotated some of his most valuable manuscripts not merely in pencil, but in ink. He cut them to pieces, re-arranged them to his own desire" (12:lxix–xx). This practice did not begin in the 1870s. To the young readers of *Sesame and Lilies* in 1865, Ruskin states, "We none of us need many books, and those which we need ought to be clearly printed, on the best paper, and strongly bound" (18:33). Presumably the books he owned were "healthy" in this way, for, twelve years earlier, his diary of 3 January 1854 reads in part, "Cut missal up in evening; hard work" (12:lxx). He chopped up books to fit shelves and ripped out pages to frame. When he bought Francesca Alexander's *Roadside Songs of Tuscany* in 1882, he scattered its 122 folio leaves among drawing schools and museums. To make the volume available to even more "people of moderate means," Ruskin had twenty of the illustrations photographed, platinotyped, and distributed with an explanatory text; it appeared in 1884 in ten parts priced at 7s. apiece. (Some years after its publication, Alexander's mother tried to reconstruct the volume but could not find 14 of the leaves. Ruskin promised to restore the book in its original order but never did so, and the editors finally reconstituted it from various sources [32:xxiii–iv, 44–47, 51–52].)

When Ruskin showed, as even his loyal editors admit, "little consideration for the integrity of a collection" (32:xxiv), he often was acting for the benefit of provincial readers. This largesse opposes the miserly streak evident in much of his interpretive and pedagogical work. But his destructive practices enact a hoarder's idea of distribution, for, in using up treasures to the point of their own dissolution or in changing their form, he kept originals from circulating; *their* worth would remain intact while the butchered versions of the whole became the exchangeable commodities. In his economy, then, dispersed objects metamorphosed to signify their altered value. By cutting up the Psalter and Alexander's manuscript, Ruskin adopted the role of the manufacturer who, with modern techniques of production or his own scissors, created numerous commodities from a single volume. The result suited a populistic program:

prints of *Roadside Songs of Tuscany* graced the rooms of a few thousand readers of indeterminate demographic status. Yet other prints or numbers ended up behind glass cases as the objects of hushed viewing in museums. In both instances, especially the latter, the hoarder's labor was on display. Moreover, the exhibit also materialized surplus value, the chief characteristic of industrial capitalism. Ruskin's own labor, with that of journeymen such as Arthur Burgess, extracted this surplus from objects in order to reach an expanded market.

In ripping apart books to give as many people as possible as much as they could absorb, Ruskin extended his educational program of Arnoldian touchstones from museums to publishing. He also continued the nineteenth-century tradition of learning through snippets or extracts. Pieces of literature, like leaves of a manuscript and copies of Venetian architecture, reached those cut off by money, location, and intellect from the real places and objects of culture. As metonymies of an unwieldy and inaccessible tradition, distributed parts offered consumers rights of possession: mastery of words through ingestion and repetition of extracts—a favorite nineteenth-century practice—and ownership of art through prints. While creating and distributing these parts, Ruskin seemed to lack the ambivalence toward audience betrayed in his plans for and execution of museums. Yet withholding and exclusion underlie his whole metonymic theory of education and interpretation. In sacrificing the complete object for the sake of a large audience, Ruskin disclosed his mixed feelings about teaching "peasants." For once a work of art became a commodity, its form and meaning must, for Ruskin, change utterly, and the original, whether destroyed or hoarded, was preserved from the eyes of unknown viewers.

In the mass marketplace, books even looked different, and Ruskin believed that a changed form signaled a changed content. In his essay on modern literature, he sneers at the "true elements of popular education," penny literature and cheap reproductions (19:210). It may be the subjects that bother him (advertisements, bill-stickers); he elaborates on this complaint some years later in *Fiction Fair and Foul*. But he justifiably linked form and content because, according to Altick, books in the last quarter of the century were often not only badly bound and printed but also sloppily edited. Many of these books, available for as little as 3d. in the 1880s, were "haphazard selections" of the works of a great author, but readers could not tell from the books' titles and publicity whether they were getting a complete text.[50] Because Ruskin wanted a stable sign system, he had to believe that a penny novel could not contain something more or better than its wrapper. Although he doubted that verbal and visual signs could retain the same iconology and referents among readers from different classes, he still believed in the congruence of outer and inner, physical and spiritual. He enforced this connection through his attention to objects, his manufacture of strong book covers and bindings, and his criticism of material cheapness, which for him was synonymous with spiritual and intellectual waste. In this light, his destruction of some books is an aberrant practice prompted by his social conscience: anticipating their sure fate in the market, Ruskin ruins his treasures for the public.

When Ruskin, in his metonymic gestures, changed these volumes to portable property, he not only anticipated the destruction of art in the circuit of exchange but also violated the ethos of labor he had professed so eloquently in *The Seven Lamps of Architecture* and *The Stones of Venice*. If the imperfect object bespeaks the life of the hand and the sincerity of the worker, Ruskin, in these dispersions, is one of the middlemen he hated, with no regard for the integrity of the substance. Besides, for a collector, art historian, enemy of restoration, and lifelong advocate of order and elegance, these methods of distribution were equally anomalous. As I have just tried to show, his careless treatment of precious acquisitions realized the fear of a miser and fetishist. So even though he continued to advance a universal economy of equivalences and unalterable signs, he recognized the presence of a market economy in which the intrinsic value of an object lay in the eyes of ignorant beholders.

When in 1885 Ruskin resigned his Slade professorship, he took his last public stand against the new aesthetic. Twelve days after the university had voted to support vivisection, Ruskin retired in protest. Were it not for the vote, he would, he wrote to the *Pall Mall Gazette,* on April 24, have "died in my harness."

His exact quarrel with Oxford is uncertain. He may have been protesting what he regarded as a diversion of funds from his art school to experimental medicine, but his published grounds were ideological.[51] In an address to the Antivivisection Society, he declared that he had to leave the university to assert not the rights of animals, but the relation of all living things to God. Vivisection tore "the great link which bound together the whole of creation"; it infected society "with a thirst for knowing things which God had concealed from them" (34:644). In this statement, Ruskin articulated the assumptions of empirical natural theology that had grounded British science since the beginning of the century. The theory, suggests Richard D. French, provides a doctrinal or theological basis for antivivisection, which was largely an ecumenical though factional movement. Natural theology "sought to establish the existence, completeness, and perfection of the Deity through inductive inference from the evidences of purpose and design in the physical universe."[52] This description matches Ruskin's beliefs in inner and outer correspondences, professed in both the early volumes of *Modern Painters,* and his comments for the antivivisectionists.

Whether Ruskin now actually believed in natural theology or God is unclear. Possibly scientific naturalism endured for him as a philosophy because it had become useful to him by the time he tried to reach an expanded audience. Through the 1870s and 1880s, particularly in his autobiography, he restated a nostalgic, some say medieval view of the universe, in various descriptions of nature at the end of each chapter of *Praeterita*.[53] The assumptions of natural theology were similarly mystical and anti-epistemological; they elided all scientific and social change after Paley. Part of the debate over vivisection centered on the ethics and dispersion of knowledge. Much of the correspondence in the *Oxford Magazine* during November 1883, for example, concerned whether discoveries in medicine for the good of the species justified painful experiments on animals. Edward P. Poulton writes on 7 November, "The essence of our defence of vivisection in its proper place as a method of research is, then, — pain may be inflicted for the acquisition of knowledge."[54] An antivivisectionist, Edward B. Nicholson, challenges Sydney J.

Hickson to cite, with references, one experiment involving vivisection that has resulted in a discovery of benefit to human beings. In response, Hickson claims that Harvey discovered the circulation of the blood and that a doctor at Cambridge discovered the contractions of the spleen.[55] Challenged further to prove that these findings could not have occurred without vivisection, Hickson moves to a larger issue:

> I cannot refrain from the remark that the question he [Nicholson] has put bears a very suspicious resemblance to a question which has met researchers into all the branches of science and literature from time immemorial. "Of what use is it all?" ask the uninitiated; and the true answer has never been one bound down to a detail and hemmed in by stipulations. If Mr. Nicholson were asked by an ignoramus, "Of what use is the reading of books," he might fail to find at once a case in which this inestimable practice has saved the life of a human being or made him healthier or even happier; and his reply would probably be, "Read books and you will understand." And in a similar manner when physiologists are asked, "What is the use of physiology?" they do not reply by giving cases, for their reply comes from a much higher standpoint which the inquirer *may* fail to understand.[56]

Nicholson is cast as an uninitiated ignoramus because he does not practice experimental medicine. Further, by forging an analogy between vivisection and reading, Hickson has insulted him from the larger grounds of philosophy. Each has its own method and objectives, but in both discourses knowledge rests on the authority of a "higher standpoint" of practitioners which the average inquirer may not comprehend but has to accept nonetheless. Hickson, like Ruskin in his reading of the Romantics, handles troublesome interpretations, opinions, and questions with the authority of a practitioner that closes the discussion to a general audience.

Hickson's analogy is unsuccessful on a practical level because one cannot answer the antivivisectionist as one can the nonreader: vivisecting, like reading books, may bring understanding, but not very many people can do it. Yet as his various lectures and essays show, Ruskin did not think that most people could really read either; it was as specialized a skill as vivisection. And if only those who actually read or vivisected could understand the benefits of each activity, people had to accept the authority of the skilled worker. They were compelled, then, to believe in an experiential epistemology. In the above passage, Hickson makes the epistemology that encompasses both science and philosophy empirical and nonempirical at the same time. Similarly, Ruskin grounded his position in the controversy in an empirical natural theology that supported the divine authority of pre-Darwinian science. He protested the scientist's search for knowledge because it probed and disrupted the perfect, actually static, design and harmony of the universe. And he extended this reverence for the authority of received knowledge over discovery in his educational programs. In his essays on Wordsworth and Byron and correspondence in *Fors,* Ruskin discouraged people from reading. As a natural theologian, he implied that the poets' texts and his own contained a truth discernible only to him. Ironically, his lack of faith in the public's ability to read turned him into a sort of vivisector of books. He began to dispense parts of many works, insisting that each of these embodied enough of his difficult and, he suspected, unpalatable aesthetic and working, to use Hickson's words, from a "much higher standpoint" for the good of the nonreading public.

Calling Ruskin a vivisector may seem farfetched because books are not living things. Yet cutting and separating are not only a desecration but also a kind of vivisection by his own standards. If art and books represented the labor of great men and women and became monuments of their culture, then tearing up even something such as *Roadside Songs of Tuscany* destroyed part of Francesca Alexander for the sake of an unknown public. (Certainly her mother thought so.) In her place, Ruskin became the creator and interpreter of her fragments, as he extracted, multiplied, and annotated leaves from her book. In packaging and explaining Alexander's work for an audience, Ruskin ensured his authority as disperser of culture, but he also encouraged the partial truths and misperceptions he associated with circulation. Because the whole, original work of art signified the labor of its creator, misreading or perceived misreading was, as Terry Eagleton notes, "an equivalent in the literary realm to grievous bodily harm."[57] Art had always represented to Ruskin a living spirit, but as his theology and theory of labor reified into things whose value lay in their material circumstances, he violated what had been the sacrosanct character of the whole. In short, Ruskin had to disregard the material integrity of art to teach an amorphous public, but the specter of the original work haunted all his statements on aesthetic value and meaning, as well as his destructive expenditure of objects.

When Ruskin celebrated the Gothic worker in *The Stones of Venice* or the life of the hand in *The Seven Lamps of Architecture,* he presupposed an unalienated labor synonymous with imaginative creation. In the 1870s and 1880s, he depicted Wordsworth, Byron, Dickens, Scott, and himself as commodity producers, but he never actually modified his theories of imagination to fit his demonstrated belief in alienated labor. Each of the three kinds of imagination Ruskin introduced in volume two of *Modern Painters* was a teleological and mystical process of only the highest minds. Imagination associative is compositional; it constructs a "governed and perfect whole" from "imperfections" (4:248, 234). Imagination penetrative reaches the truth beneath the surface of things; it is an energetic, "possession-taking faculty" (4:251). Imagination contemplative displaces memories onto metaphors coined like money to represent a desired value. Its excesses produce pathetic fallacies, but its impulse comes from trust in "the beneficence . . . of an Omnipotent Spirit" (4:288n.2). This last phrase, added to the abridged edition of *Modern Painters* compiled by Susan Beever in 1875, reasserts the religious character of creativity, which had not concerned him for a long time. Perhaps an awareness of the intended audience prompted this reversion to his former orthodoxy. For this edition, called *Frondes Agrestes,* was a digest of Ruskin's aesthetic and the version of *Modern Painters* most familiar to contemporary readers. By 1903, thirty-six thousand copies at 3s.6d or 3s. had been printed (3:lxi). Readers of these excerpts were likely to be unsophisticated in intellectual or aesthetic matters; when addressing them, it was more appropriate to attribute guidance to God or the genial powers of the artist than to the effects of circulation.

To the man who still thought in terms of "Omnipotent Spirit" when theorizing about the imagination, Ruskin's actual disregard for the material integrity of art objects seems contradictory. But in editing *Frondes Agrestes,* Ruskin was doctoring an old text for a new market; that it was, moreover, a text comprised largely of theory explains why Ruskin paid less attention to the contents of this and other collections of extracts than to their distribution. At Oxford, Ruskin had become a practitioner who often sneered at theorizing and viewed even his own writing and lecturing as action. Whereas imagination was the fulcrum of his early studies of art, distribution became the core of his late criticism. But depicting himself as a laborer and creator of surplus value involved Ruskin in the consequences that Ricardo and Marx had foreseen and that he had suffered. Specifically, Ricardian labor theory led Ruskin to realize that a commodity on the market for the profit of the manufacturer would not represent the worker's original concept or actual work. The example of alienating labor in the life of Scott, in particular, led him to seize control of his own production, but, in doing so, Ruskin did not alter the process; he merely set himself in the place of the profiting bookseller and manufacturer. In fact, he demonstrated the questionable ethics involved in commodifying art in his handling of Francesca Alexander's work.

This destructive distribution was problematical because it both manifested and justified Ruskin's own anxiety about the fate of art as a commodity. Generally, he tried to constrict what was becoming a huge, unknown audience of art-consumers by various ways of withholding. If his books were hard to get, he could be sure that those who did find them would appreciate his message. In maneuvering for a receptive audience, he guaranteed a small one. Similarly, in the published plans for Walkley, the entire exchange was mapped and controlled: the object was protected by physical or hermeneutical barriers; the reader, kept at bay, eventually perceived these boundaries as a characteristic of art. Physical distance turned into social rifts not only between the viewer and the object but also between the viewer's conception of himself and the person interpellated into the exchange—the ideal beholder he or she must become. Both of these divisions, inherent in the engagement between audience and art object, constituted Ruskin's aesthetic for the masses.

These strategies protected the value of work which Ruskin, along with believers in marginal utility, linked with scarcity. Unfortunately, like many economists under the sway of Say's Law, Ruskin tried to deal with contemporary demand that was independent of production. The desires of the heterogeneous classes he ostensibly tried to reach repelled him because he recognized that their cultural base would modify the value of his own work and all the things he revered. New audiences were not rebelling against tradition, as he had in the first volume of *Modern Painters;* they were ignoring everything about the aesthetic and perceiving in different ways. Ruskin could not be sure of their beliefs: his reference to divinely governed art in *Frondes Agrestes* and his John Bullish promotion of the "thingness" of England, its language and objects, show that he sensed a diffusion of values that would affect the worth of his own art as well as that of others. In the last decades of his productive life, Ruskin showed much of the reserve toward mass culture which we associate with some of the Modernists. Yet he had a generous, spontaneous, and populistic streak, evident in his attempts to give high culture to the classes from which, as he well knew, he had emerged.

Ruskin lived at the crossroads of aesthetics: he constructed a sort of great tradition of European art that glorified the worker; he subverted the conventional, historicist view of art history with the work of women and peasants (which he in turn used to uphold the material conditions of that old historicism); he transmuted his highly doctrinal typology into a materialism that he recognized as a parody of his beloved Greek autochthonous universe; he turned rare and valuable books into prints; he addressed working-class readers in arrogant but personal letters; he organized a system of pricing that drew a variety of readers to prestigious books. He was a demagogue and a populist. If he had lived a few decades later, one wonders in what direction his social conscience would have led him; certainly viewing him as a sinister anachronism of the twentieth-century totalitarian leader ignores the tensions in his work. Ruskin was aware of his circumstances. His efforts to be a practical man and embrace the readers of his time, and his recoil from their sensibilities, herald both popular and elitist aesthetics.

Notes

CHAPTER 1. INTRODUCTION: ECONOMIC
AND AESTHETIC CONTEXTS

1. Richard D. Altick, *The English Common Reader* (Chicago: University of Chicago Press, 1957), 383–84.

2. See Brian Maidment, "Ruskin, *Fors Clavigera* and Ruskinism, 1870–1900," in *New Approaches to Ruskin,* ed. Robert Hewison (London: Routledge and Kegan Paul, 1981), 196.

3. Alon Kadish, *The Oxford Economists in the Late Nineteenth Century* (Oxford: Clarendon Press, 1982), 3.

4. See E. J. Hobsbawm, *Industry and Empire* (London: Penguin Books, 1968), 119.

5. Quoted in Asa Briggs, *Victorian Things* (Chicago: University of Chicago Press, 1988), 174–75.

6. Gerald Reitlinger, *The Economics of Taste* (London: Barrie and Rockliff, 1961), 148–49.

7. Ibid., 157.

8. Walter Benjamin, *Illuminations,* trans. Harry Zohn (New York: Schocken Books, 1969), 243.

9. Reitlinger, 157.

10. Benjamin, 243 and 221.

11. Quoted in Briggs, 178.

12. Reitlinger, 152 and 157–58.

13. Alan Lee, "Ruskin and Political Economy: *Unto This Last,*" in *New Approaches to Ruskin,* 71,73.

14. Adam Smith, *An Inquiry into the Nature and Causes of the Wealth of Nations* (New York: Random House, 1937), 30.

15. David Ricardo, *On the Principles of Political Economy and Taxation,* vol. 1 of *The Works and Correspondence of David Ricardo,* ed. Piero Sraffa and M. H. Dobbs, 10 vols. (Cambridge: Cambridge University Press, 1951–55), 12; John Stuart Mill, *Principles of Political Economy,* vols. 2 and 3 of *Collected Works of John Stuart Mill,* 25 vols. (Toronto: University of Toronto Press, 1965), 2:25; and Karl Marx, *Capital,* ed. Frederick Engels, 3 vols. (New York: International Publishers, 1967), 1:164–72.

16. Nick Shrimpton, "'Rust and Dust': Ruskin's Pivotal Work," in *New Approaches to Ruskin,* 59; and John Ruskin, *The Library Edition of the Collected Works of John Ruskin,* ed. E. T. Cook and Alexander Wedderburn, 39 vols. (London: George Allen, 1903–12), 5:380. References of all future quotations from this edition will appear in the text by volume and page number.

17. Quoted from Pierre Bigo's *Marxisme et humanisme* (Paris, 1953), in Dirk J. Struik, "Introduction" to Karl Marx, *The Economic and Philosophic Manuscripts of 1844,* trans. Martin Milligan (New York: International Publishers, 1964), 53.

18. For arguments that Ruskin rejected elements of labor theory, see Jeffrey L. Spear, *Dreams of an English Eden: Ruskin and His Tradition in Social Criticism* (New York: Columbia University Press, 1984), 149–50; and James Clark Sherburne, *John Ruskin, or the Ambiguities of Abundance* (Cambridge, Mass.: Harvard University Press, 1972), 130–36. These critics differ on the role of price in labor theory and Ruskin's own interpretation of it, but agree that Ruskin's emphasis on demand placed his ideas outside labor theory.

19. Georg Simmel, *The Philosophy of Money,* trans. Tom Bottomore and David Frisby (London: Routledge and Kegan Paul, 1978), 423.

20. For a discussion of labor and *opera* or pleasurable exertion in *Munera Pulveris,* see P. D. Anthony, *John Ruskin's Labour: A Study of Ruskin's Social Theory* (Cambridge: Cambridge University Press, 1983), 160–66.

21. Smith, 735.

22. For a discussion of the implications of Mill's controversial idea for orthodox economics, particularly the link between his wages-fund theory and Say's Law, see Sherburne, 150–51, 156–57. Although there is no way to tell whether Ruskin annotated his copy of

Mill's *Principles,* according to John Tyree Fain (*Ruskin and the Economists* [Nashville: Vanderbilt University Press, 1956], 117), Lee says the volume was "meagerly annotated" (73).

23. Henry William Spiegel, *The Growth of Economic Thought,* rev. ed. (Durham, N.C.: Duke University Press, 1983), 511–12.

24. Spear, 144.

25. Lee, 85–86. For a discussion of the similarities between Ruskin's stated ideas and marginal utility, see Sherburne, 138–40.

26. Quoted in Spiegel, 517.

27. Ibid., 518.

28. Briggs, 15.

29. Hobsbawm, 128–29.

30. Mill, 2:203.

31. See Marcus B. Huish, *Happy England as Painted by Helen Allingham, R.W.S.* (London: Adam and Charles Black, 1904), 118–29; and Laurel Bradley, "Evocations of the Eighteenth Century in Victorian Art" (Ph.D. diss, New York University, 1986), passim.

32. T. Edmund Harvey, *Report of the Master of the Guild, 1936–37* (London: Le Play House, 1937), 8.

33. See *Works* 30:328–33; Margaret E. Spence, "The Guild of St. George: Ruskin's Attempt to Translate His Ideas into Practice," *Bulletin of the John Rylands Library* 40 (1957):181–90; and H. C. Fairfax-Cholmeley, *Report of the Master of the Guild, 1930–31* (London: Le Play House, 1931), 7.

34. Rylands English MSS. 1254/9.

35. Karl Marx, "Estranged Labor," in *The Economic and Philosophic Manuscripts of 1844,* 109.

36. Sherburne treats abundance, manifested in organicism, as the underpinning of Ruskin's economy (1–25). He does not believe that a subverting economy of scarcity informs Ruskin's aesthetics. See 139–40.

37. Quoted in Fredric Jameson, *The Political Unconscious* (Ithaca: Cornell University Press, 1981), 24.

38. Kadish, 41.

39. Jameson, 25.

40. The main studies of Ruskin's theory of political economy have been written by Fain (1956), Sherburne (1972), Anthony (1983), and Spear (1984), all cited above.

CHAPTER 2. RUSKIN AT OXFORD:
THE PROBLEM OF AUDIENCE

1. Alon Kadish, *The Oxford Economists in the Late Nineteenth Century* (Oxford: Clarendon Press, 1982), 3.

2. W. R. Ward, *Victorian Oxford* (London: Frank Cass, 1965), 280, 282; and Kadish, 85.

3. Ward, 283.

4. Ibid., 281–86.

5. *Oxford University Extension Reports* (London, 1866), 8.

6. Christopher Harvie, *The Lights of Liberalism* (London: Allen Lane, 1976), 75.

7. Quoted in ibid., 257, from G. C. Brodrick, *Report of Speeches on the Abolition of Tests,* 1866.

8. Ward, 244.

9. Harvie, 195.

10. Kadish, 95–100.

11. Harvie, 195–96.

12. Ruskin generally attacked individual freedom as an ideal of the ambitious and mocked the "self-made man" (e.g., 20:293, 293n.3).

13. See Ward, 279.

14. Harvie, 203.

15. E. T. Cook, *The Life of John Ruskin,* 2 vols. (1911; reprint, New York: Haskell House, 1968), 2:178; and Kenneth Clark, *Ruskin at Oxford* (Oxford: Clarendon Press, 1947), 3–4.

16. Clark, 9.

17. Terry Eagleton, *Literary Theory: An Introduction* (Minneapolis: University of Minnesota Press, 1983), 28–29.

18. Martin J. Wiener, *English Culture and the Decline of the Industrial Spirit, 1850–1980* (Cambridge: Cambridge University Press, 1981), 22–23.

19. Louis Menand, *Discovering Modernism* (Oxford: Oxford University Press, 1987), 107.

20. Pierre Macherey, *A Theory of Literary Production,* trans. Geoffrey Wall (London: Routledge and Kegan Paul, 1978), 71.

21. *Oxford Magazine* 1 (28 February 1883):114.

22. Clark, 9.

23. Helene E. Roberts, "Exhibition and Review: The Periodical Press and the Victorian Art Exhibition System," in *The Victorian Periodical Press: Samplings and Soundings,* ed. Joanne Shattock and Michael Wolff (Toronto: University of Toronto Press, 1982), 80.

24. Quoted in ibid., 94.

25. Jacques Derrida, "Economimesis," *Diacritics* 11, no. 1 (1981):7.

26. Julie F. Codell, "Marion Harry Spielmann and the Role of the Press in the Professionalization of Artists," *Victorian Periodicals Review* 22 (1989):9.

27. Allen Hoey, "The Name on the Coin: Metaphor, Metonymy, and Money," *Diacritics* 18, no. 2 (1988):29.

28. Cosmo Monkhouse, "A Pre-Raphaelite Collection," *Magazine of Art* 6 (1883):62–70; and Sidney Colvin, "Rossetti as a Painter," 177–83.

29. *Oxford Magazine* 1 (24 January 1883):2.

30. See Trevor Fawcett, "Scholarly Journals," in *The Art Press: Two Centuries of Art Magazines,* Art Documents, no. 1 (London: Art Book Co., 1976), 14.

31. See Anthony Burton, "Nineteenth-Century Periodicals," in *The Art Press,* 3–13. Approximate and conflicting monthly circulation figures for the *Art Journal* are given by Michael Collins (3,000) in "English Art Magazines before 1901" (*Connoisseur* 191 [1976]:199) and George P. Landow in "There Began to Be a Great Talking about the Fine Arts" (*The Mind and Art of Victorian England,* ed. Joseph Altholz [Minneapolis: University of Minnesota Press, 1976], 130). Landow gets his figure from the *Art Journal* itself (13 [1851]:301), though it seems implausibly high compared with the circulation of similar journals. See Alvar Ellegård, "The Readership of the Periodical Press in Mid-Victorian Britain," *Victorian Periodicals Newsletter* 13 (September 1971):3–22. In 1870 even *Cornhill* had an estimated circulation of only eighteen thousand, the more specialized *Fortnightly Review* had twenty-five hundred, and *Blackwood's* had seven thousand. In any case the circulation of many journals had dropped between 1860 and 1870, so the *Art Journal's* probably also had decreased.

32. *Art Journal* 48 (1886):320.

33. Bradley, 126.

34. Cook, 2:202; and John Dixon Hunt, *The Wider Sea: A Life of John Ruskin* (London: Dent, 1982), 349.

35. *Oxford Magazine* 1 (9 May 1883):203.

36. *Oxford Magazine* 1 (31 October 1883), front page.

37. Quoted in *Igdrasil* 2 (1890):267, from *St. James's Budget,* 16 March 1883; and Cook, 2:202.

38. Cook, 2:475–76.

39. Quoted in ibid., 2:477n.

40. *Oxford Magazine* 1 (7 February 1883):60.

41. Clark, 4.

42. Huish, 43.

43. For a description of Allingham as a fair-weather painter, see Huish, 193; for Tom Taylor's review, 58; and for Walker's influence on her, 182–84.

44. Ruskin's reference to the Dusseldorf School is appropriate. Its painstaking detail made painting look "manufactured rather than handmade." Robert Rosenblum and H. W. Janson, *Nineteenth-Century Art* (New York: Harry N. Abrams, 1984), 163–64. Carl Friedrich Lessing and Peter Hasenclever were prominent members of this well-known school. There are no references to either in the Index of the Library Edition.

45. P. D. Anthony, *John Ruskin's Labour: A Study of Ruskin's Social Theory* (Cambridge: Cambridge University Press, 1983), 36.

46. Brian Maidment, "Readers Fair and Foul: John Ruskin and the Periodical Press," in *The Victorian Periodical Press,* 29–58.

47. Fredric Jameson, *The Political Unconscious* (Ithaca: Cornell University Press, 1981), 249.

CHAPTER 3. RUSKIN'S ECONOMIC MODEL

1. Pierre Macherey, *A Theory of Literary Production,* trans. Geoffrey Wall (London: Routledge and Kegan Paul, 1978), 71.

2. David Ricardo, *On the Principles of Political Economy and Taxation,* vol. 1 of *The Works and Correspondence of David Ricardo,* ed. Piero Sraffa and M. H. Dobbs, 10 vols. (Cambridge: Cambridge University Press, 1951–55), 1:12.

3. John Tyree Fain (*Ruskin and the Economists* [Nashville: Vanderbilt University Press, 1956]) suggests that Ruskin copied passages from Smith in *Unto This Last* (145).

4. Ricardo, 1:11.

5. Fain, 38–69.

6. Mark Blaug, *Ricardian Economics* (New Haven: Yale University Press, 1958), 36; and Karl Marx, *Capital,* ed. Frederick Engels, 3 vols. (New York: International Publishers, 1967), 1:57, 62.

7. Fain, 105, 117–19.

8. Maxine Berg, *The Machine Question and the Making of Political Economy* (Cambridge: Cambridge University Press, 1980), 47–48; for the difference between the nineteenth-century notion of the Ricardian

school and the much more complex theories of Smith and Ricardo, see Biancamaria Fontana, *Rethinking the Politics of Commercial Society: The Edinburgh Review, 1802–1832* (Cambridge: Cambridge University Press, 1985), 80–81.

9. Michel Foucault, *The Order of Things* (New York: Random House, 1970), 261.

10. Marx, *Capital,* 1:46.

11. Ibid., 1:43–48.

12. Rylands English MSS. 1254/15.

13. Quoted in E. T. Cook, *The Life of John Ruskin,* 2 vols. (1911; reprint, New York: Haskell House, 1968), 2:429.

14. *Art Journal* 45 (1883):47.

15. Quoted in *Art Journal* 45 (1883):48.

16. James Kissane, "Victorian Mythology," *Victorian Studies* 6 (1982–83):13.

17. Jacques Derrida, "White Mythology: Metaphor in the Text of Philosophy," in *Margins of Philosophy,* trans. Alan Bass (Chicago: University of Chicago Press, 1982), 216–17.

18. *The Ethics of Aristotle,* trans. J. A. K. Thomson (Harmondsworth: Penguin, 1976), 208.

19. Ibid., 210.

20. Ibid., 209.

21. Ibid., 212.

22. Ibid., 212–13.

23. Terry Eagleton, *Literary Theory: An Introduction* (Minneapolis: University of Minnesota Press, 1983), 20.

24. Frank M. Turner, *The Greek Heritage in Victorian Britain* (New Haven: Yale University Press, 1981), 323–34, 358–68.

25. Foucault, 257.

CHAPTER 4. MONEY

1. Carol T. Christ, *The Finer Optic* (New Haven: Yale University Press, 1975).

2. Marc Shell, *The Economy of Literature* (Baltimore: Johns Hopkins University Press, 1978), 68–69, plate 16.

3. Fredric Jameson, *Marxism and Form* (Princeton: Princeton University Press, 1971), 371.

4. Herodotus connects minting with tyranny in the story of Gyges (*Histories* 1.8–14). See Marc Shell, *Money, Language, and Thought* (Berkeley: University of California Press, 1982), 2; and Shell, *The Economy of Literature,* 12–13.

5. Shell, *The Economy of Literature,* 92.

6. John Vernon, *Money and Fiction: Literary Realism in the Nineteenth and Early Twentieth Centuries* (Ithaca: Cornell University Press, 1984), 32.

7. John Tyree Fain, *Ruskin and the Economists* (Nashville: Vanderbilt University Press, 1956), 54.

8. Ibid., 137–38.

9. Ruskin challenges Henry Fawcett's theory of interest in *Fors* 22 (27:378) and criticizes Millicent Garrett Fawcett's *Political Economy for Beginners* (the "Cambridge Catechism") in *Fors* 1 and 11.

10. Shell, *The Economy of Literature,* 32–35.

11. Paul L. Sawyer, *Ruskin's Poetic Argument: The Design of the Major Works* (Ithaca: Cornell University Press, 1985), 206.

12. Vernon, 40.

13. Ibid., 36.

14. See Ruskin's debates with R. G. Sillar and W. C. Sillar on usury in *Fors* passim (particularly 28:121, 139, 186–87, 400–401); his argument about taking interest and promise to stop (29:180); lists of his expenses in published accounts attached to *Fors* and reports of the guild (vols. 27–30 passim), for example, his love of collecting art, his new posting carriage, and his brass rubbings (28:519, 531).

15. Hansli's coins are illustrated in 27, plate 14.

16. Michael McKeon, *The Origins of the English Novel, 1600–1740* (Baltimore: Johns Hopkins University Press, 1987), 3.

17. John Stuart Mill, *Principles of Political Economy,* in *Collected Works of John Stuart Mill,* 25 vols. (Toronto: University of Toronto Press, 1965), 2:214–17.

18. See 30:103–56. The last financial statement was issued in 1885.

19. The connection between Romantic humanism and political as well as mercantile economy is explored respectively in James Clark Sherburne, *John Ruskin, or the Ambiguities of Abundance* (Cambridge, Mass.: Harvard University Press, 1972), 26–55; and Colin Campbell, *The Romantic Ethic and the Spirit of Modern Consumerism* (New York: Basil Blackwell, 1987).

20. P. D. Anthony, *John Ruskin's Labour: A Study of Ruskin's Social Theory* (Cambridge: Cambridge University Press, 1983), 106–7.

21. Friedrich Nietzsche, *The Genealogy of Morals,* in *The Birth of Tragedy and The Genealogy of Morals,* trans. Francis Golffing (New York: Anchor, 1956), 160.

CHAPTER 5. CIRCULATING VALUE

1. See Dinah Birch, *Ruskin's Myths* (Oxford: Clarendon Press, 1988), 93–132.

2. Cf. David Ricardo, *On the Principles of Political Economy and Taxation*, vol. 1 of *The Works and Correspondence of David Ricardo*, ed. Piero Sraffa and M. H. Dobbs, 10 vols. (Cambridge: Cambridge University Press, 1951–55) 1:12.

3. P. D. Anthony, *John Ruskin's Labour: A Study of Ruskin's Social Theory* (Cambridge: Cambridge University Press, 1983), 118–19; and John Tyree Fain, *Ruskin and the Economists* (Nashville: Vanderbilt University Press, 1956), 110.

4. See chap. 1, n.22 above; 16:10.

5. Fain, 110.

6. Generally, "worth" refers to intrinsic value and "value" to exchange value. Marx carries this distinction from Locke, who mentions "natural worth," but links it with use rather than any inherent property of the object. See Karl Marx, *Capital*, ed. Frederick Engels (New York: International Publishers, 1967), 1:44n.

7. Karl Marx, *The Economic and Philosophic Manuscripts of 1844*, trans. Martin Milligan (New York: International Publishers, 1964), 108, 116.

8. J. A. Hobson, *Confessions of an Economic Heretic* (London: George Allen, 1938), 23–25; and Christopher Harvie, *The Lights of Liberalism* (London: Allen Lane, 1976), 202.

9. Hobson, 86.

10. Guinevere L. Griest, *Mudie's Circulating Library and the Victorian Novel* (Bloomington: Indiana University Press, 1970), 54.

11. Alan Lee, "Ruskin and Political Economy: *Unto This Last*," in *New Approaches to Ruskin*, ed. Robert Hewison (London: Routledge and Kegan Paul, 1981), 81.

12. Marx, *Capital*, 1:44.

13. John Kenneth Galbraith, *Economics in Perspective* (Boston: Houghton Mifflin, 1987), 128–29, 92–95.

14. Marx, *The Economic and Philosophic Manuscripts of 1844*, 185.

15. Henry Gay Hewlett, "The Rationale of Mythology," *Cornhill* 35 (1877):410–12; and Birch, 72–93; 19:lxvii.

16. Paul de Man, *Allegories of Reading* (New Haven: Yale University Press, 1979), 153–54; and Hewlett, 409.

17. George P. Landow, *The Aesthetic and Critical Theories of John Ruskin* (Princeton: Princeton University Press, 1971), 415.

18. Raymond E. Fitch, *The Poison Sky* (Athens: Ohio University Press, 1982), 536.

19. Richard D. Altick, *Victorian People and Ideas* (New York: Norton, 1973), 242.

20. Galbraith, 143.

21. Georg Simmel, *The Philosophy of Money,* trans. Tom Bottomore and David Frisby (London: Routledge and Kegan Paul, 1978), 278.

22. Ibid., 279.

CHAPTER 6. LEVELING DOWN: WORDS
PROPOSED AND PRACTICED

1. Hans W. Frei, *The Eclipse of Biblical Narrative: A Study in Eighteenth- and Nineteenth-Century Hermeneutics* (New Haven: Yale University Press, 1974), 9, 17–51.

2. David G. Riede, *Matthew Arnold and the Betrayal of Language* (Charlottesville: University Press of Virginia, 1988), 14–15.

3. See Elizabeth K. Helsinger, *Ruskin and the Art of the Beholder* (Cambridge, Mass.: Harvard University Press, 1982), 1–7; and John Rosenberg, "Style and Sensibility in Ruskin's Prose," in *The Art of Victorian Prose,* ed. George Levine and William Madden (New York: Oxford University Press, 1968), 181–83.

4. Jeffrey L. Spear, "Ruskin as a Prejudiced Reader," *ELH* 49 (1982):73–74.

5. Rosenberg, 197–200.

6. George P. Landow, "Reading Pre-Raphaelite Painting," *Journal of Pre-Raphaelite and Aesthetic Studies* 1, no. 1 (part 2, 1988):25–31.

7. See Robert Hewison, *John Ruskin: The Argument of the Eye* (Princeton: Princeton University Press, 1976), 46–52.

8. See Helsinger, 47.

9. Joel Snyder, "Picturing Vision," in *The Language of Images,* ed. W. J. T. Mitchell (Chicago: University of Chicago Press, 1980), 223, 224.

10. W. J. T. Mitchell, "Spatial Form in Literature: Toward a General Theory," in *The Language of Images,* 274–80.

11. Ruskin quotes from *Oeuvres Posthumes—Derniers Chants: Poëmes et Ballades sur l'Italie* (1855). Seven stanzas from the ballad appear in 5:213–14.

12. Riede, 94.

13. Terry Eagleton, *Literary Theory: An Introduction* (Minneapolis: University of Minnesota Press, 1983), 37–38.

14. Richard D. Altick, *The English Common Reader* (Chicago: University of Chicago Press, 1957), 184, 176.

15. See Spear, "Ruskin as a Prejudiced Reader," 85.

16. The symbolic grotesque is a "series of symbols . . . of which the connection is left for the beholder to work out for himself." The gaps form the "grotesque character," whose meaning is hidden, illogical, and difficult "to express in any verbal way" (5:132).

17. George Levine, *The Realistic Imagination: English Fiction from Frankenstein to Lady Chatterley* (Chicago: University of Chicago Press, 1981), 5–8.

18. Marx quotes from *Timon of Athens* and *Faust*. See *The Economic and Philosophic Manuscripts of 1844,* trans. Martin Milligan (New York: International Publishers, 1964), 166.

19. Adam Smith, *An Inquiry into the Nature and Causes of the Wealth of Nations* (New York: Random House, 1937), 643. The English quotation is from Mirabeau's *Philosophie Rurale ou économie générale et politique de l'agriculture, pour servir de suite à l'Ami des Hommes* (Amsterdam, 1766).

20. Karl Marx, *Capital,* ed. Frederick Engels, 3 vols. (New York: International Publishers, 1967), 1:76–87.

21. Brian Maidment, "Ruskin, *Fors Clavigera* and Ruskinism, 1870–1900," in *New Approaches to Ruskin,* ed. Robert Hewison (London: Routledge and Kegan Paul, 1981), 211n.

22. For membership rolls, see 39:248. In the final year of *Fors* (1884), for example, the guild had sixty-five members (30:86).

23. J. L. Austin, *How To Do Things with Words,* ed. J. O. Urmson and Marina Sbisa, 2nd ed. (Cambridge, Mass.: Harvard University Press, 1962), 18, 15.

24. P. D. Anthony, *John Ruskin's Labour: A Study of Ruskin's Social Theory* (Cambridge: Cambridge University Press, 1983), 36.

25. Austin, 93; "a long chain of the will" and the phrase following it are from Friedrich Nietzsche, *The Genealogy of Morals,* in *The Birth of Tragedy and The Genealogy of Morals,* trans. Francis Golffing (New York: Anchor, 1956), 190.

26. Nietzsche, 189.

27. Ibid., 160.

28. James Clark Sherburne, *John Ruskin, or the Ambiguities of Abundance* (Cambridge, Mass.: Harvard University Press, 1972), 136, 151.

29. Anthony, 184. See also 30:xli, and Margaret E. Spence, "The Guild of St. George: Ruskin's Attempt to Translate His Ideas into Practice," *Bulletin of the John Rylands Library* 40 (1957): passim.

30. John Tyree Fain, *Ruskin and the Economists* (Nashville: Vanderbilt University Press, 1956), 26.

31. Eagleton, 37.

CHAPTER 7. *FICTION FAIR AND FOUL* AND RUSKIN'S LATE LITERARY CRITICISM

1. The two shillings probably are a rhetorical flourish, for the recipient would not pay for a telegram. In any case, they would refer to the number of words, which had been the basis of rates since 1866. Perhaps Ruskin mistakenly wrote "telegram" instead of "letter" and intended to imply he had received one with postage due, for prepayment of mail had been compulsory since 1855. See J. C. Hemmeon, *The History of the British Post Office* (Cambridge: Harvard University Press, 1912), 203–9; and Asa Briggs, *Victorian Things* (Chicago: University of Chicago Press, 1988), 335, 376–78.

2. See Roland Barthes, "The Reality Effect," in *French Literary Theory Today,* trans. R. Carter and ed. Tzvetan Todorov (Cambridge: Cambridge University Press, 1982), 11–17. The crucial nineteenth-century texts I have in mind which link realism to details of the everyday are Wordsworth's "Preface" to the second edition of the *Lyrical Ballads* (1800) and chap. 17 of George Eliot's *Adam Bede* (1859).

3. By the end of Victoria's reign, Great Britain had four or five of the world's largest conurbations, with more than half of its population resident in cities of twenty thousand or more, and three-quarters of the population classified as urban. The highest incremental urbanization occurred in England and Wales from 1870–90. Migration to the suburbs of London peaked from 1881–91. See Eric E. Lampard, "The Urbanizing World," in *The Victorian City: Images and Realities,* ed. H. J. Dyos and Michael Wolff, 2 vols. (Boston: Routledge and Kegan Paul, 1973), 1:10–11; and E. A. Wrigley and R. S. Schofield, *The Population History of England, 1541–1871* (Cambridge: Cambridge University Press, 1981).

4. A sample of circulation statistics and prices are illustrative: by 1891, Ward's *Robert Elsmere* (1888) had appeared in three editions (31s.6d., 6s., 2s.6d.) and had sold 70,500 copies. In 1882, a 6d. edition of *Sartor Resartus* sold 70,000 copies; the circulation of the *Boy's Own Paper* was 200,000 around 1880. "Between 1885 and 1888, Tennyson's collected editions sold about 15,000 copies a year." See Richard D. Altick, *The English Common Reader* (Chicago: University of Chicago Press, 1957), 386, 390, 395, 387.

5. E. H. Gombrich, *Art and Illusion* (New York: Bollingen, 1961), 202, 382–83.

6. W. F. Axton, "Victorian Landscape Painting: A Change in Outlook," in *Nature and the Victorian Imagination,* ed. U. C. Knoepflmacher and G. B. Tennyson (Berkeley: University of California Press, 1977), 292.

7. Elizabeth Deeds Ermarth, *Realism and Consensus in the English Novel* (Princeton: Princeton University Press, 1983), ix–x.

8. Gombrich, 240.

9. F. S. Schwarzbach, *Dickens and the City* (London: Athlone Press, 1979), 1; quoted in N. N. Feltes, *Modes of Production of Victorian Novels* (Chicago: University of Chicago Press, 1986), 15.

10. Altick, 82.

11. Philip Fisher, "City Matters, City Minds," in *The Worlds of Victorian Fiction,* ed. Jerome F. Buckley, Harvard English Studies, vol. 6 (Cambridge, Mass.: Harvard University Press, 1975), 373.

12. George Levine, *The Realistic Imagination: English Fiction from Frankenstein to Lady Chatterley* (Chicago: University of Chicago Press, 1981), 12.

13. Roger Ramsey, "Ruskin's Literary Self," *Pre-Raphaelite Review* 3, no. 2 (1979):10.

14. For information about Edwardes, see 31:xxxvi–xlii. For more of the books in Ruskin's *Bibliotheca,* see 28:499–502. For the editors' sketch of the life of Bitzius, see 32:xxxiv–v.

15. See Colin Campbell's discussion of the "redrawing of the cultural lines of battle" in *The Romantic Ethic and the Spirit of Modern Consumerism* (New York: Basil Blackwell, 1987), 178–79.

16. Terry Eagleton, *Criticism and Ideology* (London: Verso, 1978), 40.

17. Altick, 306, 309–310.

18. Eagleton's phrase is "metropolitan 'pastoral' myth," 40.

19. Karl Marx, *Capital,* ed. Frederick Engels, 3 vols. (New York: International Publishers, 1967), 1:78.

20. George Levine, "High and Low: Ruskin and the Novelists," in *Nature and the Victorian Imagination,* 149, 145–46.

21. Levine, *The Realistic Imagination,* 5.

22. Katherine Mary Peek, *Wordsworth in England: Studies in the History of His Fame* (New York: Octagon, 1943), 186–87.

23. Quoted in ibid., 170, from Sir Charles Duffy's *Conversations with Carlyle* (London, 1892).

24. In his "Preface" to *Selections from the Works of Lord Byron,* in *The Complete Works of Algernon Charles Swinburne,* Bonchurch Edition, 20 vols. (London: Heinemann, 1926), 15:126. But in "Wordsworth

and Byron" (*Nineteenth Century* [April and May 1884]), he criticizes Byron's poetry and character. See *Complete Works,* 14:161–90.

25. W. E. Henley, *Athenaeum,* 25 July 1881; reprint, *Views and Reviews* (London, 1890), 59–60; see *The Works of W. E. Henley,* 7 vols. (London: David Nutt, 1908), 5:65–73; and Alfred Austin, *Quarterly* 154 (1882):53–82. Austin dismisses three-quarters of Wordsworth's writing and complains, as did Ruskin, that the poetry shows no sense of humor or action. No great subject "can be treated adequately or greatly by merely writing *about* it" (76–77).

26. Quoted in Peek, 190.

27. Quoted from *De Pace Veneta Relatio,* in John Julius Norwich, *A History of Venice* (New York: Knopf, 1982), 113–14.

28. Peek notes that Wordsworth eventually learned that the story was false and suggested a substitution: "The penance inflicted by Gregory the Seventh upon the Emperor Henry the Fourth at Canosa" (187).

29. Norwich, 116–17.

30. Karl Elze's *Lord Byron* (1870) had been translated into English in 1872; John Morley, "Byron and the French Revolution," *Fortnightly Review,* n.s. 48 (1870):650–73. Stowe's article first appeared in *Macmillan's* 20 (1869):377–96, then in expanded form in *Lady Byron Vindicated* (London, 1870); see also Samuel Chew, *Byron in England* (London: Murray, 1924), 288–300.

31. Chew, 264–68; Edward John Trelawny, *Recollections of the Last Days of Shelley and Byron* (London, 1858), ed. J. E. Morpurgo (New York: Philosophical Library, 1952); and Walter Bagehot, "Percy Bysshe Shelley" (1856), in *The Collected Works of Walter Bagehot,* ed. Norman St John Stevan, 2 vols. (Cambridge: Harvard University Press, 1965), 1:433–76.

32. Quoted in Chew, 279n.

33. For Ruskin's sympathies in all these disputes, including the Schleswig-Holstein conflict, see 18:xxii–xxv; 27:622–23.

34. In *Lectures on Architecture and Painting* (1854), 12:55; and the third volume of *Modern Painters* (1856), 5:335.

35. William Ruddick, "Byron in England," in *Byron's Political and Cultural Influence in Nineteenth-Century Europe: A Symposium,* ed. Paul Graham Trueblood (Atlantic Highlands: Humanities Press, 1981), 25.

36. Friedrich Engels, *The Condition of the Working Class in England,* trans. W. O. Henderson and W. H. Chaloner (Palo Alto: Stanford University Press, 1968), 273.

37. Alfred Austin, *The Poetry of the Period* (London, 1870); George Meredith's comments in a letter of 1864 (*Letters,* 2 vols. [Lon-

don: Constable, 1912], 1:164); and Charles Kingsley, "Thoughts on Shelley and Byron," *Fraser's* 48 (1853):568–76. "The truth is, that what has put Byron out of favour with the public of late, is not his faults, but his excellencies. His artistic good taste, his classical polish, his sound shrewd sense, his hatred of cant, his insight into humbug, above all, his shallow, pitiable habit of being always intelligible" (571).

38. Ruddick, 29.

39. Philip W. Martin, *Byron: A Poet before His Public* (Cambridge: Cambridge University Press, 1982), 3.

40. *Art Journal* 39 (1877):29.

41. Michael H. Friedman, *The Making of a Tory Humanist: Wordsworth and the Idea of Community* (New York: Columbia University Press, 1979), 297.

42. But see Guinevere L. Griest, *Mudie's Circulating Library and the Victorian Novel* (Bloomington: Indiana University Press, 1970), 43–44; books of poetry were relatively inexpensive and had a smaller audience than novels had.

43. Peek, 199–202, 209–10.

44. Matthew Arnold, "Preface" to *Poems of Wordsworth, Chosen and Edited* (1879; reprint, "Wordsworth," in *The Works of Matthew Arnold*, Edition de Luxe, 15 vols. [London: Macmillan, 1903], 4:118).

45. Matthew Arnold, "On Translating Homer: Last Words" (1862), in *The Complete Prose Works of Matthew Arnold*, ed. R. H. Super, 11 vols. (Ann Arbor: University of Michigan Press, 1960), 1:206.

46. Arnold, "Preface," in *Works*, Edition de Luxe, 4:109–10.

47. Ibid., 4:109.

48. As the editors note, Ruskin takes "Samian wine" from *Don Juan* 3.86. Compare Kingsley's comments about Byron's decline in popularity written almost three decades earlier: "Well, at least the taste of the age is more refined, if that be matter of congratulation. And there is an excuse for preferring *eau sucré* to waterside porter, heady with grains of paradise and quassia, salt and *coccum indicum*" ("Thoughts on Shelley and Byron," 570).

49. Campbell, 65, 89.

50. Arnold, "Byron," in *Works*, Edition de Luxe, 4:149.

51. Eagleton, 40.

52. Brian Maidment, "Ruskin, *Fors Clavigera* and Ruskinism, 1870–1900," in *New Approaches to Ruskin*, ed. Robert Hewison (London: Routledge and Kegan Paul, 1981), 194.

53. 33:380. In this sentence, Ruskin also says that supply is limitless; he is commenting on the diminished amount of pleasure from painting in a flooded market.

54. Marcel Proust, "Preface" to *Sésame et les lys,* in *On Reading Ruskin,* trans. Jean Autret, William Burford, and Phillip J. Wolfe (New Haven: Yale University Press, 1987), 121, 125.

55. Proust, "Notes to Preface" to *Sésame et les lys,* 138.

56. Proust, "Preface" to *Sésame et les lys,* 120.

57. Ibid., 120.

58. Ibid., 120.

59. Ibid., 114.

60. Naomi Schor, *Reading in Detail: Aesthetics and the Feminine* (New York: Methuen, 1987), 84.

61. Ibid., 84.

62. Feltes, 10.

63. Norman Bryson, *Vision and Painting* (New Haven: Yale University Press, 1983), 5.

CHAPTER 8. HOARDING AND SPENDING: RUSKIN'S EXPERIMENTS

1. Karl Marx, *Capital,* ed. Frederick Engels, 3 vols. (New York: International Publishers, 1967), 1:48.

2. John Vernon, *Money and Fiction: Literary Realism in the Nineteenth and Early Twentieth Centuries* (Ithaca: Cornell University Press, 1984), 42.

3. John Bayley, "Best and Worst," review of *Dickens: A Biography,* by Fred Kaplan, *New York Review of Books,* 19 January 1989, 12.

4. Richard D. Altick, *The English Common Reader* (Chicago: University of Chicago Press, 1957), 309. This was the price of books bought directly from Ruskin's agent. The retail bookseller was to charge twenty and thirty shillings, respectively, for plain and illustrated volumes. In 1872 Ruskin sold plain volumes directly to purchasers for 9s.6d., illustrated volumes for 19s. (18:11).

5. Altick, 262.

6. Ibid., 262–63.

7. Ibid., 274, 307, 311.

8. Ibid., 286–87.

9. Ibid., 306–7.

10. Ibid., 309–10.

11. See John Kenneth Galbraith, *Economics in Perspective* (Boston: Houghton Mifflin, 1987), 108.

12. For an explanation of Duff's remark, see 27:244n.6.

13. Brian Maidment, "Ruskin, *Fors Clavigera* and Ruskinism, 1870–1900," in *New Approaches to Ruskin,* ed. Robert Hewison (London: Routledge and Kegan Paul, 1981), 196.

14. "He was proud of the book [a Greek Testament], having obtained it by boldly writing to its London publisher, a thing he had never done before" (Thomas Hardy, *Jude the Obscure,* Part First. vii.)

15. The holdings of these libraries were published in tabular form by the Ruskin Society of Manchester: "Table of Mr. Ruskin's Works as Contained in the Free Town Libraries of the United Kingdom," in *Is It True Mr. Ruskin's Books Are "Scarce, Dear, and Difficult to Obtain"?* (Manchester: John Heywood, Excelsior Printing and Stationery Works, n.d. [probably 1880]); see Brian Maidment, "Readers Fair and Foul: John Ruskin and the Periodical Press," in *The Victorian Periodical Press: Samplings and Soundings,* ed. Joanne Shattock and Michael Wolff (Toronto: University of Toronto Press, 1982), 56.

16. George P. Landow, *Elegant Jeremiahs* (Ithaca: Cornell University Press, 1986), 18.

17. Guinevere L. Griest notes, in *Mudie's Circulating Library and the Victorian Novel* (Bloomington: Indiana University Press, 1970), that by midcentury most publishers were binding their own books (42).

18. N. N. Feltes, *Modes of Production of Victorian Novels* (Chicago: University of Chicago Press, 1986), 26.

19. Ibid., 8.

20. By 1889, for example, Ruskin had made £3,069 on the 1886 edition of *The Stones of Venice* (30:361).

21. Altick, 316–17.

22. Feltes, 80–81; and Galbraith, 179.

23. Feltes, 87.

24. Ibid., 98.

25. Maidment, "Ruskin, *Fors Clavigera* and Ruskinism, 1870–1900," 205.

26. E. T. Cook, *The Life of John Ruskin* (1911; reprint, New York: Haskell House, 1968), 2:346.

27. William C. Ward, "St. George's Museum, Sheffield," *Art Journal* 44 (1882):240.

28. *Magazine of Art* 3 (1878):57.

29. Ward, 240.

30. Robert Hewison, *Ruskin in Sheffield, 1876* (London: Bentham Press for the Guild of Saint George, 1979), 10.

31. Peter Gay, *The Bourgeois Experience: Victoria to Freud,* 2 vols. (New York: Oxford University Press, 1984), 1:439.

32. Ibid., 1:439. This sensuality is evident in *Praeterita*, in which Ruskin remembers of Paris "the soft red cushions of the armchairs" and the "polished floor" of the salon "as reflective as the mahogany table" (35:104–5), the carriage his father made for their travels to Switzerland (35:106–7), and later the sunny gallery in Turin where he gazed at Veronese's *Solomon and the Queen of Sheba* and felt, through an open window, "warm air" wafting in with "floating swells and falls of military music" (35:496).

33. Quoted in Hewison, *Ruskin in Sheffield, 1876*, 18–19.

34. Quoted in ibid., 5.

35. *Magazine of Art* 3 (1878):60.

36. Dianne Sachko Macleod, "Art Collecting and Victorian Middle-Class Taste," *Art History* 10 (1987):329.

37. See, for example, Joseph Alsop, "The Faker's Art," *New York Review of Books,* 23 October 1986, 25–31.

38. John Ruskin, "Arthur Burgess," *Century Guild Hobby Horse* 2 (1887):48, 50–51.

39. Ibid., 53.

40. Ibid., 48.

41. June Rose, *The Drawings of John Leech* (London: Art and Technics, 1950), 18.

42. Reproduced in ibid., 65.

43. Simon Houfe, *John Leech and the Victorian Scene* (Suffolk: Antique Collectors' Club, 1984), 43, 152–58.

44. Percival Leigh, *The Comic English Grammar,* illus. John Leech (London, 1840), 155–56.

45. Ibid., 157.

46. *Works* 3:192. Ruskin does not describe the subject of the picturesque in economic terms until volume four of *Modern Painters* (6:10–15). See also Robert Hewison, *John Ruskin: The Argument of the Eye* (Princeton: Princeton University Press, 1976), 46–50.

47. Macleod, 338.

48. Ibid., 332, 344.

49. Feltes, 94–97.

50. Altick, *The English Common Reader,* 309.

51. Cook, 2:481–82. Ruskin's stated reasons for resigning were printed in the *Zoophilist* of 1 January 1885, reprinted in *Works* 34:643–44. See Richard D. French, *Antivivisection and Medical Science in Victorian Society* (Princeton: Princeton University Press, 1975), 276n.; and John Dixon Hunt, *The Wider Sea: A Life of John Ruskin* (London: Dent, 1982), 392. Both suggest that lack of funding for the drawing school prompted Ruskin's decision.

52. French, 352.

53. George P. Landow, *The Aesthetic and Critical Theories of John Ruskin* (Princeton: Princeton University Press, 1971), 414.

54. *Oxford Magazine* 1 (7 November 1883):360.

55. *Oxford Magazine* 1 (7 November 1883):358; 1 (28 November 1883): 416. Nicholson refutes these arguments in his response printed in the 28 November issue. He claims that the experiments on the spleen have yielded no practical results. He goes on to contest the necessity of vivisection in the work of Harvey: because he already had described the circulation of the blood by injecting warm water into the heart of a dead man, he could have demonstrated systemic circulation in a similar way.

56. *Oxford Magazine* 1 (7 November 1883):358.

57. Terry Eagleton, *Literary Theory: An Introduction* (Minneapolis: University of Minnesota Press, 1983), 33.

Index

Designed by Joanna Hill.
Composed by The Composing Room of Michigan, Inc.,
in Garamond text and display.
Printed on 50-lb. MV Antique Cream Sebago
and bound in Holliston Roxite B grade cloth
by The Maple Press Company.

DATE DUE

~~JAN 1 3 1993~~			
			Printed in USA